The Cuisine of Alsace

The Cuisine of Alsace

by
Pierre Gaertner
and
Robert Frédérick

Translated by J. F. Bernard
Adapted by Helen Feingold
Color photographs by Pierre Ginet

with a foreword
by
Madame Fernand Point

BARRON'S
WOODBURY, NEW YORK
LONDON

Half-title page:
Woodcut from *Der Junge Knabe Spiegel*
by Jörg Wickram, Strasbourg, 1554, J. Frölich.
Colmar Municipal Library; photograph by Patrick Flesch.

First U.S Edition, 1981 by
Barron's Educational Series, Inc.

All inquiries should be addressed to:
Barron's Educational Series, Inc.
113 Crossways Park Drive
Woodbury, New York 11797

Library of Congress Catalog Card No. 81-3584

International Standard Book No. 0-8120-5403-2

Library of Congress Cataloging in Publication Data
Gaertner, Pierre.
The Cuisine of Alsace

Translation of: La cuisine alsacienne.
Includes index.
1. Cookery, French. 2. Alsace (France)—Social life
and customs. I. Frédérick, Robert, 1926-
II. Title.
TX719.G1513 641.5944'383 81-3584
ISBN 0-8120-5403-2 AACR2

PRINTED IN HONG KONG

CONTENTS

WISSEMBOURG
OBERHOFFEN-LES-WISSEMBOURG
ROTT
STEINSELTZ
CLEEBOURG
RIEDSELTZ
RHINE
FRANCE
GIMBRETT
KIENHEIM
MARLENHEIM
WANGEN
WESTHOFFEN
TRAENHEIM
STRASBOURG
ERGERSHEIM
AVOLSHEIM
WEST GERMANY
MOLSHEIM
BISCHOFFSHEIM
OBERNAI
BERNARDSWILLER
ERSTEIN
HEILIGENSTEIN
BARR
MITTELBERGHEIM
EICHHOFFEN
EPFIG
REICHSFELD
BLIENSCHWILLER
DAMBACH-LA-VILLE
SCHERWILLER
SELESTAT
KINTZHEIM
RORSCHWIHR
BERGHEIM
RIBEAUVILLE
ZELLENBERG
MARCKOLSHEIM
RIQUEWIHR
BEBLENHEIM
KIENTZHEIM
MITTELWIHR
BENNWIHR
KAYSERSBERG
AMMERSCHWIHR
SIGOLSHEIM
KATZENTHAL
NIEDERMORSCHWIHR
TURCKHEIM
COLMAR
WINTZENHEIM
WALBACH
WETTOLSHEIM
NEUF-BRISACH
VOEGTLINSHOFFEN
HATTSTATT
RHINE RIVER
ROUFFACH
ORSCHWIHR
GUEBWILLER
SOULTZ
HARTMANNSWILLER
UFFHOLTZ
CERNAY
THANN
MULHOUSE
BASEL
SWITZERLAND

FOREWORD

Of all the regional cuisines of France, that of Alsace is one of the richest and most varied. It combines the tastes of the region and the habits acquired through the centuries with the highest degree of gastronomic subtlety. And it continues to evolve with respect to quality. Its talent for accommodating both fishes and meats, the opulence of its pork dishes as well as of its desserts—all enhanced by local wines of incomparable bouquet—have made Alsatian cooking famous in Europe and throughout the world.

There are no others more qualified than Pierre Gaertner, chef of the celebrated Aux Armes de France restaurant at Ammerschwihr and a former student of Fernand Point, and Robert Frédérick, himself an Alsatian as well as a journalist and writer, to describe Alsatian cuisine: its history, its traditions, and its future.

The authors describe in detail some easy recipes that will delight you because they reflect both simplicity and fidelity to the traditions of Alsace.

They deserve our gratitude—the gratitude of all who love good eating and good drinking and who still adhere to the good life.

Madame F. Point

Madame F. Point

INTRODUCTION

The Alsatian plain is extraordinarily rich. It has been nourished by all the alluvial wealth carried by the Rhine to the Alpine chain from Saint-Gothard, and by all the dusts brought by the winds. Among the latter, we might mention especially the precious loess, a powdery and fertile sand brought, it is said, from China.

It is here that dwells that race of humans known as Alsatians. Here despite invasions, wars, and the continuous military floods that have swept back and forth across the countryside, the people have created a garden—a haven where, throughout the centuries, it has been good to live.

Today if you glide over the Alsatian plain—flying, for example, from Paris to Strasbourg to Mulhouse—you will see what we mean. Once over the crests of the Vosges, you see beneath you a neat and delightfully orderly garden surrounding the villages. Everywhere there are flowers, and everywhere there are smiling faces to welcome visitors to Alsatian territory.

"It is a happy land," said Victor Hugo. And so it is. But it is happy only because of the inflexible will of the Alsatian people; their unceasing efforts; their optimistic acceptance of misfortune; their courage; their ability to walk the middle path between conflicting and contradictory pressures, whether from the two powerful nations which have done battle over Alsace, or from the battle for religious dominance among Catholics, Protestants, and even Jews (who, in some areas, are quite numerous).

It is said that, in a given region, everything is cut from the same bolt of cloth. That the geological nature of an area; the structure of the very rocks and the climate form the character of men. That the mode of life and the activities that result from these factors shape one's tools, movements, traditions, and language. That one's furniture as well as artistic masterpieces are the result of these things; clothing as well as legends; cooking as well as dreams. . . .

Alsace however is not a hinterland, difficult in access and climate, as Frenchmen from the interior often think. It is a welcoming land, a land where life is good. It is a place where people have learned to shape their future in accordance with reason—that is to say, with an eye to happiness.

It is with wish, this same sense of balance and moderation, this "serious joy," this spirit of epicurean humanism, that you should approach Alsatian cuisine.

PART I
TRADITIONS

Cologne has her cathedral.
So does Strasbourg!
But Alsace also has her wine,
her Kirsch, and her good food.
Ernst Moritz Arndt,
German writer and poet

CULINARY TRADITIONS

In the year 1449, on the feast of Saint Valentine, a Tuesday, Robert of Bavaria, bishop of Strasbourg, took possession of his residence. When the religious ceremonies were over, a sumptuous banquet was served, comprising three courses of five dishes each:

First course:	Cabbage
	Boiled beef
	Ragout of chicken with blanched almonds
	Fish in a black gelatin
	Flan
Second course:	Shoulder of venison
	Venison pâté
	Boiled young crane with caramel sauce
	An illuminated pastry
	Blanc-mange
Third course:	Rice sprinkled with sugar
	Roasted capons, chickens, and pork
	Aspic of fowl and veal with a sauce
	Pastry with the appearance of a pear (fritters)
	Prune compote

This memorable feast of the mid-fifteenth century serves as an introduction to the gastronomy—or at least to the feeding—of Alsatians in the Middle Ages, and it allows us to go back to the culinary traditions of that province.

There are not a great many original sources available to enlighten us with respect to the kind of food eaten in the Middle Ages. Those that do exist usually deal only with the eating habits of the nobility and the ecclesiastical princes.

So far as earlier epochs are concerned, we know very little. One bit of information that has come down to us—from Roman texts describing the life of the legionnaires guarding the marshes of "Germania" in Alsace—is that it was a "land abounding in delicious pork" and in "succulent pastries of honey and of aromatic resins."

Alsatian Cooking in the Middle Ages

The Middle Ages were a difficult time for Alsace. The peasants, to escape the roving horde of bandits and mercenary soldiers, frequently were obliged to leave everything they had and take refuge in the mountains. Famine was endemic, caused by alternating rainy years and severe winters with torrid summers. The production of grains of various kinds was minimal and extremely irregular.

The basic food was bread and, during the proper season, a few vegetables: peas and green beans in summer and lentils in winter. Meat was rare; fowl and pork were reserved for feast days. During the winter, fat bacon and meat—salted and smoked with wood from the fire—was popular when available.

During the grape-harvesting season, the lot of the peasants working in the vineyards was somewhat better. At Ammerschwihr, for instance, at the end of the fifteenth century the workers at Meywihr, which belonged to the counts of Ribeaupierre, were fed bread, cabbage and turnips, blood sausage, and tripe. On Sundays, Tuesdays, and Thursdays, they were served dishes each containing "five to six pounds of meat." An "ordinary white wine" was served at lunch, and an "old wine" at dinner.

Fish, on the other hand, was abundant. The waters of the Rhine were clear and fresh, as were all the streams of the Vosges, and fishing was easy. Fish were boiled in lightly seasoned water or were braised. At Strasbourg, during the fifteenth century, there were meals composed entirely of fish dishes. They were known as *fischmohl.*

Members of the various religious communities, who were the only ones who knew how to read and write, have left us many bits of information on their eating habits in the medieval period. One twelfth-century manuscript describes the food of the monks at the Abbey of Murbach, in the Guebwiller Valley: daily, there was rye bread; two cups of wine (three during the spring and summer); two dishes of seasoned vegetables (one with salt, the other with lard or oil according to the season and with cheese). During Lent, the latter was replaced by a dish of herring. Beans and fish were the staples. The cathedral chapter of Strasbourg, however, ate somewhat better: two meals per day, with meat, beer, eggs, bread, and honey cakes.

The feast of Easter was appropriately celebrated with "Soup, three portions of boiled meat, four of roasted meat, chickens, lamb with fritters and cakes, and three breads besides the ordinary bread, as well as wine."

So far as the nobles were concerned, their tables were opulent for the time and evidence the beginnings of gastronomic research. In 1469, the Archduke Sigismond turned over the county of Ferrette to the commissioners of Charles the Bold. On that occasion supper consisted of, among other

Kuchenmeisterei, Strasbourg 1519. Municipal Museum of Colmar; photograph by Patrick Flesch.

Carp, tench, perch, eel, bream, and pike were excellent food, as well as the crayfish which abounded in the streams of plain and mountain.

Jerome Guebwiller, a Renaissance humanist, describes the market at Strasbourg as follows: "The market abounds in fishes both expensive and common, so that the rich man may satisfy his greedy appetite and the poor man his hunger. Also offered for sale there are all the delicacies which too often lead to excess, and the expense of which seduces people of moderate means to ruin themselves."

Meats were represented chiefly by pork, beef, and fowl. Game in many cases was reserved for the gentry. Onc head chef of the seventeenth century tells us that "pheasant, hazel grouse, quail, rock partridge, and white grouse are regarded as both tasty and healthful. But they are not for everyone. They are left for the lords; and the rest of us content ourselves with domestic birds." Pork, which was a favorite, was either salted or smoked, and was accompanied by various vegetables, including salt cabbage in the form of sauerkraut. Along with these meats, tripe and, above all, blood sausage was always highly prized.

Certain financial reports of the time mention particularly sumptuous banquets given by cities of the Empire and by high dignitaries. But the peasant, the artisan, and the ordinary workman did not eat equally well. Farmers and woodcutters often made do with black bread, vegetables, cheeses, and whatever could be gathered from the fields. For them, meat was rarely available and generally was kept for feast days. Wine was conspicuously absent.

Eighteenth Century: A Touch of French Finesse

At the end of the Thirty Years' War, Alsace passed into the hands of the king of France, and a royal administration took over the affairs of the province. At that point, France discovered—not without a touch of contempt—the eating habits of the Alsatians. One Frenchman of the era, a medical man named Mauge, compiled a *Natural History of the Province of Alsace,* and noted:

> The food is like the climate in which it is grown. It is, as such, coarse and clammy—spinach, radish, turnips (both cooked and raw), beans, peas, rice, Schnitzen, hulled barley, and cabbage of every kind. . . .
>
> Alsatians are not appreciative of delicacies. The meats are

> badly prepared, their stews without subtlety, their roasted meats dry. They eat little meat, in fact, and they will make a soup by taking two pounds of beef and leaving it in a pot of boiling water for a while. They do not cook herbs in the soup, but put them on the slices of bread that they eat with the soup. If they eat little good meat, they eat a great deal of bad meat. . . . They love dry roasts; and the latter are usually half-cold when they are served because the roast gets cold while the Alsatians eat their first course, a salad, which is eaten alone. . . .

A French gourmet, M. de l'Hermine, made two voyages to Alsace, one in 1674–1676, and the other in 1681. On one occasion, he was invited to a wedding near Altkirch, at Sundgau. He did not have a happy memory of the occasion and tells us that he was fed only cabbage, turnips, and beets; various fritters; and "meatballs in a buttered dough."

Public dignitaries and nobles imported French chefs, but ordinary Alsatians were determined to retain their culinary identity which little by little improved along traditional lines, especially in the area of sauces and of the preparation of meats and fishes.

It is to the experimentation and gastronomic evolution of this era that Alsace developed a specialty of which the area may be justly proud: *foie gras.* Foie gras came into being at Strasbourg, in 1780. Its creator was a chef from Lorraine, Jean-Pierre Clause, who was in the service of the Marshal de Contades, governor of Alsace.

Clause made "a crust in the shape of a round box, which he filled with whole foie gras and topped off with a stuffing of veal and freshly chopped bacon. The whole was covered with a lid of the same crust and was baked in a moderate oven." The result was a phenomenal success. One of these pâtés was sent to Versailles, where King Louis XVI greatly enjoyed it. During the Revolution, Nicolas Francois Doyen, a chef from Bordeaux traveling through Alsace, suggested to Clause that he add a truffle to his foie gras.

In this way, what was till then known as Pâté à la Contades was transformed into Pâté de Foie Gras de Strasbourg, aux Truffles du Périgord, and its fortune was made.

It was also during the eighteenth century that the potato began to appear on the plain, and, despite several setbacks, to appear everywhere in the province. It was nonetheless already popular since, beginning in the sixteenth century, several *Kraüterbücher,* or botanical treatises, described its cultivation. By the seventeenth century, it was the basic foodstuff of certain high valleys of the Vosges.

By then, Alsatian food had improved considerably, as witnessed by several documents of the period. It was then that, gastronomically speaking, Alsace became a "blessed land." It is true that Alsatian cooking had benefited

from the influence of French cooking, but also by the infiltration of certain influences from the other side of the Rhine. Chefs—and recipes—were constantly arriving from Worms, Cologne, Trier, and Heidelberg. Stasbourg was, of all cities, "the city of good living."

The Nineteenth Century and the Golden Age

The Alsatians had learned to eat well, but they retained their old habit of "being moderate in their excesses." At banquets and feasts their food was grand indeed, but in everyday life their meals were more simple.

Here is the menu prepared by J. Sarger, innkeeper of L'Agneau d'Or at Colmar, for the agricultural convention held at Kayserberg on September 2, 1868:

Hors d'oeuvre:	Soup à la reine
	Filet of beef with tomato sauce
	Puff pastry pie financière
	Pike à la Chambord
Entrées:	Green cabbage à la Flûamande
	Jugged hare with croutons
	Duck with turnips
	Leg of venison with black pepper sauce
Roast:	Pullets from Mans
	Cold pâtés
	Salads
Desserts:	Jellies of mixed fruit and others
	Various cakes
	Assorted pastries

Local wines

What appetites they must have had in those days! The people at the banquet obviously were expected to spend the entire afternoon and evening at the table. But that was not an unusual expectation in wine-growing country.

Below is another menu typical of the late nineteenth century, served during festivities at Ammerschwihr and Ribeauvillé, also in wine-growing districts:

Bacon soup
Cream of chicken soup
Grouse in aspic

Grape sherbet

Broiled blue trout
Venison in brown sauce
Champagne sherbet

Roasted pullets
Beef in spice sauce

Salad

Various cakes
Macaroons

Local wines

Between certain dishes, one managed to sneak in a shot of some *eau-de-vie*—usually made from Gewürztraminer grape skins—to help in digesting the greasy food. This was known as "the Alsatian Hole."

This golden age of Alsatian cooking was noted, and recorded, in 1862, by the publication at Colmar (and its re-issue in Nancy in 1877) of *L'Ancienne Alsace à table* (Old Alsace at the Table), a remarkable book by Charles Gérard, a lawyer practicing in the Court of Colmar and, later, at Nancy.

Since 1918

November 1918. Marshal Philippe Pétain entered Strasbourg at the head of the French army. It is said that "more sausages were eaten, and more kegs of beer and bottles of Riesling were drunk in Alsace, than during the entire forty-eight years preceeding."

The Paris government's respect for certain Alsatian peculiarities as a means of unifying France, had the effect of creating a favorable climate for the development of the province. There was industrialization, modernization of agriculture, a raising of the standard of living at all social levels, while maintaining essential Alsatian traditions.

Gourmet cooking spread, both because of the great restaurants located from the Rhine to the crests of the Vosges, and because of the thousands of household kitchens where the aromas of stews, sauerkraut, and trout wafted through the air. Despite the drama and tragedy of the period between 1939

and 1945, Alsace remained united, homogeneous—and mindful of its basic needs: the beautiful, the good, and the tasty *(le beau, le bien, le bon)*.

Alsatian cooking is still resisting a trend toward internationalizing culinary art, which seems to be part of the trend toward a European culture. Strasbourg, capital of the European community and an international metropolis, still cherishes its traditional dishes. And this determination is even more evident in Colmar.

In the whole of Alsace, whether on the plain or in the mountains, regional cooking is still being refined and perpetuated. From the banks of the Rhine to the heights of the Vosges, the butcher shops are pouring out an unprecedented and diversified wealth of products. The *boulangeries* have an infinite variety of Alsatian rolls of every kind. And so far as Alsatian pastries are concerned, if they often have the creamy thickness of Anglo-Saxon desserts, they also have their very own special refinement, their own particular subtlety of aroma or taste.

The culinary traditions of Alsace, although open to the products of other regions, nonetheless repose essentially on local goods: the fields and gardens of the plain, the asparagus and early vegetables of the Strasbourg area, the domestic and wild fruits, the game of the forests, and the goods of the fish merchants. (Unfortunately the Rhine has long been empty of salmon and trout are becoming more and more rare in the Fecht and in the upper waters of the Thur and the Bruche.)

Now, in the latter part of the twentieth century, Alsatian cuisine has attained, not its apex (because all things are open to improvement) but an astonishing balance of variety and quality.

Table 1: POPULAR GASTRONOMIC CELEBRATIONS IN ALSACE

Date	Celebration
Upper Rhine	
April (entire month)	Ammerschwihr: wine market
May 24	Guebwiller: wine market
June 8	Ribeauvillé: Kougelhopf Festival
June (end)	Orbey: Cheese Festival
July 28–29	Riquewihr: Riesling Festival
August 4–15	Colmar: wine market
August 18–19	Gueberschwihr: Friendship Festival ("open doors and cellars")
August and September	Colmar: Sauerkraut Days
September 1	Ribeauvillé: Fiddler Festival
September 28–October 7	Mulhouse: October Days
September	Riquewihr: New-wine Festival
October (end)	Munster: Pie Festival
Lower Rhine	
May 1	Molsheim: Spring Celebration and regional wine market
June 17	Westhoffen: Cherry Festival
June 30	Grandfontaine: Huckleberry Festival and St. John's Fire
July 7–8 and 13–15	Karkolsheim: Pâté Festival
July 8	Dambach-la-Ville: wine market
July 8	Wanger: Festival of the Wine Fountain
July 12–15	Barr: wine market
July 29	Dambach: Wine Festival, Grape-harvest Festival
August 4–5	Dambach: Wine Festival
August 11–12 and 14	Dambach: Wine Festival
August (entire month)	Andlaus: Trout Festival
August 19	Erstein: Sugar Festival
August 25–September 2	Haguenau: Hop Festival with Gastronomic Week
September 1–2 and 15	Geispolsheim: Sauerkraut Festival
September 2	Mutzig: Beer Festival
September 23	Brumath: onion market
October 6	Plobsheim: Gastronomy Festival
October 7	Barr: Grape-harvest Festival

October 13–14 and 20–21	Geispolsheim: Grape Festival ("open doors and cellars")
October 14	Obernai: Grape-harvest Festival
October 21	Marlenheim: Grape-harvest Festival
October 21	Merkwiller-Pechelbronn: village festival and Alsatian Specialties Festival
November 10 and 17	Lipsheim: Salt Turnip Days

Von der Kutz der Ding, Pierre de Crecentius, Strasbourg, 1518. Municipal Museum of Colmar; photograph by Patrick Flesch.

THE WINES OF ALSACE

Here ripens an agreeable wine on the
sun-blessed hills called Alsace. . . .
Mathias Ringmann Philesius,
1482–1551

For anyone who knows anything about wine, it is impossible to think of Alsace without thinking of wine, for this rich area has an astonishing variety of wine grapes.

Alsatian wines, nonetheless, have been slow to become known elsewhere in France, or even on the other side of the Rhine. It used to be said that they did not travel well, but the main reason was that Alsatian wines are particularly dry, and sweeter wines were more in demand. Robert Browning noted, "You know that I love good wine. Well, I know some Alsatian wines that are not sweet, but which are nonetheless very agreeable."

Today, having finally obtained legal recognition of their rights and laws forbidding Alsatian wine to be bottled anywhere but in Alsace, the vintners are happy. The demand for Alsatian wine increases every year. In 1976, for example, sales in Germany rose 27 percent, and almost as much in Great Britain. So far as the Americans are concerned, they will bear watching. Americans do things in a big way and, having taken a liking to Riesling and Gewürztraminer, they may buy not only the wines, but the vineyards as well.

There are three roads crossing Alsace from north to south. There is the plain road, which follows the Rhine; the wine route, clearly marked on the maps and easy to follow because of the directional signs on the road; and the cheese road (see page 43). Of the three, the middle road, the road of the wine and the slopes, is incontestably the most precious; indeed it is almost sacred.

The History of Grape-Growing in Alsace

The wine of Alsace, although it may appear to be of relatively recent

development, has ancient origins. Recent archeological research tells us that grapes were growing in Alsace during prehistoric times, several thousand years before the Christian era. These grapes grew wild, and their juice was used as a form of nourishment by local inhabitants and by wandering tribes.

It may be that these wild grapes grew simply by chance in the Rhine plain, or they may have been brought by one or another of the innumerable peoples who drifted into the area from the East—from the Hungarian plains or from much further away, from the plateaux of Mongolia. It is not known for certain.

The ancient Gauls were familiar with the lambrusque grape, or Lambrusco wine, another species of wild grape which was smaller and less sweet. They fermented the juice of these grapes, but they did not know how to cultivate the grapes or how to preserve the wine.

When Gaul was invaded by the soldiers of Rome, grapes were under cultivation only in the extreme south of the country, in the area of Narbonne. The Romans maintained particularly large garrisons in Alsace along the Rhine to protect the northern boundaries of the Empire against the German tribes. The patricians and officers of these garrisons were fond of wine, and wine was supplied to them by wagons carrying amphoras, or jugs. Such supply trains were of long duration, difficult to move, and often fell victim to marauding Gauls. Specialists from Narbonne were then imported to teach the local populace how to cultivate and care for the lambrusque vines.

When the Roman Empire in the west fell to barbarian invasions in the fifth century, the wines of Alsace were already of some repute. Their fame was spread thereafter by religious communities. In 509, St. Gregory of Tours was already singing the praises of the wines of Marlenheim.

A Thousand Years of Commercial Expansion

For a thousand years, through alternating periods of war and peace, invasions and cultural development, misery for many and comfort for a few, Alsace developed and worked its vineyards.

We know comparatively little about the medieval period, but contemporary sources reveal the existence, beginning in the late Middle Ages, of ordinary vines *(hunische weine)* and noble vines *(edel weine)*. White wines dominated the market, but red wines were even then of considerable importance. There was a major motivation for the Alsatians to make their wines: there was a market for them. The exportation of these wines began in the late medieval period, and reached its peak in the fifteenth and sixteenth centuries.

When the Roman Empire fell, there was a halt to the free circulation of thousands of products throughout the Empire, from Asia Minor and Africa to Rome and even to Britain. The international economy of the Empire was replaced by a local economy, with each region of Europe attempting, of necessity, to become self-sufficient. The commercial spirit of the ancients did not regain its vigor until the rise of the cities of Europe.

Before that, vintners owed whatever prosperity they enjoyed to the Church. Certain monasteries were located in regions where there were no grapes, and yet wine was indispensable to the celebration of the mass. Also the priests and monks were not ignorant of the qualities of wine, and they were fond of it. Monasteries began buying vineyards in Alsace. Among these were the vineyards of Fulda in Franconia; Saint Gall in Switzerland; Etival in Lorraine; Reims and Saint Denis in France. The grape-growing monks hauled their wines in barrels by wagon to their mother-houses. And the latter, sometimes, redistributed them among their dependent monasteries.

From a commercial standpoint, Alsace occupies an advantageous geographic situation. By virtue of the Rhine Valley, she is the link between the north and south of Western Europe. Throughout the Middle Ages, pilgrims traveling to and from Rome, from the Netherlands and Scandanavia, carried the fame of Alsatian wines throughout Europe.

The commercial routes followed by the wines of Alsace were diverse. Beginning in the time of Charlemagne, the Swiss were the traditional buyers. Despite competition from local French and Italian wines, the Colmar region was the supplier for the important market centering on Basel, Zurich, Lucerne, and Berne. The northern vineyards around Strasbourg sold their produce in southern Germany, toward Ratisbon, Nuremberg, Breslau, and even in Vienna and Prague in central Europe. Some bills of lading for Alsatian wine have been found in Poland, at Kraków! This is indisputable proof of a quality of wine that was able to withstand competition from Austrian and Hungarian vineyards, even on their own home territory.

Most of the wine of Alsace was exported northward, by means of barges on the Rhine. Frankfort, the transportation center of the area, re-exported barrels of wine to Leipzig and Hamburg. Cologne also re-exported it, to the Netherlands and to England. The English knew it as Sussay or Osaye wine.

There were even times when the cities of the Hanseatic League, such as Lubeck, bought large quantities of Alsatian wines for export to the Baltic countries: Denmark, Sweden, Latvia, and Lithuania. There exists a letter, written in 1416, from a Latvian baron to a friend in Prussia: "I have just had the best dinner of my life, washed down with that wine of Elsatz that I had ordered at Lubeck and that I recommend to you because there is no other wine I know of that goes so well with roasts, ragouts, and game!"

Another important customer of Alsace's vintners was the neighboring duchy of Lorraine. The duke and his court at Nancy, the noble families of the

slopes of the Moselle, of Barrois and the Meuse, the abbeys and monasteries, ordered numerous casks of wine, especially from Ammerschwihr and Kayserberg. These were delivered over the hills of Bonhomme, Saint Amarin, and Saverne and reached as far as Brabant and Luxemburg.

At the beginning of the fifteenth century, it is estimated that a yearly total of 15 to 26 million gallons (58,000 to 100,000 hectoliters) of Alsatian wines were exported; that is, were sent across the Vosges and the Rhine. The people of the slopes prospered accordingly. The corporations and the grape-growing middle class were taking on an increased importance. The living standards of the vintners was markedly superior to that of the farmers of the plain or of the mountain. The wine road had already distinguished itself by its prosperity.

Beginning in the sixteenth century, the botanical treatises, or *Kraüterbücher,* give us specific information on the various vines cultivated. Muscat appeard in 1552. But we know, by means of various municipal regulations, that excellent red, white, and gray Pinots were already being cultivated in Alsace. The vintners also continued to devote important vineyards to ordinary grapes, the *heunisch.*

The Black Years

The prosperity of Alsace and its vineyards continued until the eve of the Thirty Years' War, in 1618.

Then came the apocalypse. As in Lorraine and other Rhine regions devastated by the passage of armies, many villages and hamlets were wiped from the face of the earth. Alsace was deprived of its population and of its vigor. The little town of Ammerschwihr, for instance, in the heart of the grape-growing country, had a population of 1,300 at the beginning of the war. By 1637, there were barely 200 people left. More than a thousand had died between 1633 and 1637.

As a consequence of this wholesale depopulation, the cultivation of the vineyards was virtually abandoned. In 1631 in the Ribeauvillé vicinity, another important vineyard region, half of the cultivated land had been abandoned. Wine production dropped to almost nothing. The formerly opulent vineyards of Riquewihr sold only about 40 measures of wine (about 2000 liters) between 1636 and 1645.

For all practical purposes, the export of wine ceased altogether. Neither the roads nor the rivers were safe. The wagons were often confiscated and their drivers imprisoned or forcibly recruited. The same held true for barges along the Rhine.

The Peace of Munster, in 1648, arbitrarily gave Alsace back to the French crown. It was a sad gift, for the province was desolate and in ruins. It was not long before the vineyards had been reestablished. But Holland was still at war with France, and this prevented exports to the North; for, before the war, the merchants of Batavia had been the pipeline through which wine flowed from Alsace into Scandinavia. The English market was closed for the same reason. As for the former buyers of Alsatian wine in Lorraine and Germany, they had their own demographic and economic wounds to lick.

The Anarchy of the Eighteenth Century

Fortunately Switzerland remained a faithful customer. In 1725, the Colmar vintners exported a total of 30,576 measures of wine, half of which was destined for the towns of the federated cantons.

Southern Germany also was beginning to drink Alsatian wine again. By wagon and boat, it made its way toward Swabia, Bavaria, and Austria. The barges of the Rhine began once more to carry casks to Frankfort and Cologne. But commerce in the north, in the Baltic, remained impossible, as did trade with Holland. On August 18, 1722, a royal edict forbad Hollanders to buy wood for construction in Alsace. In retaliation, Holland blocked all imports of wine from France.

Alsace was now paying the price for its attachment to France. This was especially true as of 1748, when the new tariff-war policy was implemented. At that time, the wines of Alsace—one of the principal sources of income for the province and its natural resource of the future—were difficult to export. It is true that Lorraine, as a state of the Holy Roman Empire, and Luxembourg, were once more ordering wine from Kaysersberg, Ammerschwihr, and Turckheim; but it is equally true that it was impossible to export any wine toward the west. The fact was that Alsatian wines were too dry for the French palate; and France itself was saturated by the products of Champagne and Burgundy. These problems, however, were not immediately obvious to all Alsatians. Vine planting continued everywhere, even on the plain.

The archives of the period are surprising in that they attest to an astonishing development of variety in these vines. We find mention of Heunisch, Burger, Olber, several Klevners, Riesling and Traminer, and also of a Grostz Schlitzer which appears to have been a Chasselas. Süssling was also cultivated in several parts of the wine country.

In order to maintain some sense of order in this proliferation of grapes, many municipalities passed laws intended to promote the cultivation of noble

grapes to the detriment of the more common varieties. Among the many documents that have come down to us is a map of the Weinbach domain, at Kientzheim, which belonged to the Capuchin monks. The map was drawn in 1750 and contains information on the variety of grapes planted in a large vineyard:

3,000 plants of Gentil Rouge (Rottraminer)
2,000 plants of Rouge (Burgunder)
3,000 plants of Muscat
700 plants of Tokay (Grauklevner) and Chasselas
7,700 plants of Raeuschling

On January 16, 1731, an order from the Council of State, ratified by the king, prohibited any new planting of vines. It was the intention of France to reserve the plain for the planting of grain. The anarchic proliferation of vineyards had also had a disasterous effect on the forest of the middle slopes of the Vosges, above the belt of traditional vineyards. The forests were being seriously damaged by uncontrolled use of chestnut vine-props. Moreover, the wines from the plain, which were of inferior quality, were hurting the reputation and the sales of the better wines of the slopes.

The provisions of the order, however, were not complied with by everyone. In 1766, we find the law being strengthened, and mandating a fine of 3,000 livres for violators. It was now specified that the prohibition against planting any new vines applied to the whole of Alsace.

At this point, the vintners of the slopes became alarmed. Their vineyards had never fully recovered from the calamities of the Thirty Years' War. Some of the former vineyards were still meadows and chestnut groves, and the vintners were eager to reclaim these lands for grape-growing. Moreover, the villages were being suffocated within their walls. It was expedient to begin building beyond the walls, to build larger granges and stables, to dig larger cellars to accommodate new kinds of wine. But, in order to do that, it was necessary to reclaim some of the fallow land of the slopes.

The problems of the traditional vintners must be distinguished from those of the new planters on the plain. This was especially true in that, despite prohibitions and laws, the vineyards on the plain continued to flourish. Then, several years of overproduction were followed by a drastic fall in prices.

The Nineteenth Century: Stagnation and Crisis

Paradoxically, the uncontrolled and illegal development of vineyards on the

plain was responsible for the prosperity of the first decade of the nineteenth century in Alsace.

In 1803, the annual report of the Haut-Rhin (Upper Rhine) Department concluded regretfully that vineyards of the plain were developing to the detriment of wheat production in the area. It listed in great detail all the varieties of vines in the areas of Strasbourg, Marlenheim, Obernai: the ordinary white grape; another white grape christened Oberlander; Olber; Thalburger; Pinot Gris (or gray grape); Riesling; a black grape of good quality; Edelrother; Farbtrauben (a black grape); white Muscat and black Muscat; Chasselas; red Chasselas (Süssling); greater and lesser Rischling; Grauklevner (a gray grape); white Gentil (Grünedel); Rotklevner (a red grape); white and red Frauentrauben.

This seems to be an enormous variety but, in reality, some of these varieties were cultivated only on small plots of land. In 1833, the annual report listed only the following: Thalburger; white and red Gentil; white and red Chasselas; Riesling; Pinot Gris; the Muscats; the two Rischlings; and the Frauentraubens.

In 1808, the vineyards of Alsace covered 58,800 acres (23,000 hectares); in 1822, 72,000 acres (29,390 hectares); and, in 1828, 74,000 acres (30,000 hectares).

In 1812, a great year for wines, the environs of Colmar produced 76.6 million gallons (290,000 hectoliters) of wine, of which 30.6 million gallons (116,000 hectoliters) were exported to faithful customers such as Switzerland, Baden, Wurtemberg, Bavaria, and other regions of Central Germany. Prosperity had come, and the price of wine stabilized at what was then between 15 to 20 francs per hectoliter. It did not hurt that the Napoleonic armies—and later, the armies of the Allies—drank a great deal of wine as they swept across Alsace.

In 1815, however, it became obvious that the market was dropping. The fall of Napoleon had much to do with this phenomenon. So did the appearance, even in Alsace, of a formidable competitor: beer. More and more, one began to see beer on Alsatian tables, accompanying certain traditional dishes such as sauerkraut. It was also drunk in the coffeehouses; and, in a few years, the production of beer increased tenfold. Finally, under the Restoration, severe tariff laws were passed in order to protect France's economy, with consequences that proved to be serious for Alsatians.

In 1821, Paris increased the tariff on imported wines. What would become of Alsace if the Grand Duchy of Baden, for example, retaliated in a kind? For, with the exception of Napoleon's soldiers, Frenchmen still did not drink Alsatian wines, and any market for these products lay beyond France's borders.

On July 27, 1822, still with the intention of protecting French products, the government increased the tariff on livestock imported from abroad. As it

happened, the largest exporters of cattle to France were also the best customers for Alsatian wines. Switzerland and the German principalities retaliated by increasing their own import tariffs on French wines. It was a catastrophe. At the time of the grape harvest of 1828, the wines of 1825 still had not been sold. There was so much wine on hand that there was no place to store it. At Ammerschwihr, one of the most important producers of Alsatian wine, a vintner who had sold 1.3 million gallons (5,000 hectoliters) in 1810 could, only with great difficulty, sell 760 thousand gallons (2,950 hectoliters) in 1824. Orders from Switzerland, always Alsace's most faithful customer, arrived only rarely now, and by 1850 they had ceased altogether.

Under the Second Empire, the situation remained the same, and even got worse. Alsace was invaded by wines of middling quality from the south of France. The governmental fees for shipping Alsatian wines to the interior of France were fixed at 70 francs per hectoliter in 1864. They were subsequently lowered to 35 francs, but without any notable improvement in the situation. This was still too expensive, even for quality wines, since foreign wines imported into France had to pay only 25 centimes per hectoliter. Germany had turned her back on Alsatian wine. The Swiss ignored them completely. All markets were blocked. The more enterprising vintners, so as not to be limited wholly to local markets, began growing grapes with some success in the neighboring regions of Lorraine and Franche-Comté.

These rare successes could not hide the disastrous condition of the Alsatian wine industry. Prices, which had gone down to 5 francs, and even to 3 francs per hectoliter in 1825, did not rise. Many vintners on the slopes gave up their vineyards. Alsace no longer believed in its own wines.

Sixty Years of Annexation

The annexation of Alsace in 1870, in the wake of the Franco-Prussian War, gave hope once more to the vintners of the province. Alsace was now part of the domains of Wilhelm I, Emperor of the Germans. Now, perhaps, there would once more be a German market for Alsatian wines. By then however Germans had lost their taste for the wines of Alsace. Their own, from the Rhineland, were perfectly adequate for them. And of course the Germans drank a great deal of beer. It was only with great difficulty that Alsace was able to sell between 39.6 and 44.9 million gallons (150,000 and 170,000 hectoliters) a year of her wine in Germany.

In 1880, to make matters worse, the most serious crisis in the history of Alsatian wine-making got under way. Bad year followed bad year, and there

seemed to be no end in sight. But the worse was yet to come. Beginning in 1893, vineyards—which still comprised an area of 60,000 acres (24,835 hectares)—were infected by a variety of blights. Mildew, oidium, peronospora, phylloxera, and cochylis attacked the vines, infesting them and causing enormous damage. (We still do not know how to fight effectively against these scourges.)

But the vintners were not willing to lay down and die. Instead they organized. A specialist in vine cultivation, Charles Oberlin established a Viticultural Institute at Colmar. With the help of a number of vintners, he experimented with crossing Alsatian vines with those of other European vineyards which were capable of resisting these mysterious diseases. To some extent, Oberlin was successful, but his success was qualified by the fact that the wines produced from these vines were of inferior quality. Another specialist, Paul Grenier, conscious of the risks involved with hybrids, attempted to graft vines, immune to phylloxera, onto the old local vines.

When World War I broke out in 1914, the vineyards were in deplorable condition and the experts were still fighting among themselves as to the best way to save them.

French Once More

In 1918, when the young grape-growers were demobilized from the German army and returned to Alsace, they found a deplorable situation. The vineyards were ravaged. Only certain hybrids created by Oberlin were resistant to disease, especially a red hybrid, known as Oberlin 595.

For a while it seemed that some progress was being made, but by 1921 everything seemed to be falling apart again. The Oberlin 595 vines produced only a mediocre wine that was unable to compete with the red wines from the south of France; that is, from the area known to the ancients as Narbonne, with which the vintners of Alsace had had some contact in Roman Times. On the other hand, the old vines, when grafted in accordance with the methods developed by Paul Grenier, were healthy and supplied an excellent wine, with the old Alsatian taste.

From then on, the situation improved steadily. In 1925, the Vintners Association decided to reconstitute the vineyards by means of grafted vines. Thus the old vines were reestablished, and, in order to compete in the marketplace with the other wine-growing regions of France, it was decided to reduce the number of varieties of wine.

Starting in 1925 Sylvaner, Gutedel, and the different kinds of Chasselas took up two-thirds of the vineyards. The remaining one-third was planted

with "noble" grapes: Riesling, Muscat, Pinot, and Traminer. Certain villages also cultivated Pinot Gris and Knipperlé grapes.

Having resolved the problem of production, Alsace now had to take on the problem of finding a market for its wines. Beginning in 1920, villages began to set up their own grape-growing syndicates. Alsatians living and working elsewhere in France began to promote the wine of their native province by word of mouth, in an effort to excite the interest of Frenchmen.

In 1922, Ammerschwihr inaugurated its Wine Market. Colmar, where such a market had been under discussion since 1904, had to wait until the end of World War II before actually realizing its dream. The first Regional Market for Alsatian wines was formally opened on June 1, 1948, by Pierre Pfimlin, mayor of Strasbourg and later minister of agriculture.

This annual event quickly became a success. Today it is the financial and commercial focus of the Alsatian wine industry and it brings to Colmar, in addition to buyers from all nations, large numbers of tourists attracted to the wine-tastings and the various collorary festivals.

The Alsatian Wine Industry Today

Today the vineyards of Alsace appear to be stable with respect both to their extent and to the variety of wines produced. They prosper on soil that varies greatly according to location and to their situation on the upper and lower slopes. From Marlenheim in the north to Rouffach in the south, the soil runs the gamut from shale and sand to clay and limestone, each with its special virtues appropriate for the cultivation of this or that variety of grape. Thus Turckheim, which has sandstone slopes, produces a Pinot Noir known as Turk's Blood *(Sang des Turcs)* in commemoration of the exploits of some local lord at the time of the Crusades.

The Alsatian wine industry comprises 25,880 planted acres (10,400 hectares), all qualified as Appellation Contrôlées although the industry has been a member of the Institut National des Appellations d'Origine (National Institute of Name Brands) only since 1962. The vineyards stretch from north to south for a length of about 60 miles (100 kilometers) and a maximum width of 2½ miles (4 kilometers); from Marlenheim, to the west of Strasbourg, to Thann in the south. There is also a small enclave at Cleebourg, to the south of Wissembourg, in the southern part of the Bas-Rhin, which is all that remains of a very old vineyard that has now virtually disappeared.

The grape-growing country consists of 7,500 growers, of which only 1,000 grow grapes exclusively. These are essentially family businesses, a structure which ensures the maintenance of quality by meticulous and

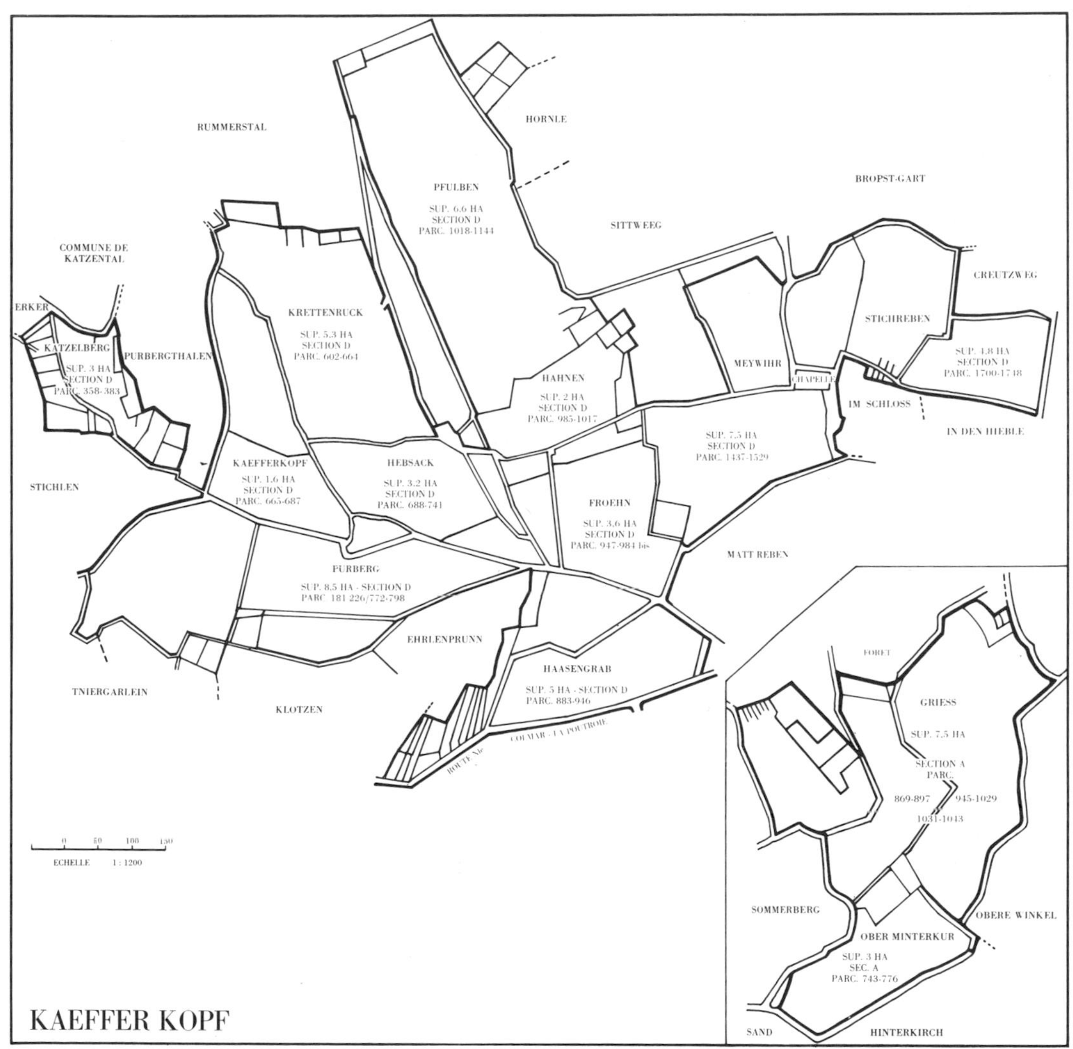

Example of an official map of an "exceptional vineyard." The wines produced by this vineyard are authorized to bear the supplementary name of *Kaefferkopf*. Ammerschwihr is in the middle of the map.

regular work, both in the vineyards and in the storage areas. There are no cooperatives and no bureaucratic network to stiffle these family enterprises. There are only old friends collaborating at all levels in the use of tractors and the sharing of markets. The results are proof that this system works: an average production of 211 million gallons (800,000 hectoliters), three-fourths of which is sold in France (partly for export to other countries). In the past twenty years, Alsatian wines have succeeded in being adopted in a dozen new markets including Portugal and Greece, both of which are themselves major wine-producing countries.

In relation to overall production of wines in France, Alsace accounts for 10 percent of the Appellations Contrôlées. Alsatian wines make up 40 percent of the white wine sold for use in homes in the domestic market, and 80 percent of the white wine sold in bars, restaurants, and coffeehouses. And, in accordance with a law of 1972, bottling takes place only in Alsace, in its characteristic elongated bottle.

In order to keep up with the increasing demand for Alsatian wines, both in France and abroad, the Alsatian Vintners Association decided, with the approval of the authorities, to increase cultivation by almost 5,000 acres (2,000 hectares).

These new acres represented 20 percent of the total land then under cultivation. It was stipulated that the new vineyards must be within the territory which had the right to use a particular brand name. A first assemblage of 2,500 acres (1,000 hectares) was planted in 1974 and 1975. The rest is to be planted over a minimum of five years. It was also agreed that the new plantings must be of noble variety, with the intention of improving the quality of the wine. The planting of Chasselas is prohibited, in accordance with a law intended to enhance the noble varieties.

The Vines

The wines of Alsace are unique in France in that they are not sold under the name of their places of origin. Instead they carry the name of the vines that produced the grapes from which they were made.

Today the best known wine is Sylvaner, which accounts for 27 percent of production, and the most famous of which are those produced in the vineyards stretching toward Marlenheim.

Next is Chasselas, a white or pink grape, which comprises 17 percent of production.

Gewürztraminer (20 percent) stands apart gastronomically because it is

a fruity wine used especially as an apéritif or a dessert wine. Those of Mittelbergheim, Heiligenstein, and Barr are justly famous.

Next comes the lordly Riesling, accounting for 14 percent of production, the best of which comes from the area situated between Ammerschwihr and Ribeauvillé in a line between Mittelwihr, Riquewihr, Sigolsheim, Zellenberg, and Nunawihr.

The balance of production is divided among the Pinot Gris (commonly called Tokay d'Alsace), the Muscat, the Pinot Noir, and the Pinot Blanc.

With the exception of a few red and rosé wines (Chasselas rosé, Pinot Noir), all of the above are dry white wines.

The Zwicker (discontinued) and the Edelzwicker belong in a separate category since they are not pure wines, but an assemblage of different vines. They are of lesser quality and quite variable from year to year.

We should mention that, by way of exception, some Alsatian wines carry, along with the name of their respective vines, that of the slope of the place from which they come. In such cases, the quality of the ground in their places of origin explains their remarkable bouquet. This is the case, for instance, among some of the vintners in the "noble triangle" formed by Ammerschwihr, Riquewihr, and Turckheim, who market Kaefferkopf Riesling, Eichberg Gewürztraminer, Schoenenburg Riesling, or a Bebleheim wine produced on a certain slope and known as Sonnerglanz.

A Few Traditions That Have Survived

GOURMETTAGE

The wines of Alsace have their own selling traditions and have never been marketed in the same way as the wines of France, Italy, Spain, and Greece. The selling of wines in Alsace follows certain precisely defined rites, all hinging on a practice known as *gourmettage* which goes back to the Middle Ages. In the latter period, one did not buy and sell wine in a free market. The responsibility for such transactions rested with a *gourmet,* a connoisseur or expert, who served as intermediary between buyer and seller. Every town or village of Alsace had one or more gourmets, according to their size, who were appointed by the Municipal Council and held to a rigid accountability for all wine transactions.

There were benefits to be derived from such a system. It freed the vintners themselves from having to market their wine. They were able to devote themselves full time to their vineyards and their cellars. The gourmet was responsible for finding outlets for the vintners' products. He was often the owner of an inn or hostelry—which made it possible for him

psychologically to condition his customers, in the interest of a future transaction, while he lodged and fed them.

Part of the gourmet's duties was to find out how much wine a vintner had to sell from each vineyard, and to test the quality of the wine. All sale papers had to carry a description of the quantity of wine, price, name of buyer, and name of seller. These records are what make it possible for us today to know the history of Alsatian vineyards in such detail. When a potential customer appeared on the scene—a Swiss, German, Frenchman, or a "city" Alsatian—the gourmet, or *weinsticher,* led him from cellar to cellar, tasting the various wines until a choice was made.

Obviously the gourmet's services were not provided free of charge. He received two kinds of fee. The *stichwein* was paid in kind and consisted of about 2 liters of wine for every 1,000 liters sold. This was paid by the seller. The *stichgeld,* paid in currency, depended on the time and place of the sale. In the Colmar region, at the beginning of the eighteenth century, for instance, the fee was 13 sols and 4 deniers for every transaction, one-third of which was paid by the buyer and the balance by the seller.

The role of the gourmet was over as soon as the buyer had made his choice and given his order. At that point, other municipal officers came upon the scene.

The cask-inspector *(tonnelier-juré),* ensured that the wine casks sold were not damaged. If necessary, he also reinforced the casks to make sure that they remained intact during shipment. He handled the gague, or dip-rod, if it was necessary to transfer the wine from one cask to another of smaller capacity.

The wine-porters *(porteurs de vin* or *leiterer),* as their name implies, carried the wine casks on their backs to the wagons. The latter were either brought by the buyer or rented by him with drivers. Each wagon could transport several casks with an average capacity of 600 liters each.

The tenders *(tendeurs* or *spanner)* were responsible for insuring that the casks rested on straw in the wagons, to absorb the bumps from the rough roads, and that they were solidly anchored with ropes or chains.

THE CONFRATERNITY OF SAINT STEPHEN

Two or three centuries ago, throughout Alsace, there were a large number of societies of prominent citizens, especially in the grape-growing villages. Only one has survived: the *Confrérie die Saint-Étienne* (Confraternity of Saint Stephen), which has become a sort of gourmet society.

In 1561, a municipal law of Ammerschwihr legalized the *Herrenstuben-gesellschaft,* or Society of Prominent Citizens. In 1780, Ammerschwihr's Society of Prominent Citizens became the Confraternity of Saint Stephen. Its annual banquet was held on the day after Christmas—the feast of Saint Stephen.

ALSACE
APPELLATION ALSACE CONTROLÉE

Gewurztraminer
1964

CONFRÉRIE ST-ETIENNE ✶ ALSACE
au Château de Kientzheim (Ht-Rhin)
Oenothèque No 37 G 1964

The first article of the Confraternity's bylaws was: "No one shall be allowed to become a member of the Confraternity of Saint Stephen unless he loves good fellowship, good food, and the wine of Alsace."

The grand master and the permanent membership chairman were in charge of supervising the tests imposed on those seeking membership. First there was an ordinary wine test, in which the applicant was expected to be able to distinguish and identify ordinary wine, semifine wine, and fine wine. If successful, he was admitted to the Confraternity as a Brother Apprentice. The apprenticeship lasted at least one year.

The next step conferred the title Brother Companion, and required that the candidate distinguish among the four noble wines: Riesling, Gewürztraminer, Pinot Gris, and Muscat.

Then, after one year, the candidate for the title of Master could ask to take the final test, in which he had to recognize and identify any Alsatian wine and to distinguish all the Alsatian vine stocks.

The members of the Grand Council had the privilege of wearing a red cape, striped with blue, red, or green according to their rank. The ordinary members could wear only a red, blue, or green ribbon. The Grand Council members, moreover, wore a black three-cornered hat.

The Confraternity fell into abeyance in 1848. It was revived in 1941 however and, in 1947 at Ammerschwihr, was "restored to its ancient rights and privileges." Its headquarters were originally at Colmar, but in 1977 they were transferred to a restored chateau at Kientzheim, where there is a museum devoted to the vineyards and wines of Alsace.

After almost a century of sleep, the new Confraternity has found new vigor in keeping with the prosperity of the Alsatian vineyards. Every year it organizes various ceremonies and festivities: a general meeting, in the vineyards, on the third Saturday of June; an executive meeting of the two Councils in the chateau at Kientzheim; an official wine tasting of the wines of the preceding year; wine tastings to honor distinguished visitors and "true friends of the wines of Alsace."

The Confraternity of Saint Stephen has become a recognized jury with respect to the quality of Alsatian wines and, by extension, of Alsatian cuisine. The Confraternity created, in 1957, the *sigille* (seal), a highly prized distinction awarded each year to the best wines of the preceding year. The *sigille* is awarded in the course of the official wine tasting ceremony. The winners are allowed to display a gold ribbon on the bottle, the ends of which are attached to the bottle with the red seal of the Confraternity just beneath the label. This distinction is regarded as more desirable than any other, including medals awarded even at the Concours Agricole (Agriculture Competition) in Paris.

THE FIDDLERS FESTIVAL OF RIBEAUVILLÉ

If by chance or intention you should be at Ribeauvillé on the first day of September, you will be pleasantly surprised to discover that the wine is free! There is a Wine Fountain, set up in the public square in front of the Hotel de Ville, during the celebrations marking the Pfifferdaï, or Fiddlers Festival. This ceremony commemorates the time when, every year on September 1, the Alsatian guild of wandering musicians came to render homage to the lord of Ribeauvillé.

THE PISTOL WINE OF OBERNAI

In the sixteenth century, one of the Holy Roman Emperors—Ferdinand, or Maximilian II—visited Obernai. There was a reception at the town hall and a wine tasting with much praise for the wine. Suddenly the *stettmeister* (mayor) exclaimed:

"Your Majesty, this wine is good; but we have some even better wine that we're keeping for ourselves."

Everyone held their breath. But the Emperor only smiled, removed a pair of pistols from his belt, and held them out to the mayor.

"Here," he said. "Take these pistols. If ever you meet anyone with worse manners than yourself, I give you permission to shoot him."

It is not recorded whether the mayor ever had a chance to use his pistols, but ever since then the best wine of Obernai is known as "pistol wine."

From the Cellar to the Table

I have often gone down into the cellars in the period before Christmas when the new wine is being made. I've tasted wine after wine during fermentation, and I've observed the serious looks and the satisfied smiles of my vintner friends. I know therefore that for an Alsatian the making of wine is a serious business, and one to which he devotes all his care.

THE CELLAR SCHEDULE

The grapes are gathered at the end of September or the beginning of October. They are then trampled and pressed.

The grapes are then stocked in casks and the juice stands for twenty-four hours. The must deposits its sediment.

It is treated to prevent oxydation.

Then it is fermented.

The first drawing of the wine takes place in January. The lees or dregs of the wine are drained off (and often kept to distill and make an excellent and very disgestible alcohol). The wine is then filtered to remove any impurities.

It is bottled in the spring. It is then ready to be drunk.

THE BOTTLE

The famous Alsatian bottle, slender and long-necked, is known locally as *la flûte* (the flute). It was officially recognized in 1930, by a decree.

THE GLASS

The Oeuvre Notre-Dame museum at Strasbourg exhibits among its masterpieces a painting by Stoskopff (1597–1657) entitled "Basket and Glasses," which testifies as to the ancient use of wine glasses designed specifically for Alsatian wines.

The form of these glasses appears to have been developed by small crystal-makers, at the request of members of the higher clergy (particularly the clergy of Worms). And in fact these glasses do serve to display the limpid purity and absolute transparency of the wines of Alsace.

During the centuries following, each noble family, every bishop or abbot, wanted a service of wine glasses personalized with his own coat-of-arms. During the nineteenth century the great merchant princes

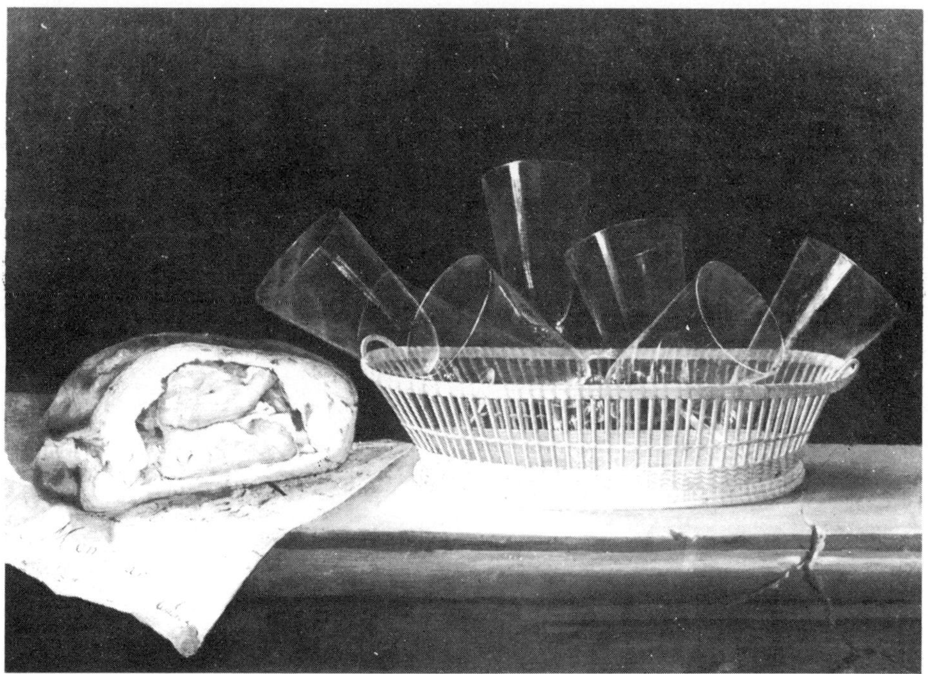

Basket and Glasses. Stoskopff, Musée des Beaux-Arts, Strasbourg. Photograph by Giraudon.

ordered such services etched with their initials, and the four major crystal-makers of France and those of Bohemia continue to make services of this kind.

All of the great crystal-makers of Europe include glasses for Alsatian wines in their services.

How to Serve Alsatian Wines

Alsatian wines generally are white and dry; as such, they take their place in the order of dinner wines. Nonetheless some of them have certain peculiarities which it is well to know.

Sylvaner is appropriate for the whole meal, and especially for the hors d'oeuvre, for sausages, and for shellfish.

Pinot Gris is essentially an apéritif, for appetizers, for chicken with sauce, for pork, and for game.

Muscat is an apéritif and for between meals.

Edelzwicker may be served throughout the meal, but it should not be served with red meats or game, or with elaborate dishes. It is a very thirst-slaking wine that may be drunk throughout the day.

Riesling, true lord of Alsatian wines, may very well be served throughout a meal, from the beginning to the end. It goes marvelously well with oysters and other seafood. A really fine Riesling goes perfectly with a foie gras. The only time not to serve it is with a dish that was prepared with another wine.

Pinot Noir is particularly valuable for enhancing the taste of red meat or game.

Gewürztraminer has an exceptionally fruity flavor and poses a very delicate problem. It is a wine for between meals, and also a good dessert wine. It also goes well with cheese. But it has been discovered to be a perfect companion for foie gras and serves to emphasize the flavor of the foie gras. Foie gras usually is eaten at the beginning of a meal, and it is impossible, because of the Gewürztraminer's bouquet, to use other Alsatian wines—white and dry as they are—for the remainder of the meal. What should one do?

Recently someone in Alsace arrived at a solution. The foie gras, with Gewürztraminer, was served at the *end* of the meal, immediately before the dessert. It was a veritable revolution, and some of the excitement generated has not quite subsided yet. For the diner from the interior of France—who is perhaps too attached to the old way of doing things—the problem remains.

In any event, there is one inflexible rule: in order for the bouquet of the Gewürztraminer to develop fully, it must be drunk cold, very cold: between 46° to 50°F (8° to 10°C). Finally, you should avoid exposing it to widely varying temperatures. Keep it in a cool cellar and put it into the refrigerator several hours before serving. Carry it to the table only at the moment that you are about to pour it.

The wines served at an Alsatian meal—depending on the food—are typically as follows: Muscat, Sylvaner, Pinot Gris, Riesling, Pinot Noir, and Gewürztraminer.

Quality of Alsatian Wines since 1945

1945	Good year
1946	Average year
1947	Very great year
1948	Good year
1949	Good year
1950	Good year

1951	Mediocre year
1952	Good year, well rounded wine
1953	Very good year
1954	Good year, wine with character
1955	Very good year
1956	Average year
1957	Good year
1958	Relatively good year
1959	Excellent year
1960	Good year
1961	Great year
1962	Good year
1963	Mediocre year
1964	Great year
1965	Passable year
1966	Good year
1967	Good year, fruity wine
1968	Average year, light wine
1969	Very good year
1970	Average year
1971	Exceptional year
1972	Passable year
1973	Good year
1974	Average year
1975	Average year
1976	Good year
1977	Average year
1978	Good year
1979	Good year
1980	Good year

I love this wine that one drinks almost without knowing it, but which leaves its incomparable bouquet in one's mouth just as a fine poem leaves a dream in one's heart.

Paul Valéry

EAUX-DE-VIE AND LIQUEURS

Give me another glass
Of that Alsatian Kirsch,
Of that clear water from the slopes
Which inebriates the body
and gladdens the soul.
Heinrich Heine

Of all the regions of France, Alsace is incontestably the richest and most diverse with respect to its *eaux-de-vie* and liqueurs. This is because of the richness of its orchards and the extraordinary variety of wild fruits and berries that can be picked on the slopes of the Vosges.

The Origins

Alsatians have been making *eaux-de-vie* and liqueurs from time immemorial. The names of several Alsatian villages are derived from distilleries established there in the Middle Ages: Brennenhüttle, for instance, and Brennenbachlein (*brennen* means "to distill").

SPICED WINES
From the earliest Middle Ages, back to Carolignian times, Alsatians were drinking wine mixed with honey, the proportions varying according to the region. These sweetened wines, taken after meals, were first made in the monasteries and reserved for the use of the monks who made them. But very soon the ordinary people developed a taste for them and discovered how to improve both their flavor and their ability to keep. People were also fond of a before-dinner drink, and this is perhaps the origin of the actual apéritifs,

which are herb wines; that is, wines in which wild plants, carefully selected and picked on the prairies and in the underbrush, are soaked in the wine for a certain length of time.

It appears that this taste had been introduced into Alsace before the decline of the Roman Empire and the barbarian invasions, by the Roman legionnaires who had earlier served in Africa or in Asia Minor. There, they had developed a liking for very spicy food and drink.

During the Renaissance the taste for spiced wines, or *würzweine,* spread. These wines were prepared from the best grapes and were steeped with established proportions of sugar, nutmeg, cinnamon, and other "foreign" and odiferous plants. Spiced wines, for which every large town had its own recipe, were not imbibed daily, but were kept for religious or municipal holidays and for family occasions. They were then served at the end of a meal, as digéstifs, or as after-dinner wines.

Gradually over the centuries the spiced wines evolved into liqueurs. Today they are practically unknown.

In some of the villages of the grape-growing country some very ancient liqueur recipes are still preserved, and good housewives every year make a "family drink" by pouring several bottles of their best Pinot Noir or Muscat into a little barrel and letting it steep with certain local herbs and spices. The curious traveler may get further information from the pharmacists of the towns and villages along the wine route in Alsace. These practitioners often know the secret of the local spiced wine.

STRAW WINE (VINS DE PAILLE)

Today when someone says "straw wine," he is often thinking of certain delicious Arbois wines. But this ignores the fact that straw wine undoubtedly originated in Alsace. In the seventeenth century, and still more in the eighteenth century, Alsace was exporting straw wine to France and as far away as Russia. In Paris and Moscow, it had a place on the tables of kings, princes, and emperors.

Alsatian straw wine, or *strohwein,* was a white wine made from grapes that were dried on straw mats until they became raisins. The resulting sweet, golden wine had to be aged eight to twelve years under very special conditions. It was then properly fermented and fit to drink. This wine was produced in the eighteenth century especially between Ammerschwihr and Ribeauvillé, and it was very expensive. As a wine, it may be classed somewhere between a dinner wine and a digéstif.

EAUX-DE-VIE

The family pratice of distilling alcohol developed during the Middle Ages and in the following centuries. Most family stills were set up on farms and in

houses near a stream or river, so that the water could be used as a coolant to condense the alcohol.

In Alsace, from the twelfth to the seventeenth centuries, these stills produced only "little" wines of small worth, along with brandy made from the lees of the wine and the skins of the crushed grapes. Sometimes the lees and the skins were mixed together and the product was called *drusenbrantwein*. But the best brandies came from the direct distillation of good-quality grapes.

The chief *valet de chambre* of King Louis XIV said that he "often prevented the king from getting a stomach ache, as a consequence of his robust appetite, by suggesting that he drink, in small doses, the fruit alcohols that Alsatians make so well."

From the sixteenth century onward, the reputation of Alsatian *eaux-de-vie* was such that it was difficult to keep up with the demand for it in all parts of Europe. The archives reveal how these shipments of *eaux-de-vie* were dispatched from Strasbourg and Colmar, where casks from all the valleys and slopes were stockpiled. In 1583 Strasbourg exported 530,000 gallons (2,057 hectoliters) of *eaux-de-vie*. The northern Germans, Dutch, and English at that time were particularly addicted to such liquors.

Exports of *eaux-de-vie,* like that of Alsatian wine, ceased almost completely at the beginning of the seventeenth century. Stocks were pillaged by roaming hordes of mercenary soldiers during the Thirty Years' War. And the plagues which beset Alsace at that time—the burning of towns and villages, the destruction of farms—put an end to over 90 percent of the stills. In the eighteenth century, royal decrees forbad any "making of *eau-de-vie* of corn or any other grain," and any distillation of fruits, which prevented any revival of Alsatian alcoholic drinks.

The making of *eaux-de-vie* did not develop again until the nineteenth century, with Kirsch taking the lead as the most popular by far. At that time, almost all skins of crushed grapes were distilled, and especially those of the Gewürztraminer grapes because they were more aromatic and more noble. This distilling was mostly a family affair. A small town such as Ammerschwihr had only 2,000 inhabitants at the time, but it had 180 stills!

Toward the end of his life Georg Cantor (1845–1918), the great German mathematician, regularly drank a small glass of Alsatian Kirsch after dinner. "It cleanses my mind to dream about equations."

Liqueurs and *Eaux-de-vie* Today

Eaux-de-vie or white brandies include Kirsch, Mirabelle, eau-de-vie de Marc, and others. These must not be confused with fruit-flavored liqueurs such as

raspberry, pear, and so on. They are totally different things. What they have in common is that they all contain alcohol, even though some of the liqueurs are more syrupy and sweeter.

Nonetheless both kinds may be designated as digéstifs since their role—except when used in cooking—is to facilitate digestion, especially of fatty foods, either during or after a meal (see the description of the Alsatian Hole on page 11).

In Alsace, most of the larger growers produce *eaux-de-vie* and, often, fruit liqueurs. The quality is always good, although somewhat uneven and specialized. The best and most consistent quality is achieved by some of the small private distilleries, such as that at Lapoutroie.

LIQUEURS

Alsatian liqueurs, which are generally prepared by steeping fruit in alcohol, often have an alcohol content of 60 percent. They must have at least 30 percent alcohol (60 proof).

They are extremely aromatic. Here are the most common liqueurs: strawberry, wild strawberry, plum, wild prune, huckleberry, raspberry, pear, black currant, apricot, quince, and—no doubt the most original of them all—fir-bud liqueur, which encloses in each bottle the impenetrable depths of the forests of the Vosges.

EAUX-DE-VIE

These are obtained by distilling fruit and catching each precious drop of the liquid that falls from the coil. *Eaux-de-vie* are clear, which differentiates them from liqueurs, which are always more or less colored, and from aged brandies, which are usually amber.

Legally, *eaux-de-vie* must have an alcohol content of about 50 percent (100 proof). Special products sometimes have a content of 60 percent, such as dog-rose brandy, commonly known as *gratte-cul* (fanny scraper).

The most digestible *eau-de-vie* is that of the lee, which was very popular until the beginning of the twentieth century. It is rarely made any longer; being only slightly perfumed, it proved to be almost unmarketable.

There is a large variety of Alsatian *eaux-de-vie*. Some of them are astonishing in their originality. Certainly you should taste them when an occasion is offered. Their aromas are far from the beaten path and they lack neither charm nor taste. Here are some of these possibilities: prune, pear, raspberry, wild raspberry, Alsatian purple plum, wild blue plum, Mirabelle plum, gentian, fir-bud, quince, strawberry, wild strawberry, dog-rose, elderberry, sorb, blackberry, wild prune, huckleberry, shadbush, holly, black currant, golden apple and—Kirsch, of course, which is made from wild cherries, mashed and distilled with their stones.

To this list we should add one of the most prestigious flowers of Alsatian *eaux-de-vie,* the *Marc de Gewürztraminer,* which is made from the husks of the crushed Gewürztraminer grapes. It is considered very salubrious and an effective aid to digestion.

Among the *eaux-de-vie,* the Mirabelle (yellow plum), and especially those from Lorraine, is that which most captures the perfume of fruit. Next comes the William Pear, which has been cultivated in Alsace for several decades now. The raspberry, grown in the upper valleys of the Vosges, produces a delicate, subtle, and very agreeable liquor. Its perfume, however, is less penetrating and less durable than that of the wild raspberry, which is gathered in forests at altitudes from 1,600 to 3,000 feet (500 to 900 meters). Plums flourish in Alsace, where they are very popular and produce excellent *eaux-de-vie.* In addition to the wild blue plum, which grows on slopes and which has all the savor of a free life, the Quetsche, a purple fruit with a strong perfume, also produces a very popular brandy. The most widely known *eau-de-vie,* however, is Kirsch.

Leaving aside commercially manufactured Kirsch, we may say that the accent in Alsatian Kirsch is on quality. Among the varieties available, we may mention the Lapoutroie Kirsch, which is distilled from Merises, half-wild black cherries which grow in a lovely valley running from Ammerschwihr and Kaysersberg toward the Bonhomme pass.

Elderberry and blackberry *eaux-de-vie* are useful in aiding digestion. And huckleberry boasts of two almost miraculous properties: it can cure certain intestinal disorders and soothe intestinal pain while reestablishing the internal flora of the intestine; and it is said to improve eyesight—particularly night-vision, "giving those who drink it the eyes of a cat."

The *eau-de-vie* of wild juniper berries sometimes leaves a rather surprising taste. That of the sorb and the shadbush are pleasant to the taste. And dog-rose is said to be a stimulant of the heart.

The *eaux-de-vie* exude a very particular bouquet. Holly is redolent of the stubble fields of the Vosges, and fir-bud gives off the scent of the great forest. Fir-bud *eau-de-vie* must be prepared carefully and often is cut with a neutral alcohol so as to lessen its strong resin aroma.

Alsatian distillers also produce bottles, sometimes of crystal, in which "a fruit" is preserved in its own alcohol; a William pear for instance, or a bunch of Gewürztraminer grapes. In such cases, the fruit is selected as soon as it begins to form. The bottle is placed over the fruit on the plant or tree, and the fruit grows and ripens inside the bottle. It is then plucked and the bottle is filled with alcohol made from the same kind of fruit. These "bottled" grapes or pears obviously are not made to be eaten, for this would necessitate breaking the bottle. Its purpose is essentially esthetic; that is, to stimulate our taste for the liquor. Whenever the bottle is empty, it has only to be filled again with the same *eau-de-vie.*

HOW TO SERVE *EAUX-DE-VIE*

Alsatian white brandies, more than any others, should be served very cool. It is suggested that you also cool the glass beforehand by putting a piece of ice into it and swirling the ice around until the glass is frosted. Then throw out the ice and pour in the *eau-de-vie*. Take small sips of the liquor, keeping it in your mouth for a fairly long time so as better to appreciate the bouquet.

During ceremonial dinners or family occasions, even in the best restaurants, Alsatians take advantage of the custom of the Alsatian Hole by sipping a very small quantity of *eau-de-vie*—usually Gewürztraminer—to help in digesting rather heavy or greasy dishes.

Pierre Gaertner has a very elegant way, and one that will appeal to gourmets, of making the Alsatian Hole. He serves the Gewürztraminer *eau-de-vie* as a sherbet (see page 264).

ALSATIAN BEER

There is no worthy poet without sane pleasure;
No sane pleasure without joyous cellars;
No enjoyment without good beer;
And no good beer except in Strasbourg!
Novalis

In medieval times, in both northern Alsace and in the Palatinate, it was a common practice for people to eat the tips of the stalks of a plant which the Germans called *hoppe.* It was usual, even in the Carolignian age, to aromatize the fermented juice of barley with the cones of this plant.

Beer originated in the Rhine valley and, probably, in northern Alsace. The term *bier,* as applied to this new drink, appeared in The Netherlands around 1435, and quickly spread to the Germanic and Anglo-Saxon countries. In France, it was gallicized into *bière.*

Alsatians fell into the habit of drinking beer as well as the good wines of their province, for outside of the villages of the grape-growing region the price of wine placed it beyond the reach of the peasants of the plain and the upper valleys of the Vosges. It would be misleading, however, to say that the common people drank beer in Alsace and that the nobility and the clergy drank wine. The monks, canons, bishops, barons, and knights loved beer just as much as the peasants did.

As late as the twelfth century, beer was brewed only on family properties or in convents and monasteries. Which is not to say that production was necessarily small; in 1160, the cathedral chapter of Strasbourg alone produced over 265,000 gallons (1,000 hectoliters).

The first professional brewery was founded in 1259 at Strasbourg, which then became the acknowledged capital of the industry. In the fourteenth century, there were eight brewers in the city. In 1723, with family production lessening, there were twenty-six; and by 1763, there were thirty-five.

The production of the professional brewers of Strasbourg totalled 11 million gallons (41,598 hectoliters) by 1769. Quality was strictly controlled. Any beer that did not contain the proper proportions of malt, water, hops,

and yeast was withdrawn from the market and thrown into the Rhine or the Ill.

In the period 1825–1828, there were sixty-three brewers at Strasbourg, twelve at Mulhouse, seven at Colmar, and ten at Saint-Marie-aux-Mines. There was stiff competition between Alsatian beer and Alsatian wine, with beer having the edge since it cost less than half as much. The peak of production was reached in 1829 when 37 million gallons (142,150 hectoliters) were brewed in the Bas-Rhin, and 10 million (38,975) in the Haut-Rhin.

Thereafter, production declined somewhat but began to increase once more toward the end of the nineteenth century. Since then, it has multiplied enormously, reaching 11 billion gallons (4,200,000 hectoliters) in 1964, and 14 billion (5,617,000) in 1970. Ninety percent of this beer is sold outside Alsace, and Alsatian beer is found the world over.

Beer, depending as it does on the cultivation of hops, was brewed and drunk more in lower Alsace than in upper Alsace. It is significant perhaps that the wine industry is much less important in the former area than in the latter. Although it remains above all a producer of wine, upper Alsace nonetheless has some very reputable breweries. Alsatian beer is popular not only in Alsace but also in the rest of France and—despite stiff competition—in foreign countries as well.

Strasbourg rivals Munich as the beer capital of the world, and among the great breweries to which Alsace owes its fame in this regard, are Meteor, Schutzenberger, Mutzig, and Kronenborg—to mention only a few.

Bottled in 75-cl (24-ounce) containers, the so-called table beer of Alsace has a low alcoholic content (around 40 percent) and is drunk with meals. Stronger beer (8 to 12 percent) is consumed at other times and is bottled in smaller containers—about 33 cl (12 ounces). Beer is also used in cooking, as in Beer Soup (page 118); and it is served with certain traditional dishes, such as sauerkraut.

Traditionally beer is drunk in steins in Alsace. The use of steins goes back to the Middle Ages when, as now, they were made of terra cotta, enameled and elaborately decorated. They also have lids, which are supposed to help the beer retain its flavor. Some of these mugs are preserved in our museums and bear the arms of celebrated religious communities, bishops, nobles, municipalities, and guilds. Such steins are still much preferred to glass mugs in Alsace, and visitors may see them in use in the cozy and welcoming *brasseries* of the province as they make their choice of beer from the thirty-or-so varieties available.

REGIONAL CHEESES

From the first centuries of the Christian era, the people of Alsace knew how to clabber milk, and they ate a great deal of uncured white cheese. They quickly learned also the secrets of herb or spiced cheese, using especially chives, chervil, mint, and cumin for such purposes.

This cheese was crude and easy to make, and along with black bread it was a staple food of the farmers when they were driven into the mountains to escape famine, epidemics, or invasions. They could have done much worse, for primitive as it may sound, this white cheese (fromage blanc) was identical to that made at present in all other dairy regions of Europe.

The second cheese to appear in Alsace seems to have been that known as *Fleuri*. It received its name in some of the villages of the upper slopes and on isolated mountain farms, because of the spots of mildew, or "flowers," which formed on its crust. Today it is known as Carré de l'Est.

Next came the greatest of them all, the Munster cheese. As early as the eighth century, Munster was made and used along the whole of the Alsatian Vosges. It even penetrated along the Vosges into Lorraine, where it was called Gérômé and later Gérardmer. Munster was, and remains, the specifically Alsatian cheese.

We have already pointed out that Alsace, from north to south, is crossed by three roads: the plain route, the wine route, and the cheese route. The cheese route, the highest of the three, twists and turns along the crests of the upper valleys at an altitude of between 1,900 and 3,000 feet (600 and 1000 meters). Along this road are the large farms where Munster Fermier (Farmer's Munster)—the best Munster—is made. The quality of Munster depends on the herbs used.

This route is considered to begin, to the north at Signal de Grendelbruch, to the east at Schirmeck and Donon, and runs southward to Hartmannswillerkopf, between Grand Ballon and Cernay. The route may be followed by automobile, along charming little forest roads, but it is suggested that you try it on foot during the summer and on skis during the winter.

What a joy it is then to sit in a huge rustic hall on crude wooden benches, before a monumental table spread with freshly-baked bread, a bottle of Pinot Noir, and a slab of fragrant Munster before you. These are the ideal surroundings for enjoying the tastiest cheese made anywhere.

Among the farms open year-round on the cheese route, we might mention the Lac Blanc Inn and the Trois Fours farm, opposite the Hohneck massif and the Frankenthal cliffs.

Carré de l'Est

This cheese is made in the whole of northeastern France, as well as in Alsace (the southern part of the Vosges massif). It is a square cheese, weighing about 6½ ounces (200 g) with a side of 3½ to 4 inches (9 to 10 cm). It is soft, slightly salted, uncooked, and unpressed. It develops its flavor between mid-September and mid-May, and is reminiscent of a good Camembert in flavor. In fact, it gives Camembert stiff competition.

This is a quality cheese. Today it is essentially an industrial product, but it is still made at home on many isolated farms. The best wines to drink with it are Gewürztraminer and Pinot Gris.

Munster

Munster was invented in the seventh century by monks who had established monasteries in the upper valleys of the Vosges. The name Munster—which appeared in the time of Charlemagne and designated the principal city of the region, at the foot of the Schlucht and the Hohneck where the cheese was produced—is said in fact to be a corruption of the word *monastere* (monastery).

Production of Munster cheese, however, did not remain long in the hands of the monks. In the eleventh century it was part of the diet of the peasants of the Alsatian slopes. There are fifteenth-century documents showing that wine occasionally was bartered for Munster cheese. And, at the same time, the cheese was being exported to Switzerland, Baden, Wurtemberg, and the Palatinate. In the sixteenth century, Munster cheese followed the same trade routes as Alsatian wine and was known and appreciated in the Low Countries, the cities of the Hanseatic League, and as far away as Sweden.

Munster is a soft, highly flavored cheese. It owes its particular bouquet to the milk of cows grazing on plants which grow in soil peculiar to the Vosges region. The cheese is uncooked and unpressed. The crust, red or ocre in color, is lightly washed and abounds in the microbiotic life which hastens the

ripening in depth of the cheese. The cheese then becomes creamy, mellow, and fragrant.

The finished Munster is round in shape, with a diameter ranging (according to the region in which it was made) from 6 to 8 inches (11 to 20 cm). The thickness is from 1 to 2 inches (3 to 5 cm).

The best season for Munster, say the connoiseurs, is from November to May. Even so, it remains tasty and fragrant throughout the summer. The best cheese comes from the upper Munster valley toward Hohneck, Schlucht Pass, and also from the Metzeral Valley and Orbey. Other good cheese is ripened in the Saint-Marie-aux-Mines Valley and in the Lapoutroie Valley which leads to the Bonhomme Pass.

For some time now, industrially produced Munster Laitier has been made from pasteurized milk. There is nothing wrong with it, except that it has little in common with the real Munster Fermier which is made from the famous milk of Vosgian cows grazing during the summer in stubble-fields at high altitudes. During the winter, the cows come down to their stables in the valleys.

Munster is considered to be one of France's great cheeses. It is eaten with white bread or sometimes with rye, but never in combination with butter, for the Munster is sufficiently rich of itself and the flavor of the butter lessens that of the cheese. Suitable wine to accompany this cheese is a fruity Gewürztraminer.

Cumin Munster

In the fifteenth century, at a time when Alsatians tended to make an exaggerated use of spices, many people developed a taste for Munster seasoned with cumin, or even with anise. This Cumin Munster is often asked for by visitors who come to Alsace. Cumin Munster cannot compare to real Munster, but, compared to the industrially produced Munster, it is certainly edible and even good. A good wine to go with this is Gewürztraminer.

Lorraine

The Alsatian monks who produced Munster made a gift of their product to religious communities in neighboring Lorraine, and particularly to the canonesses of the Chapter of Remiremont, who appreciated the gift so much that they adopted it as their everyday cheese.

The peasants of the west slope of the Vosges showed their appreciation to their Alsatian neighbors by sending them a Lorraine cheese, as they called it, which is actually a very large Munster, with a diameter of from 7½ to 10 inches (20 to 25 cm) and weighing from 4½ to 11 pounds (2 to 5 kg). It is a particularly mellow cheese.

PORK BUTCHERY

There is nothing more appetizing than the displays of Alsatian pork butchers which adorn the streets of towns and villages in the province. One hardly knows what to look at first: plain sausages and cumin sausages, pâtés enveloped in delicious crusts, saveloys. . . . One feels like a child in a candy store, wanting to sample everything.

For many connoisseurs, nothing is more representative of Alsatian gastronomy than the number and variety of its pork products. And yet the whole of France is rich in this respect. There is not a province, not a single little region, that does not have its own specialties, its hams smoked in this or that manner. Alsace however seems to be the heaven of pork addicts; it is a place invented to make everyone succumb to the sin of gluttony.

Apart from that dry, flat, almost hard sausage that is known as a *gendarme* (which naturally originated in Switzerland but has been adopted by Alsace), there is nothing actually very special about Alsatian pork except that spices are often used in preparing the saveloys, the large and small sausages, and the pâtés. Cumin, black pepper, and cinnamon are all used to give fragrances to these pork preparations.

Nonetheless there are certain regional specialties that should not be forgotten, such as the *knackwurst* of Strasbourg, a little sausage traditional to Strasbourg that is known the world over as the equal of *foie gras*. There is also the *mettwurst,* a sausage used in sandwiches and devoured by everyone from schoolchildren to workers in the vineyards and fields. In Alsace, the mettwurst takes the place of the usual snack composed of Camembert and a dry sausage.

Characteristic of the region also is the *waedele,* or liver sausage, which is succulent and aromatic. The waedele, the gendarme, mettwurst, and knackwurst are only a few of the fifty-or-so varieties of pork products that have been developed in the course of Alsatian history so that they may be available today to the discerning palate.

It would be unforgivable, in speaking of Alsatian pork, not to speak of the salting and smoking of hams, bacon (usually lean rather than fat), pork shoulders, knuckles, and so on. In some regions, bacon and knuckles are preferred salted; in others, semi-salted; and in still others, smoked. Generally speaking however all of these are used pretty much everywhere in the province.

The use of salted and smoked pork originated in the farms of the upper valleys which were, in past centuries, completely cut off from the outside world during the winter months. According to tradition, on the slopes fir is used for smoking pork and on the plain, cherry wood or wild cherry. The wood used gives a very special flavor to the meat which is left hanging—often for weeks—in the smoke.

We cannot close without mentioning Colmar sausage—so delicious with sauerkraut—and Thann sausages and blood sausages. These are only a few of the marvels to be discovered, little by little, as you gaze into the windows of the pork butchers of Alsace.

BREADS AND PASTRIES

To go for a walk in Alsace, in the humblest villages as well as in Strasbourg or Colmar, is to treat oneself to a fascinating display of half-timbered houses, carved wood, ornately sculptured stone and, from spring to fall, masses of flowers cascading from balconies, lighting up the façades of buildings and brightening entire towns. It is also an opportunity to stand in ecstasy before the shop windows of the bakeries.

Alsatian bakery products are astonishingly opulent and varied. There are literally dozens of kinds of breads in every shape and of every fragrance: cinnamon, cumin, almond, and so on. There is milk bread, rye bread, white bread, and so forth. But it is especially in the area of the sweet or breakfast rolls that Alsatian baking distinguishes itself—so much so that in 1977, for instance, fully 10 percent of the rolls produced were exported to Germany and Switzerland. The richness and variety of Alsatian baking is illustrated particularly in the confection of these rolls, which are showcases for the use of spices of which Alsatian bakers are past masters.

Most of these varieties of rolls date back several centuries, usually to a village celebrating a particular holiday; from there it spread to the rest of the province.

In Alsace, in addition to religious festivals, the feast day of a village's patron saint has always been an occasion for celebration. On such occasions, the local baker was much in demand; even today he is overwhelmed with work as the feast day approaches. He must work day and night for a week before the great day so as to stock the shop adequately. On the feast day itself, his business doubles and triples. Everyone eats and drinks in astonishing quantities. His regular customers—families, mostly—order kougelhopfs, cherry and huckleberry tarts, pies, and hot pastries of every kind; the baker's oven is never empty.

Today as in the past in certain villages the baker's customers bring him milk, butter, and eggs from their own farms and *eau-de-vie* from their own cellars. They also provide a kougelhopf mold. The baker provides the rest: flour, sugar, raisins, almonds, and yeast. This was an almost universal practice until World War II.

New Year's Bread

In accordance with a very old Alsatian custom, on New Year's Day children went to wish a Happy New Year to their close relatives: uncles, aunts, cousins, godfather, and godmother. They would bring a brioche-shaped bread called a *Neyjohrweka,* or New Year's Bread. The children in turn were given some *Beerawecka* (page 219), along with a small glass of nut or currant liqueur; or, if the children were older, they had a small glass of *schnaps.*

This custom continued to be observed until World War II. Even today it continues in many villages of upper Alsace and along the wine route.

Saint Agatha's Bread

The feast of Saint Agatha, the patron saint of bread bakers, is on February 5. On that occasion, every family in the village bought (and still buys, where the custom is still observed) a Saint Agatha's Bread: a round loaf weighing 1 or 2 pounds (500 g or 1 kg). The bread had to be bought early in the morning, because the children took it to Mass with them at 7 A.M. and placed it on the altar of the Virgin.

After Mass, the pastor recited a prayer to Saint Agatha and blessed the bread with holy water. The children then reclaimed their breads, which were still hot and fragrant, and hurried home to enjoy a piece of it before leaving for school.

Every member of the family ate a piece of the bread during the day. The domestic animals were also given a piece, and this was supposed to ensure prosperity, an abundance of food, and peace for the village, the region, and the whole of the province.

Lenten Onions

After the First World War, Alsace, and especially Catholic Alsace, enjoyed a revival of faith. During Lent, the laws of fasting and abstinence from meat were observed by most families.

On Ash Wednesday after the joys of carnival and every Friday until Easter, lunch consisted generally of a bean soup and an Onion Tart (page 96).

The poorer families brought their onions already prepared to the baker, and the latter contributed the bread dough. The dough was spread out on a large pan 3½ × 3½ inches (40 × 40 cm), and its edges turned up to hold the onions on the dough. The onion tart was baked after the baker's last oven bread.

This custom is still observed in some villages.

White Easter Lamb

Since the eighteenth century, it is customary to give children a symbol of the Pascal lamb, a lamb made of kougelhopf dough.

These lambs are made in terra-cotta molds comprising two pieces held together by a spring.

After baking, the lambs are whitened with sugar.

Cremation of Saint John

In some villages of Alsace, on the feast of Saint John, crumbs of bread are thrown on the fire to symbolize a willingness to sacrifice earthly food in order to purify and elevate the soul.

Mannala of Saint Nicholas

The feast of Saint Nicholas, December 6, is the feast of the children in Alsace. Christmas is a holy day and a family day.

It is the saint, accompanied by his redoubtable companion Father Fouettard, who distributes gifts to good children on the night of December 5.

It is the job of the village baker to make the *mannala*—little men shaped in special molds and made of brioche dough—that the children later discover in their plates or their shoes, surrounded by apples, dried pears, and nuts.

PART II
RECIPES

The traditional Alsatian Choucroute (p. 160), with Quenelles of Pork Liver (p. 158).

A Note to Readers

You'll find recipes in this section that are characteristic of Alsatian cooking. First we present some basic recipes, then we give you some samples from this most exquisite cuisine.

So as to enable you to select recipes that correspond to the amount of time you have to prepare a meal, we have given you, for each recipe, the time required for preparing the dish and also for cooking it. Occasionally, when necessary, we also indicate the approximate time required for soaking, marinating, or resting the foods.

Naturally, we are talking about *average* time. It may vary anywhere from 5 to 25 percent, depending on your own work habits, the way your kitchen is set up, and the accessibility of the various ingredients. Also, since no two stoves or ovens heat at exactly the same rate, you should make some allowance for the peculiarities of your own equipment.

We have divided the recipes into three categories:

Easy
Delicate
Grand Cuisine

These categories do not refer to the degree of difficulty of each recipe, but rather to the degree of care that must be exercised in following all the details and complexities of any given recipe.

The Grand Cuisine recipes, for instance, should not frighten you, even though you may be just a beginner in the kitchen. On the contrary, you'll find that as you gain experience with them you'll also gain self-confidence and a fairly good idea of what you are capable of doing.

Also, do not think that the Grand Cuisine recipes are reserved for special occasions and that the Easy ones are for everyday meals. A well-balanced menu and good eating depend more on the combination of dishes and on their quality than on how difficult they are to prepare and how elaborate they look.

Unless otherwise noted, all of the recipes in the following chapters are for SIX persons.

For American Kitchens

In several recipes, fresh *foie gras* is used. This is a type of fatty goose liver not produced in the United States, owing to certain laws. It is imported during the Christmas holiday season and can be purchased at a few gourmet shops in very large cities. For example, in New York City it can be found at Dean & DeLuca, William Poll, or E.A.T. It is very expensive and it spoils after about

ten days, so use it quickly. At other times of the year, or in other parts of the country, you can substitute either fresh regular goose livers (with a somewhat different flavor and color) or tinned *bloc de foie gras trufflé* (with a different texture).

Écrevisses are also a primary ingredient in Alsatian cooking. These are very much like small lobsters, and in this country they are called freshwater crayfish or crawfish. Specialty shops carry them in the larger cities and in the South and Midwest. They come to the stores fresh around February, or are sold frozen at other times. If you cannot find them, langostinos (saltwater crayfish) can be substituted, but the flavor is not the same. Also, for some recipes you might find that small shrimp are satisfactory substitutes.

In all the recipes using *crème fraîche,* heavy cream can be substituted. Crème fraîche is available here in gourmet stores or you can make it easily by adding one teaspoon of buttermilk to a cup of heavy cream. Cover the jar and allow to sit out at room temperature (60 to 80° F) for a few hours or a day, depending upon the time of year. The cream will stiffen and develop a slightly sour taste; in summer that will happen in a matter of hours, while in winter it may take twelve hours. Heavy cream has a flavor and consistency different from crème fraîche, so if you substitute it, remember that the heavy cream requires a little more cooking time to thicken sauces.

The ingredients indicate at certain times when a large or small item (such as an onion or a carrot) is to be used; otherwise, you can assume that a medium-sized one is intended. Quantities for herbs presume that fresh herbs will be used, but if dried herbs are preferred, that has been indicated. If you wish to substitute dried herbs for fresh, remember that the dried versions are generally stronger and therefore you should use a smaller quantity.

Throughout the book, *sifted* all-purpose flour is used unless otherwise specified. Note, for example, in the dessert recipes often unsifted flour is preferred. In all recipes, unsalted butter is used, although you can easily substitute salted butter, remembering to cut the quantity of salt accordingly.

The measurements indicated in these recipes are for both U.S. customary quantities and metric. The original versions of these recipes had metric quantities, but in preparing the book for U.S. readers, some adjustments were made in amounts to simplify the transition. Therefore, in these recipes you will find that we have used approximate conversions rather than exact ones. For our purposes, 1 liter is equal to 1 quart and—for the most part—400 to 500 grams is equal to 1 pound.

Likewise, we have chosen to use fractional quantities of larger measures than to resort to giving measurements in milliliters. It is a lot easier to remember that 1 cup equals ¼ liter than 240 milliliters.

You should have no problems with these recipes, since they have been adapted for American ingredients and American kitchens. As always, however, the publisher would appreciate receiving your comments and questions pertaining to individual recipes.

BASIC RECIPES

In this chapter you will find recipes for items that are then used as ingredients in the preparation of Alsatian dishes or recipes for foods that are served alongside some Alsatian specialties.

In each case, the cooking and preparation times are given, as well as the approximate quantity produced. Some of these items may be made ahead of time and kept ready for use in special dishes.

White Butter
Crayfish Butter

Chicken Stock
Brown Veal Stock
Game Stock
Fish Stock
Meat Glaze

Sauce Béchamel
Crayfish Sauce
Sauce Hollandaise
Black Pepper Sauce

Pinot Noir Sauce
Horseradish Sauce
Sauce Rémoulade
Sauce Mayonnaise

Alsatian Four Spices
Spiced Salt

Mustard Cucumbers
Pickled Gherkins or Onions
Peasant-Style Baby Onions
Sweet and Sour Huckleberries
Pickled Plums

Compound Butters

Beurre Blanc

White butter

Preparation time: 15 min.
Cooking time: 20 min.
Yield: 2 cups

½ cup (1 dL) water
½ cup (1 dL) vinegar or white wine such as Sylvaner
1 tablespoon chopped shallots
1½ cups (300 g) butter, cut into small pieces
Pinch of salt
1 mill-turn black pepper
Juice of ½ lemon

Combine the water, vinegar, and shallots in a saucepan. Cook over medium heat until two-thirds of the liquid has evaporated.

Remove the saucepan from the heat and allow to cool for 5 minutes. Then place over low heat and mix in pieces of butter, stirring constantly with a whisk.

Season butter with salt and pepper. Whisk in lemon juice. Do not heat sauce too hot or butter will not emulsify and form a sauce; it will just melt.

The sauce is now ready to serve.

Buerre d'Écrevisses

Crayfish butter

30 crayfish (bodies only; tails may be reserved for another use)
1 pound (500 g) butter, softened

Preparation time: 20 min.
Cooking time: 1 hr.
Yield: 1½ cups

Preheat the oven to 350° F (180° C).

Crush or grind the crayfish bodies and mix together thoroughly with the butter. Place in an ovenproof saucepan and bake slowly in a moderate oven for about 1 hour.

Remove pan from oven and fill two-thirds full with hot water. Bring to a boil and boil steadily for 1 minute. Remove from heat and let stand.

Using a large spoon, skim butter off the top and place it in a pan two-thirds full of ice water. Chill until the butter sets.

When the butter is cold, remove it from the water and melt it in a saucepan. Pour off clear liquid. This is the clarified butter with all the flavor. The milky residue will separate from the butter in the saucepan and remain on the bottom; this should be discarded. Strain the clear butter and chill until ready to use.

This butter can be used in place of fresh butter in a crayfish ragout. It can also be used as a sauce for fish, bisques, and so forth.

Stocks

Fond Blanc de Volaille

Chicken stock

Preparation time: 30 min.
Cooking time: 3 to 3½ hr.
Yield: 3 to 4 quarts (3 to 4 L)

5 pounds (2 kg) chicken bones (necks, backs, giblets, wings) or 1 large chicken, cut up
6 quarts (6 L) water
Salt
2 carrots, chopped
2 onions, chopped
½ celeriac, shredded
2 leeks, sliced
3 cloves garlic, chopped
Bouquet garni (celery leaves, thyme sprigs, bay leaf, rosemary sprigs, leeks)

Place the chicken parts in a large pot. Add the water and bring to a boil. Spoon off the foam and salt lightly. Add remaining ingredients and simmer for 3 hours. Skim off the foam frequently to keep broth clear.

Strain the broth and carefully skim off the fat. Chill or freeze until ready to use. When cold, remove any remaining fat from top.

This stock is used for preparing Tripe in Riesling (page 159) and Cream of Frogs' Legs Soup (page 117).

Fond de Veau Brun

Brown veal stock

5 pounds (2 kg) veal trimmings
8 pounds (4 kg) veal bones, broken into pieces
2 carrots, chopped
2 onions, chopped
½ celeriac, shredded
3 cloves garlic, chopped
10 ounces (300 g) fresh pork fat, diced
6 quarts (6 L) water
Bouquet garni (leeks, bay leaves, thyme, parsley)

Preparation time: 30 min.
Cooking time: 7 to 8 hr.
Yield: 3 to 4 quarts (3 to 4 L)

Preheat the oven to 400° F (200° C).

Cut up the veal trimmings and mix them with the bones.

Grease a roasting pan. Arrange the trimmings and bones in the bottom of the pan. Cook, turning frequently, in a hot oven until golden brown, about 1 to 1½ hours.

While veal and bones are browning, place vegetables and pork fat in a large stock pot.

When ready, add the meat and bones and sauté together over very high heat, stirring frequently. Drain off the fat, then add the water and bouquet garni and bring to a boil. Simmer gently for 6 hours, carefully spooning off the foam from time to time to keep broth clear.

While the broth is cooking, add additional water from time to time to keep up the level of liquid.

Strain and chill. Remove the fat layer from top. Chill or freeze until needed.

This stock is used in many meat recipes, especially those for braised meat.

Fond de Gibier

Game stock

Preparation time: 30 min.
Cooking time: 3½ hr.
Yield: 3 cups (¾ L)

¼ cup (50 g) butter
5 pounds (2 kg) game bones, cut into small pieces
1 carrot, diced
1 onion, diced
3 cloves garlic, unpeeled
½ cup (50 g) all-purpose flour
2 cups (5 dL) dry red wine
2 quarts (2 L) Brown Veal Stock (page 61)
Pinch of thyme
1 bay leaf
6 juniper berries
1 mill-turn black pepper

Preheat the oven to 450° F (230° C).

In a heatproof saucepan, melt the butter and sauté the bones for 5 to 10 minutes. Add the vegetables and garlic. Sprinkle the flour over the bones and vegetables and mix well. Bake in a very hot oven until richly browned, about 30 minutes.

Place saucepan over heat and add the wine. Simmer until most of the wine has evaporated. Add the stock and the spices, then simmer for 3 hours, occasionally spooning off the foam.

Strain and pour stock into an earthenware container to cool. It is important to stir occasionally during cooling.

This stock is used in the preparation of game sauces, Black Pepper Sauce (page 68), and so on, and is also served with pheasant, grouse, venison, wild boar, and hare.

Fumet de Poisson

Fish stock

5 pounds (2 kg) fish bones (whitefish, such as sole, turbot, hake, whiting)
1 onion, chopped
1 leek, chopped
¼ cup (50 g) butter
3 quarts (3 L) water
Juice of ½ lemon
Bouquet garni (dill, lemon peel, celery leaves, thyme, bay leaf)
½ cup (50 g) chopped mushrooms

Preparation time: 10 min.
Cooking time: 35 min.
Yield: 2 to 3 quarts (2 to 3 L)

Cut the fish bones into pieces and combine with the vegetables. Melt the butter in a large pan and lightly sauté the bones and vegetables. Add the water, lemon juice, bouquet garni, and mushrooms.

Bring to a boil and continue to boil gently for 25 minutes. Remove foam constantly while cooking.

Strain, then chill or freeze stock until needed.

This stock is used in the preparation of, among other things, Alsatian Crayfish (page 123), Riesling Fish Stew (page 133), Sole Traminer (page 140), and Filet of Sole with Noodles (page 139).

Glace de Viande

Meat glaze

4 quarts (4 L) Chicken Stock (page 60) or Brown Veal Stock (page 61)

Preparation time: 2 min.
Cooking time: 90 min.
Yield: 2 cups (½ L)

Over low heat, bring the stock to a boil. Spoon off the foam carefully and very frequently.

As the broth evaporates, pour the residue into progressively smaller pots. Keep close watch and continue to remove the foam.

The meat glaze is ready when it has attained the consistency of a thick syrup and is shiny.

A meat glaze is obtained by reducing chicken or veal stock until it becomes thick and syrupy. These glazes are used to thicken and enrich the flavor of sauces, stews, gravies, and soups.

Sauces

auce Béchamel

½ cup + 3 tablespoons (140 g) butter
½ cup (50 g) all-purpose flour
1 quart (1 L) milk
Salt and white pepper
Pinch of grated nutmeg
1 cup (2 dL) crème fraîche or heavy cream

Preparation time: 5 min.
Cooking time: 40 min.
Yield: 4 cups

Melt ½ cup (100 g) butter in a pan. Add the flour and mix with a whisk. Allow the mixture to cook without changing color, then remove from heat and cool.

When the mixture has cooled, bring the milk to a boil and pour into the mixture of butter and flour (the *roux*), stirring thoroughly. Add salt, pepper, and nutmeg.

Bring sauce to a boil and let cook over low heat for 30 minutes. It is important to stir frequently so as to obtain a perfectly smooth sauce. Finally, stir in cream and remaining butter. Season to taste with salt and pepper.

Note that it may be necessary to use more milk than indicated above, since the quality of flour varies and some batches tend to absorb more liquid than others.

Béchamel Sauce is used with many hot vegetables, in casseroles, and for preparing Horseradish Sauce (page 70).

Sauce aux Écrevisses

Crayfish sauce

24 crayfish
½ cup (100 g) butter
⅓ cup (5 cL) oil
½ celeriac, shredded
1 carrot, chopped
1 leek, chopped
3 shallots, chopped
2 cups (½ L) Sylvaner wine
1 cup (2 dL) Fish Stock (page 63)
1 tablespoon chopped tomato
Salt and black pepper
1 teaspoon chopped parsley
1 teaspoon chopped tarragon
1½ cups (3 dL) crème fraîche or heavy cream

Preparation time: 40 min.
Cooking time: 1 hr.
Yield: 4 cups

Prepare and cook the crayfish as in the recipe for Alsatian Crayfish (page 123) using half the butter and oil and all the celeriac, carrot, leek, shallots, wine, and stock given above. Add tomato, salt, and pepper.

Using a strainer, remove the crayfish from the cooking liquid. Remove the shell from the tails and reserve the tail meat.

Crush the bodies of the crayfish along with the tail shells in a saucepan. Sprinkle with parsley and tarragon. Sauté lightly in remaining oil. Add the cooking liquid and cook until one-third of the liquid has evaporated.

Add the cream and let boil for 5 minutes longer. Strain, pressing out all liquid. Stir in remaining butter and correct seasonings. Add the crayfish tails to this sauce.

This sauce is used for Pâté of Trout and Pike (page 130), Crayfish Flan (page 124), and Stuffed Trout Baked in Riesling (page 127).

Sauce Hollandaise

1 tablespoon white wine vinegar
Pinch of black pepper
3 egg yolks
2 tablespoons water
1 generous cup (250 g) soft butter, cut into 8 pieces
Salt
Juice of ½ lemon

Preparation time: 25 min.
Cooking time: 15 min.
Yield: 2 cups

In a small saucepan, place the vinegar and season with pepper. Cook until some of the liquid has evaporated.

Allow to cool, then add the egg yolks and water. Mix well. Warm over low heat, or in the top part of a double boiler set over simmering water, stirring constantly.

When the mixture has the consistency of heavy cream, add the butter 1 piece at a time while continuing to whisk vigorously. When all the butter has been incorporated into the mixture and the sauce is sufficiently thick, taste for seasoning. Add salt if necessary.

Add the lemon juice and keep hot in a double boiler. Serve this sauce as soon as possible, as it will separate if allowed to stand long.

Sauce Poivrade

Black pepper sauce

Preparation time: 15 min.
Cooking time: 2 hr., 15 min.
Yield: 4 cups

2 cups game trimmings (skin, bones, scraps of meat)
1 carrot, chopped
1 onion, chopped
¼ cup (½ dL) oil
1 cup (2 dL) red wine vinegar
1 cup (2 dL) dry red wine
2 quarts (2 L) Game Stock (page 62)
Sprig of thyme
1 bay leaf
10 black peppercorns, coarsely crushed
½ cup (100 g) butter

Cook the game trimmings, carrot, and onion in oil until they begin to brown.

Add the vinegar and the wine and continue cooking until some of the liquid has evaporated.

Add the stock, thyme, and bay leaf and cook for 2 hours, frequently removing the foam. About 10 minutes before the sauce is done, add the peppercorns.

Strain and taste for seasoning. Stir in butter.

Sauce au Pinot Noir

Pinot Noir sauce

6 tablespoons (80 g) butter
8 shallots, chopped
1 cup (2 dL) Pinot Noir wine
½ bay leaf
Pinch of thyme
1 cup (2 dL) Brown Veal Stock (page 61)
Pinch of salt
1 mill-turn black pepper

Preparation time: 10 min.
Cooking time: 15 min.
Yield: 2 cups

Heat half the butter in a saucepan and lightly sauté the shallots. Add wine and cook over high heat. Using a whisk, thoroughly scrape the bottom of the saucepan.

Add the bay leaf, thyme, and stock, and cook for 8 to 10 minutes longer.

Strain the sauce and add remaining butter. Adjust seasonings and add salt and pepper.

Sauce au Raifort

Horseradish sauce

¼ cup + 2 tablespoons (70 g) butter
¼ cup (20 g) all-purpose flour
1 cup (2 dL) milk
1 cup (200 g) grated fresh horseradish
Pinch of salt
1 mill-turn black pepper
½ cup (1 dL) crème fraîche or heavy cream
Juice of ½ lemon
Dash of vinegar (optional)

Preparation time: 15 min.
Cooking time: 25 min.
Yield: 3 cups

In a saucepan, melt 2 tablespoons (28 g) butter and stir in flour. Cook over low heat for 5 minutes. Add milk and stir until sauce thickens.

Stir horseradish into the sauce and bring to a boil. Simmer for 10 minutes, stirring occasionally.

Season with salt and pepper, then add the cream and simmer for 5 minutes more.

Stir in remaining butter and the lemon juice. A dash of vinegar may also be added to the seasoning.

Note: You can also, and more easily, prepare a cold horseradish sauce by mixing 2 parts grated horseradish and 1 part unsweetened whipped cream. Horseradish has always been very popular in Alsace, where it is used in the preparation of both hot and cold dishes. It is used with boiled beef but also with salted and smoked meats or with cold meats (in which case it may be served cold).

Sauce Rémoulade

2 shallots, chopped
1 teaspoon chopped parsley
1 teaspoon chopped chervil
¼ cup (50 g) chopped dill gherkins
1 teaspoon chopped capers
1 heaping tablespoon Dijon mustard
1 cup Sauce Mayonnaise (page 72)

Preparation time: 5 min.
Yield: 1⅓ cups

Mix together in a bowl the shallots, parsley, chervil, gherkins, and capers. Add the mustard and Mayonnaise.

Mix thoroughly until well blended.

This sauce is used with many dishes, particularly with Fried Carp (page 138).

Sauce Mayonnaise

2 large eggs
Pinch of salt
2 cups (½ L) olive or corn oil
5 tablespoons wine vinegar
1 tablespoon prepared mustard (optional)

Preparation time: 10 min.
Cooking time: 3 min.
Yield: 3 cups

Carefully separate the egg whites from the yolks. Reserve the whites for another usc.

Combine the yolks and the salt in a bowl or blender. Beat with mixer or blender for 1 minute, then, while continuing to beat vigorously, add the oil—one drop at a time at first, then in a slow, steady stream.

When all the oil has been added, pour the vinegar into a small pan and bring to a boil. Incorporate the boiling vinegar into the mayonnaise and continue to beat for another 2 or 3 minutes to homogenize the mixture. Allow to cool.

You may add a tablespoon of mustard at the same time as the vinegar; this is a matter of personal taste.

This mayonnaise recipe appears to be of Alsatian origin and dates from the end of the eighteenth century.

Spices

Quatre Épices Alsacien, or Viergewuerzmischung

Alsatian four spices 

2 teaspoons black pepper
1 teaspoon grated nutmeg
½ teaspoon ground cloves
¼ teaspoon ground ginger

Preparation time: 5 min.
Yield: 3¾ teaspoons

Combine all the spices and store in a tightly sealed jar.

You may also add, depending on what dish you are going to season, a pinch of cinnamon.

The formula for this mixture of spices varies substantially when it is bought ready-made at the grocer's. In Alsace, people generally prefer to make it themselves and keep a supply handy on the spice rack.

Sel Épicé

Spiced salt 

1 cup (250 g) fine-grained salt
2 tablespoons (20 g) Four Spices (page 73)

Preparation time: 5 min.
Yield: 1⅛ cups

Mix thoroughly and store in a sealed container.

Garnishes

Concombres à la Moutarde

Mustard cucumbers

3 large cucumbers
Pinch of coarse salt
1 tablespoon Dijon mustard
1 cup (2 dL) distilled white vinegar
1 cup (2 dL) water
1 tablespoon granulated sugar
1 teaspoon whole pickling spices

Preparation time: 30 min.
Draining time: 1 hr.
Cooking time: 5 min.
Yield: 1 quart

Peel cucumbers, halve lengthwise, and scoop out seeds. Quarter them lengthwise, then cut them into strips about 1½ inches (4 cm) long.

Place the cucumber strips in a colander and mix with salt, then let drain for about 1 hour.

Place the cucumbers in a bowl. Add the mustard and mix thoroughly.

Bring the vinegar and water to a boil. Add the sugar and spices.

Pour the boiling vinegar mixture over the cucumbers. Spoon into sterilized jars and seal.

This pickle keeps very well in the refrigerator and goes well with all cold dishes and with pork.

Cornichons au Vinaigre or Oignons au Vinaigre

Pickled gherkins or pickled onions

Preparation time: 30 min.
Curing time: 1 to 2 mon.
Yield: 3 quarts

2 pounds (1 kg) tiny gherkin cucumbers or small white pearl onions
2 handfuls coarse salt
2 large sprigs tarragon
20 black peppercorns
1½ cups (3 dL) white vinegar (approximate)

Trim the ends off the gherkins or peel the onions. Wash and wipe them dry.

Place gherkins or onions in a bowl and sprinkle with the coarse salt. Let stand at room temperature for 24 hours. (If you are using larger cucumbers, it may be necessary to repeat this step.)

Wipe the gherkins or onions dry.

At the bottom of a storage container, place a sprig of tarragon. Then make successive layers of gherkins, or of onions, or of both combined, dividing peppercorns among the layers.

Cover contents with vinegar, then add the second tarragon branch. When the container is full, seal tightly.

Refrigerate. Check once a week during the first month of soaking and add vinegar as needed so as to keep all the ingredients covered.

These are served cold with many dishes of pork, roasted or braised meats, or stews.

Petits Oignons à la Paysanne

Peasant-style baby onions

1 pound (1 kg) tiny white onions
1 cup (2 dL) distilled white vinegar
1 cup (2 dL) water
1 tablespoon granulated sugar
Pinch of salt
¼ cup (50 g) dried currants
1 tablespoon tomato paste
1 tablespoon whole pickling spices
Pinch of black pepper
Pinch of cayenne

Preparation time: 30 min.
Cooking time: 5 min.
Yield: 1 quart

Peel the onions. (To keep from crying, peel onions in a bowl of water mixed with 1 tablespoon vinegar.)

Place onions in a saucepan and add vinegar, water, sugar, salt, currants, tomato paste, and spices. Bring to a boil and simmer 5 minutes, or until onions are still crisp. Add pepper and cayenne.

Spoon onions and liquid while still hot into sterilized jars and seal tightly. Store in refrigerator until ready to serve.

Serve onions as a side dish with meats, sausages, or terrines.

Airelles à l'Aigre-Doux

Sweet and sour huckleberries

2 pounds (1 kg) huckleberries
2 cups (500 g) granulated sugar
1 cup (2 dL) distilled white vinegar

Preparation time: 10 min.
Cooking time: 10 min.
Yield: 3 pints

If possible, use freshly picked huckleberries. If using frozen or canned, discard any packing liquid.

Place the berries in a preserving pot or a large stainless steel pot. Add the sugar and vinegar and cook for 10 minutes.

Place the berries in sterilized containers while they are hot. Seal and cool. Refrigerate until needed.

Huckleberries are an excellent side dish, especially with game.

Prunes au Vinaigre

Pickled plums

5 pounds (2 kg) small Italian prune plums
Pinch of ground cinnamon
8 to 10 cloves
½ bay leaf
4 cups (1 kg) granulated sugar
1 quart (1 L) distilled white vinegar

Marinating time: 2 days
Preparation time: 30 min. over 3 days
Cooking time: 20 to 30 min.
Yield: 5 quarts

Select plums that are quite ripe and still have their stems. Wipe with a clean dry cloth. Pierce each plum several times with toothpick of wood or silver. (A skewer of any other material will adversely affect the taste and the durability of the fruit.)

Place the plums in a deep porcelain or earthenware bowl. Sprinkle with cinnamon and add the cloves and bay leaf.

Combine the sugar with the vinegar in a saucepan and bring to a boil. Pour the boiling vinegar over the plums. Cover and allow to marinate for 2 days.

On the third day, drain plums and bring marinade to a boil. Then pour liquid over the plums once more.

On the fourth day, put the mixture—plums and marinade—into a copper or enamel cast-iron pot and cook for about 20 minutes; that is, until the plums begin to split.

Remove the plums with a wooden or silver spoon and place in sterilized jars. Strain the syrup and pour over the plums. Seal the containers and store in a cool dry place.

This recipe originated on the Alsatian plain. The plums go ideally with boiled beef, stew, or game.

HORS D'OEUVRE AND SAVORY LIGHT MEALS

These are recipes for a combination of purposes. Some are excellent as hors d'oeuvre or appetizers, while others can form the basis for a light supper or luncheon.

Of special note in this chapter are the pâtés and terrines, made from the famous foie gras of Strasbourg. Also in this part is a sampling of tarts, kin to nearby Lorraine's famous quiche.

Unless otherwise noted, all recipes serve six persons.

Alsatian Snails
Fresh Marinated Herring Filets
Knockwurst Salad
Country-Style Pork Head Cheese
Beefmuzzle Salad
Cabbage Salad
May Onion Salad
Beet Salad

Pheasant Terrine
Foie Gras Terrine
Scallops of Foie Gras with Apples
Pâté de Foie Gras en Croute

Onion Tart
Pork and Cheese Tart
Alsatian Mushroom Tart

Munster Pork and Veal Tourte
Hot Pâté

Escargots à l'Alsacienne

Alsatian snails

6 dozen large Burgundy snails, prepared as described, or canned
¼ cup (50 g) butter
1 cup (2 dL) Sylvaner wine
1 cup (2 dL) Brown Veal Stock (page 61)

Snail Butter:
½ cup (30 g) chopped parsley
2 shallots, chopped
2 cloves garlic, chopped
1 pound (450 g) butter, softened
1 teaspoon salt

Preparation time: 15 min.
Cooking time: 20 min.
(plus additional cooking time and standing time if snails are prepared at home)
Suggested Wine: Sylvaner or Riesling

Follow the directions given after the recipe should you wish to prepare the snails from scratch.

Drain snails. Melt the butter in a skillet. Add the snails and sauté for 5 minutes. Add the wine and the stock and boil for 5 minutes. Remove pan from the heat and let the snails cool in the broth.

Preheat the oven to 350° F (180° C).

When snails are cool, put them back into their shells, along with a small spoonful of the gelatinous broth.

Prepare the snail butter by mixing together the parsley, shallots, and garlic. Blend with the butter and add the salt.

Seal the snail shells with the mixture and place shells in the depressions of a snail plate. Bake in a moderate oven for about 10 minutes.

Snails prepared with local wine have always been much appreciated in Alsace. This family recipe is still in use today.

To Prepare the Snails

3 cups (¾ L) Sylvaner wine
2 cups (½ L) water
1 carrot
1 turnip
1 leek
1 stalk celery
1 onion
Generous pinch of salt
2 mill-turns black pepper

Place the snails (in their shells) in a container. Cover and let stand for 5 or 6 days. Wash, changing the water several times. This will purge the snails and clean them.

Parboil the snails for 15 minutes, then cool in cold water and drain.

Remove the snails from their shells with a small fork. Cut off the black ends, then place the snails in a saucepan with wine and water.

Peel the vegetables and cut them into pieces. Combine vegetables with the snails. Season with salt and pepper. Bring to a boil, skim foam, and cook snails for 4 hours. Add a mixture of half-wine and half-water as needed during the cooking, so that snails remain covered at all times.

Remove snails from the heat and allow to cool in the cooking liquid. While they are cooling, wash the shells thoroughly and boil for 30 minutes in water to cover. Rinse in cold water and drain and dry.

Filets de Harengs Frais Marinés

Fresh marinated herring filets

Preparation time: 20 min.
Curing time: 2 days twice

12 fresh herring filets
3 tablespoons coarse salt
2 cups (½ L) Sylvaner wine
2 carrots, chopped
2 onions, chopped
1 leek, white part only, chopped
4 cloves garlic, crushed
Pinch of granulated sugar
½ bay leaf
2 cloves
1 tablespoon black peppercorns

Arrange the herring filets close together in an earthenware pot and cover with coarse salt. Let stand for 2 days.

Remove the filets from the pot, wash in cold running water, and drain thoroughly. Place them back in the pot and marinate in a mixture of the wine, carrots, onions, leek, garlic, sugar, bay leaf, cloves, and black pepper.

Wait 2 days, then serve.

VARIATION

Filets de Harengs à la Sauce de Moutarde (Herring Filets in Mustard Sauce)

Dilute 2 teaspoons of Dijon mustard with 2 teaspoons of heavy cream or crème fraîche and 2 tablespoons of the marinade.

Drain the filets and pour this sauce over them. On the serving platter, sprinkle with finely chopped onions.

These 2 recipes date from the Middle Ages. Herring has been prized in Alsace since it was first brought there during the time of the Hanseatic League, when ships from the North Sea plied the Rhine. Alsatian-style herring was so appreciated that it appeared regularly on the imperial, noble, and ecclesiastical tables of the Holy Roman Empire.

Cervelas en Salade

Knockwurst salad

6 cooked knockwurst
3 lettuce leaves
3 hard-cooked eggs, cut in half lengthwise
2 tomatoes
½ cup (1 dL) vinaigrette dressing
1 onion, chopped
Pinch of chopped parsley

Preparation time: 20 min.
Suggested Wines:
Sylvaner or Traminer

Remove the casings from the knockwurst, cut them in half lengthwise, and, on the convex side of each half, make several diagonal cuts.

Arrange knockwurst on a round or oval platter. Garnish the inner edge of the platter with the lettuce leaves and the egg halves.

Wash the tomatoes and core them. Cut into quarters and arrange on the platter.

Prepare your favorite vinaigrette dressing and sprinkle over the tomatoes, eggs, and knockwurst. Finish it off by sprinkling the entire salad with the onion and parsley.

Note: In Alsace this salad is made with saveloys—a short, thick pork sausage not available in the United States.

Presskoph Ménagère

Country-style pork head cheese

Marinating time: 2 days
Preparation time: 1 hr.
Cooking time: 2 hr.
Suggested Wine: Sylvaner

1 pig's head with tongue and ears
Generous pinch of coarse salt
2 mill-turns black pepper
8 cloves garlic, finely chopped
1 cup (2 dL) white wine vinegar
3 carrots, chopped
½ celeriac, shredded
2 leeks, sliced
5 cloves
1 teaspoon thyme
½ bay leaf
6 sprigs parsley
6 juniper berries
1 onion, sliced
10 black peppercorns
6 Pickled Gherkins (page 75), diced or bottled cornichons

Vinaigrette:
6 tablespoons oil
4 tablespoons white wine vinegar
2 teaspoons prepared mustard
Generous pinch of salt
4 mill-turns black pepper

Cut the pig's head in half lengthwise (or have the butcher do this for you). Wash the head and rub with coarse salt, black pepper, and 4 cloves of garlic. Let stand for 2 days, rubbing occasionally with salt, pepper, and garlic.

After 2 days, place the pig's head and tongue in a large pot and pour in vinegar and enough water to cover the head entirely. Bring to a boil, carefully spooning off any foam.

Add the carrots, celeriac, leeks, cloves, thyme, bay leaf, 2 or 3 sprigs parsley, juniper berries, onion, remaining garlic, and the peppercorns.

Cook over low heat, covered, and boil gently for approximately 2 hours, until the meat is cooked.

Remove the head from the broth, bone, and cut meat into small cubes. Dice tongue and sliver ears. Place the diced meats into a pot. Strain broth and pour into the pot, covering the meat. Bring to a gentle boil for 10 minutes.

Add Pickled Gherkins or cornichons.

Taste for seasoning. Pour meat and broth into several loaf pans or into a large round bowl. Chill until firm.

Dip pans into lukewarm water for a few seconds and unmold the loaves. Cut into slices, and arrange on a serving platter.

Preparc vinaigrette by mixing all ingredients together and beating until thick. Drizzle dressing over meats and garnish with additional sprigs of parsley.

This dish may be served with salad greens, cucumbers, tomatoes, or radishes. It was traditional among farmers during the pre-Christmas season when the pig was slaughtered; it has since become one of the dishes characteristic of Alsace as a whole. It is a popular family meal.

Salade de Museau de Boeuf

Beefmuzzle salad

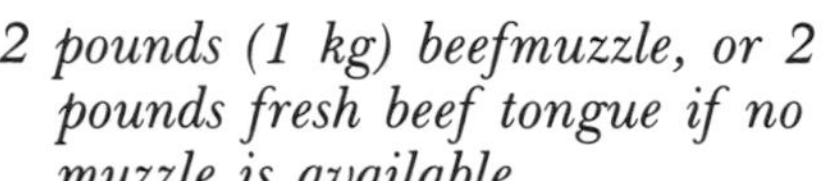

Preparation time: 15 min.
Cooking time: 2–2½ hr.

2 pounds (1 kg) beefmuzzle, or 2 pounds fresh beef tongue if no muzzle is available
2 tomatoes, quartered
3 hard-cooked eggs, halved

Dressing:
1 teaspoon Dijon mustard
½ cup (1 dL) white wine vinegar
1 cup (2 dL) oil
Pinch of salt
2 mill-turns black pepper
1 onion, chopped
1 tablespoon mixed chopped parsley and chervil

Cook beefmuzzle or tongue in salted water to cover until tender, about 2 to 2½ hours. Cool and dice.

Prepare a vinaigrette dressing with mustard, vinegar, oil, salt, and pepper. Add onion and herbs and beat until thick.

Pour the dressing into a salad bowl and add beefmuzzle. Mix well. Arrange the mixture on several salad dishes. Garnish with alternating tomato quarters and egg halves.

This is a classic recipe also found in provinces other than Alsace. It is possible, however, that it originated in Alsace, where it has been popular both on the plain and in the mountains since the beginning of the Middle Ages.

Scallops of Foie Gras with Apples (p. 93); Foie Gras Terrine (p. 92).

Chou Blanc en Salade

Cabbage salad
photo page 134

1 medium green cabbage
Pinch of salt
2 mill-turns black pepper
1 cup (2 dL) white wine vinegar
8 ounces (200 g) smoked or salted bacon, or 4 ounces (100 g) of each

Preparation time: 30 min.
Cooking time: 45 min.
Suggested Wine: Sylvaner

Core the cabbage and remove tough outer leaves. Cut into thin strips, julienne-style. Sprinkle with salt and pepper.

Bring the vinegar to a boil and cook the cabbage in it for 30 to 35 minutes or until wilted.

Cut the bacon into thin strips, julienne-style, and brown in a skillet. Drain.

Add bacon to the cabbage. Season with salt and pepper. Serve hot or cold.

This salad, which originated on the plain of lower Alsace, is particularly appropriate with a country-style main dish.

Salade d'Oignons de Mai

May onion salad

Generous 2 pounds (1 kg) small white onions
Pinch of salt
2 mill-turns black pepper
1 tablespoon granulated sugar
½ cup (1 dL) olive oil
½ cup (1 dL) white wine vinegar

Preparation time: 20 min.
Cooking time: 5 min.

Peel the onions. (Their skin is almost nonexistent, and they peel easily.) Chop finely and place in a sieve. Pour boiling water over onions.

Cool onions under cold running water and drain. Pour them into a bowl and sprinkle with salt, pepper, and sugar. Add oil and vinegar. Mix.

This unusual little salad, very popular on the plain, is a pleasant companion for cold dishes and pork.

Salade de Petites Betteraves Rouges

Beet salad

2 bunches small red beets
Pinch of salt
2 quarts (2 L) water
1 tablespoon coarse salt
2 mill-turns black pepper
2 onions, chopped
½ cup (1 dL) red wine vinegar
Pinch of granulated sugar
½ bay leaf
1 clove
1 tablespoon chopped parsley

Preparation time: 10 min.
Cooking time: 30 min.
Curing time: 12 hr.
Suggested Wine: Sylvaner

Trim the greens from the beets, but without cutting into the beets themselves.

Place the water, salt, and beets into a pot. Cook for 20 to 30 minutes depending on size of beets. Check frequently to ensure that the beets do not overcook but remain somewhat firm (use a needle to test for firmness). Remove the beets and cool in cold water. Peel under running water.

Put the beets in a bowl and season with coarse salt and pepper. Add the onions, vinegar, sugar, bay leaf, and clove. Let marinate overnight. Add more vinegar, if necessary, to ensure that the beets remain entirely covered.

Drain off some of the marinade and remove clove and bay leaf just before serving. Garnish with a sprinkling of chopped parsley.

This is a dish of the plain, apparently originating in lower Alsace. It has a very fresh taste and goes well at the beginning of a meal.

Pâtés and Terrines

Terrine de Faisan

Pheasant terrine

Preparation time: 1 hr.
Cooking time: 90 min.
Resting time: 1 day
Suggested Wine: Riesling or Pinot Noir

1 pheasant (thawed, if frozen)
3 tablespoons (40 g) butter
2 shallots, chopped
¼ cup (½ dL) Madeira wine
¼ cup (½ dL) brandy
¼ cup (½ dL) dry white wine
3 tablespoons Brown Veal Stock (page 61) or beef broth

Ground Meat Mixture:
¼ cup (50 g) butter
1 pheasant liver
2 chicken livers
Salt and pepper
¼ cup (½ dL) brandy
¼ cup (½ dL) Madeira wine
4 ounces (100 g) fresh mushrooms, chopped
4 ounces (100 g) boneless pork
4 ounces (100 g) boneless veal, cut from leg
1 slice fat bacon
2 teaspoons Spiced Salt (page 73)
8 ounces (200 g) sliced fat bacon
1 sprig thyme
½ bay leaf

Seasoning:
8 ounces (200 g) fresh foie gras, diced (See note, page 55)
½ cup (100 g) diced cooked ham
½ cup (100 g) diced fat bacon
3 ounces (80 g) truffles, diced
½ cup (50 g) shelled and hulled pistachio nuts
2 teaspoons (10 g) Spiced Salt (page 73)

First prepare the seasoning. In a bowl, mix the foie gras, ham, bacon, truffles, and pistachio nuts. Season with Spiced Salt. Set aside.

Bone the pheasant (or have your butcher do it). Reserve the carcass and the liver. Remove the skin from the meat, remove the tendons from the thighs, and dice the meat finely. Add the meat to a bowl with the seasonings.

Chop the carcass into small pieces and brown in the butter.

Add the shallots to the bones and pour in the Madeira, brandy, white wine, and stock. Boil down until only about ½ cup (1 dL) liquid is left.

Cool the liquid, pass it through a fine strainer, and mix it with the pheasant meat and seasoning.

Prepare the ground meat mixture. In a skillet, melt 1 tablespoon of the butter and cook the pheasant liver and chicken livers enough for them to be done but retain their pinkish color. Season lightly with salt and pepper and add the brandy and Madeira.

Sauté the mushrooms in the remaining butter.

In a meat grinder or food processor, grind the livers and their juices with the mushrooms, pork, veal, and bacon. Grind 3 or 4 times until mixture is very fine.

Mix ground meat with the Spiced Salt and blend with the pheasant meat mixture. Add more spiced salt if necessary.

Preheat the oven to 350° F (180° C).

Line a 1½-quart (1½ L) terrine with bacon slices, allowing excess bacon to hang out sides of terrine. Fill the terrine with pheasant mixture and top with thyme and bay leaf. Place bacon over top of terrine and smooth top.

Cover terrine and place in a water-bath, with water coming halfway up the sides of the terrine. Bake terrine in a moderate oven for 1½ hours. When terrine is cooked, juices will run clear.

Remove cover and place foil on top of pâté. Place an 8-ounce weight on top and chill until ready to serve.

Terrine de Foie Gras

Foie gras terrine
photo page 86

1 fresh foie gras, 1 to 1¼ pounds (500 to 600 g) (See note, page 55)
2 teaspoons Spiced Salt (page 73)
2 tablespoons Kirsch
2 tablespoons brandy
1 ounce (30 g) truffles
2 to 3 tablespoons rendered goose fat
Toast slices

Aspic:
¼ cup (½ dL) Madeira wine
2 teaspoons unflavored gelatin
1 cup (¼ L) beef or chicken broth

Preparation time: 15 min.
Marinating time: 12 hr.
Cooking time: 35 min.
Suggested Wines:
Gewürztraminer or
Riesling

Remove the membranes from the liver, being careful not to tear or gouge the liver itself. Season thoroughly with Spiced Salt, then marinate in a mixture of the Kirsch and brandy for several hours or overnight.

Drain the liver. Cut the truffles into strips and insert, spikelike, into the liver.

Preheat the oven to 350° F (180° C).

Select a small earthenware terrine, or one of enamel-coated cast-iron, large enough to just hold the liver. Grease it heavily with goose fat (or a good-quality butter if goose fat is not available).

Press the liver into the terrine and smear with goose fat to cover completely. Cover the terrine with foil and hold the foil in place with a lid.

Place the terrine in a roasting pan with hot water. Water should come two-thirds of the way up the sides of the terrine. Cook the terrine in a moderate oven for about 35 minutes.

Cool the terrine slowly while it is still in the roasting pan. When cold, put the terrine in the refrigerator and chill.

To prepare the aspic, mix the wine and gelatin. Stir over low heat until gelatin is dissolved, then stir in the broth and chill until firm.

The terrine is ready to serve the next day and it will keep in the refrigerator for about a month if covered with additional goose fat and with a tight-fitting lid. Serve with slices of toast and cubes of aspic.

Escalopes de Foie Gras d'Oie aux Reinettes

Scallops of foie gras with apples

photo page 86

Marinating time: 2 hr.	
Preparation time: 30 min.	
Cooking time: 20 min.	
Suggested Wines: Gewürztraminer or Riesling	

1 fresh foie gras, about 1-1¼ pounds (600 g) (See note, page 55)
Pinch of salt
1 mill-turn black pepper
2 tablespoons brandy
2 pippin or delicious apples
⅔ cup (150 g) butter
Flour for dredging
½ cup (1 dL) Gewürztraminer wine
½ cup (1 dL) Brown Veal Stock (page 61)
truffle (optional)

Cut the liver into ½-inch (1½-cm) thick slices, then flatten the slices with the flat edge of a knife.

Season liver with salt and pepper and marinate in the brandy for 2 hours.

Meanwhile, peel and core the apples and quarter them. Cook in ¼ cup (50 g) of the butter in a saucepan for 5 minutes, stirring frequently. The apple quarters should remain firm.

Drain liver slices and dredge with flour. In same pan as for apples, sauté liver in ¼ cup (50 g) butter until brown outside and pink inside, about 2 to 3 minutes.

Place apples and liver on a warmed serving platter.

Add the wine to the pan juices from cooking apples and liver. Reduce until pan is almost dry. Stir in stock and heat until bubbly.

Stir remaining butter into pan. Pour sauce over liver and apples. Serve garnished, if desired, with thin slices of truffle.

Note: In choosing goose livers, remember that those weighing between 1 and 1¼ pounds (450–500g) have the most velvety texture. Also, be sure that the livers are oily and have a nice pink color.

Pâté de Foie Gras en Croute

2 fresh foie gras, 1 pound (500 g) each (See note, page 55)
1 tablespoon Spiced Salt (page 73)
3 tablespoons Kirsch
3 tablespoons brandy
8 ounces (250 g) boneless pork filet
8 ounces (250 g) veal filet
1 tablespoon olive oil
1 recipe Pie Dough (page 210)
8 ounces (200 g) truffles
1 egg yolk

Aspic:
¼ cup (½ dL) Madeira wine
2 teaspoons unflavored gelatin
1 cup (¼ L) beef or chicken broth

Marinating time: 12 hr.
Preparation time: 1 hr.
Cooking time: 50 min.
Resting time: 5 hr.
Suggested Wine: Pinot Gris

Remove the membranes without tearing or otherwise injuring the liver. Season inside and out with some of the Spiced Salt.

Marinate the livers for several hours—preferably overnight—in the Kirsch and brandy. Drain.

Grind the pork and the veal coarsely and mix until well blended. Season with remaining Spiced Salt, and mix in the olive oil.

Preheat the oven to 350° F (180° C).

Prepare the dough as directed in the recipe, then roll out three-fourths of it on a floured surface. Line the bottom and sides of a 1½-quart (1½ L) buttered metal pâté mold.

Cover the pastry with half the veal-and-pork mixture.

Cut the truffles into strips and insert into the livers. Arrange the livers close together on the meat mixture and then spread the remainder of the ground meat over the livers.

Roll out the remaining dough and cover top of mold. Brush edges of the pastry with water and press together to seal. Trim excess dough and cut 2 round holes, 1 inch (2½ cm) in diameter, in the top of the pastry to allow steam to escape.

Brush the dough with beaten egg yolk and decorate with designs made with the tines of a fork.

Bake pâté in a moderate oven for 1 hour. When a knitting needle inserted into the pâté comes out warm, the pâté is cooked. Let stand until almost cold.

Prepare the aspic while the pâté cools. Mix the wine and the gelatin, then stir over low heat until the gelatin is dissolved. Add the broth and stir. Pour the aspic slowly into the 2 steam holes and chill pâté overnight.

Unmold pâté and cut into slices to serve.

This is a very traditional dish, perfected in the nineteenth century and served at banquets and festive meals since then. Since it is quite expensive to prepare, it is usually not served at regular family meals, but is reserved for special occasions.

Note: The best livers for this recipe are those weighing between 1 and 1¼ pounds (450–500 g). Pick those that are oily and of a pure pink color.

Tarts

Tarte à l'Oignon

Onion tart
photo page 102

4 large onions
⅔ cup (150 g) butter
1 tablespoon oil
1 tablespoon all-purpose flour
4 large eggs
1 cup (¼ L) crème fraîche or heavy cream
1 cup (¼ L) milk
Pinch of salt
1 mill-turn black pepper
Dash of grated nutmeg
1 recipe Pie Dough (page 210)

Preparation time: 30 min.
Cooking time: 1 hr.
Suggested Wines:
Sylvaner or Riesling

Peel and cut the onions into thin slices. Sauté onions in butter and oil without allowing them to brown, about 20 minutes. Sprinkle with flour. Mix well and sauté for a few moments longer.

In a bowl beat eggs with cream, milk, salt, pepper, and nutmeg.

Preheat the oven to 350°F (180°C).

Roll out dough on a floured surface. Line the bottom and sides of an 11-inch (27.5 cm) quiche pan or flan ring set on a cookie sheet.

Fill crust with egg mixture, then scatter onions over that, leaving a few rings on top.

Bake tart in a moderate oven for 30 to 40 minutes or until richly browned and puffed.

Unmold and serve hot.

Tarte Flambée, or Flammen Kuechen

Pork and cheese tart

photo page 102

- *6 ounces (150 g) prepared Basic Bread Dough (page 206)*
- *½ cup (100 g) pot cheese, sieved*
- *½ cup (1 dL) crème fraîche or heavy cream*
- *1 tablespoon all-purpose flour*
- *1 teaspoon salt*
- *2 tablespoons peanut oil*
- *3 ounces (80 g) lean cooked breast of pork, cut in strips*
- *⅔ cup (80 g) thinly sliced onions*

Preparation time: 15 min.
Cooking time: 20 min.
Serves: 2 to 3 persons
Suggested Wines:
Riesling
or Sylvaner, preferably from the Barr

Preheat the oven to 400°F (200°C).

Roll out the dough very thinly to form a 7 × 10-inch (17.5 × 25-cm) rectangle. Place it on a buttered cookie sheet. Pinch up an edge around the dough.

Mix the pot cheese, cream, flour, salt, and oil until the mixture is smooth and thick. Using a spatula, spread the cheese mixture over the dough.

Mix the pork with the onions. Sprinkle evenly over the tart.

Bake in a hot oven for 15 to 20 minutes, or until the dough is a lovely golden color.

This is a very old recipe from the lower Rhine area. The name Tarte Flambée (Flaming Tart) was originally given because it was baked very near the embers in an intensely hot baker's oven.

Tarte aux Champignons à l'Alsacienne

Alsatian mushroom tart

¼ cup (50 g) butter
2 shallots, chopped
12 ounces (300 g) fresh mushrooms, chopped
½ cup (100 g) diced ham
2 tomatoes, diced
Pinch of salt
Pinch of black pepper
½ cup (1 dL) Sylvaner wine
3 large eggs
1 cup (¼ L) crème fraîche or heavy cream
1 tablespoon chopped leeks
1 teaspoon chopped tarragon
1 recipe Pie Dough (page 210)

Preparation time: 30 min.
Cooking time: 45 min.
Suggested Wines: Sylvaner, Pinot Blanc, or an Edelzwicker (blended wine of superior grape)

Melt the butter and gently sauté the shallots and mushrooms. Add the ham and the tomatoes and cook for a few moments.

Add salt to pan (very cautiously, since the ham itself is salted) and black pepper. Add the wine and simmer until wine evaporates to half its original volume. Remove from heat.

Preheat the oven to 350°F (180°C).

Separate the egg yolks and whites. Beat the yolks with the cream. Add the leeks and tarragon. Stir in ham and mushroom mixture. Taste for seasoning.

Roll out dough on a floured surface. Line the bottom and sides of a 10-inch (25-cm) tart pan. Flute the edge. Use a fork to prick the bottom.

Prebake the crust for 10 minutes—just until the shell begins to brown.

Beat egg whites until stiff and fold gently into mushroom mixture. Fill tart shell with the mushroom mixture and bake in a moderate oven for 30 to 35 minutes or until richly browned and firm.

Serve piping hot cut into wedges.

This is a traditional, excellent Alsatian dish.

Tourte de la Vallée de Munster

Munster pork and veal tourte
photo page 102

2 crusty dinner rolls
1 cup (2 dL) milk
1 pound (400 g) pork filet
1 pound (400 g) leg of veal
2 tablespoons (20 g) butter
2 onions, chopped
1 cup (¼ L) Sylvaner wine
1 tablespoon chopped parsley
1 teaspoon salt
2 mill-turns black pepper
1 recipe Pie Dough (page 210) or ⅓ recipe Puff Pastry (page 212)
1 egg yolk, beaten

Preparation time: 30 min.
Chilling time: 12 hr.
Cooking time: 1 hr., 10 min.
Suggested Wines:
Sylvaner or Riesling

Break rolls into large pieces and soak in the milk. Drain the rolls, squeezing out liquid. Chop.

Grind the meats coarsely.

Heat butter and sauté onions. Add bread and meats and continue cooking for 10 minutes.

Stir in wine, parsley, salt, and pepper. Chill overnight.

Preheat the oven to 350°F (180°C).

Roll out on a floured surface 2 rounds of dough 9 inches (22.5 cm) in diameter. Place 1 round on a greased cookie sheet. Cover with meat mixture, mounding it up.

Top with second round. Brush edges of dough with water and press with your fingers to seal edges. Cut a round hole in the center of the pastry to allow steam to escape.

Brush crust with egg yolk. If using Puff Pastry, cut a design, as pictured, ⅛ inch (0.3 cm) into the dough using the tip of a sharp knife.

Bake in a moderate oven for 1 hour. Serve hot.

Pâté Chaud

Hot pâté

Marinating time: 12 hr.
Preparation time: 45 min.
Cooking time: 75 min.
Suggested Wines:
Riesling or Pinot Blanc

12 ounces (300 g) filet of pork
12 ounces (300 g) leg of veal
1 cup (¼ L) Riesling wine
Pinch of salt
2 mill-turns black pepper
½ cup (100 g) butter
2 onions, chopped
2 cups (150 g) chopped parsley
1 recipe (1 pound or 400 g) Pie Dough (page 210)
1½ cups (150 g) soft bread crumbs
⅓ recipe (12 ounces or 300 g) Puff Pastry (page 212)
1 egg yolk

Cut the meats into thin strips and let marinate overnight in the wine, salt, and pepper.

Melt the butter in a skillet and sauté the onions.

Drain meats and combine with the onions and the parsley.

Roll out the dough on a floured surface forming a rectangular form about 16 × 8 inches (40 cm × 20 cm).

Sprinkle the bread crumbs lengthwise down the center of the dough, covering an area about 10 inches (25 cm) long and 4 inches (10 cm) wide. Spread the strips of meat mixed with onion and parsley over this layer of bread crumbs.

Preheat the oven to 350°F (180°C).

Fold the edges of the dough over the meat, forming a rectangular box of pastry 10 × 4 inches (25 × 10 cm). Place seam-side down on greased cookie sheet.

Roll out the Puff Pastry into a rectangular shape of the same size as the top and sides of the pâté, about 12 × 6 inches (30 × 15 cm). Brush pâté top and sides with water. Cover the pâté with Puff Pastry. With your fingers, seal the pastry to the vertical sides of the pie dough.

Brush the pastry with egg yolk, and pierce here and there with the tines of a fork. Cut 2 round holes in top through both layers of dough to allow steam to escape.

Bake in a moderate oven 60 to 75 minutes or until very brown.

Serve pâté very hot, as soon as it comes out of the oven.

This is a dish for festive and ceremonial occasions. In Ammerschwihr, for instance, it is traditionally served at family functions.

Pork and Cheese Tart (p. 97); Munster Pork and Veal Tourte (p. 99); Onion Tart (p. 96).

EGGS

The egg recipes in this chapter consist primarily of omelettes in the Alsatian fashion. In the countryside of Alsace, and especially in the valleys lying among the steep slopes, omelettes are much appreciated. There are a hundred ways of preparing them: smoked bacon omelettes, herb omelettes, potato omelettes, sausage omelettes, and so forth. No matter what the other ingredients, the cook almost always adds one tablespoon of beer for every two eggs used. This makes the omelette more bubbly and lighter, as well as easier to digest.

Since there is considerable fluctuation among the recipes, the number of portions is given for each recipe.

rêpes Salées, or Eierkuchen

Savory crêpes

2½ cups (300 g) all-purpose flour
Pinch of salt
1 mill-turn black pepper
Pinch of grated nutmeg
6 large eggs, well beaten
1½ cups (3 dL) milk
½ cup (1 dL) crème fraîche or heavy cream
½ cup (100 g) butter, melted
1 teaspoon chopped parsley
1 teaspoon chopped chives

Preparation time: 10 min.
Cooking time: 2 min. per crêpe
Serves: 6
Suggested Wine: Sylvaner

In a bowl, mix the flour, salt, pepper, and nutmeg. Add eggs, milk, and cream, mixing thoroughly. Beat in half the butter, the parsley and the chives. Stir the mixture until it is a very smooth batter. Strain batter if necessary to remove any lumps.

Melt a bit of the remaining butter in an 8-inch (20-cm) omelette or crêpe pan. Pour a small ladleful of the batter (about ¼ cup or ½ dL) into the pan. Rotate pan to cover bottom evenly with batter. Cook one side until golden, then turn and cook the other side.

Continue making crêpes until batter is used up. Add more butter to pan when it seems dry.

Serve crêpes hot, with a green salad.

This is an excellent dish, thicker and more bubbly than the usual crêpe because of the cream and more aromatic because of the herbs. It is a favorite family dish for winter evenings, and also among the mountain people at Mardi Gras.

Oeufs au Plat au Foie Gras

Baked eggs with foie gras

6 tablespoons (120 g) butter
8 ounces (250 g) fresh foie gras (See note, page 55), diced
½ cup (1 dL) Port wine
12 large eggs
Pinch of salt
1 mill-turn black pepper
½ cup (1 dL) Pinot Noir Sauce (page 69)

Preparation time: 5 min.
Cooking time: 5 min.
Serves: 6
Suggested Wine: Pinot Noir or Sylvaner

Preheat oven to 400°F (200°C).

Using 6 custard cups or 1-cup ramekins, place in each 1 tablespoon of butter. Divide foie gras equally among the dishes.

Place dishes in oven for 2 to 3 minutes to melt butter.

Divide wine among dishes, and break 2 eggs into each one. Place dishes in oven and bake for about 3 to 5 minutes, or until eggs are cooked.

Remove dishes from oven and sprinkle lightly with salt and pepper. Before serving, spoon Pinot Noir Sauce over eggs.

This is a very simple gourmet recipe.

Basic Omelette

2 or 3 large eggs
Pinch of salt
1 mill-turn black pepper
1 tablespoon beer or water
2 tablespoons (28 g) butter, rendered meat, or chicken fat

Preparation time: 2 min.
Cooking time: 5 min.
Serves: 1

Break the eggs into a bowl and beat lightly. Add the seasonings and stir in beer or water. Do not over-beat, as this will impair the lightness of the omelette.

Melt butter in an 8-inch (20-cm) skillet and heat until sizzling.

Pour the eggs into the heated pan. Cook without stirring, lifting edges with a spatula to allow uncooked portion to run underneath. Cook until top is firm but moist.

Fold omelette in skillet using a spatula. Tilt pan and slide out onto a plate.

For the best results, do not use more than 6 eggs per omelette (use a 10-inch (25-cm) skillet). It is better to have several omelette pans and prepare them individually.

Omelette aux Fines Herbes

Herb omelette

1 recipe Basic Omelette (page 106)
1 tablespoon chopped parsley
1 tablespoon chopped chives

Preparation time: 5 min.
Cooking time: 5 min.
Serves: 1
Suggested Wines:
Sylvaner and Pinot Noir

Combine omelette mixture with parsley and chives. Pour into pan and prepare as for Basic Omelette.

Serve hot, on a heated plate.

An herb omelette is especially appreciated in hot weather because it is fresh and quite fragrant. At this time, fresh herbs can be grown in the garden and any favorite combination can be used in the Herb Omelette. Use 2 tablespoons chopped mixed herbs—tarragon, chervil, thyme, marjoram, dill, and so forth.

Omelette au Lard

Bacon omelette

1 recipe Basic Omelette (page 106), but excluding the butter
3 slices (40 g) lean smoked bacon

Preparation time: 10 min.
Cooking time: 8 min.
Serves: 1
Suggested Wines: Pinot Gris or Pinot Noir

Prepare omelette mixture as directed, using slightly less salt because of the salt in bacon.

Cut the bacon into small pieces and place into boiling water for 1 minute. Drain and immediately put the bacon into a hot omelette pan.

Cook bacon for 2 to 3 minutes or until brown, then add the egg mixture. Cook as for Basic Omelette. (You eliminate butter from the recipe because bacon fat is enough for preparation of omelette.)

Some regions of Alsace prefer smoked bacon, and some prefer salted bacon. This preference is also found with respect to other bacon dishes and to pork dishes generally, such as stew and sauerkraut dishes.

Omelette aux Queues d'Écrevisses

Crayfish-tail omelette

6 recipes Basic Omelette (page 106)
1 recipe Crayfish-Tail Ragoût with 24 crayfish (page 125)

Preparation time: 15 min.
Cooking time: 30 min.
Serves: 6
Suggested Wines:
Sylvaner, Riesling, or
Pinot Gris

Prepare omelette mixture as directed and make 6 omelettes.

Before folding the omelettes, fill them with two-thirds of the ragoût.

Arrange the omelettes on heated plates and spoon the remaining ragoût around them.

Omelette aux Cuisses de Grenouilles

Frogs'-leg omelette

¼ cup + 2 tablespoons (80 g) butter
18 frogs' legs
Pinch of salt
1 mill-turn black pepper
1 shallot, chopped
½ cup (1 dL) Sylvaner wine
½ cup (1 dL) crème fraîche or heavy cream
1 tablespoon chopped chives
6 recipes Basic Omelette (page 106)

Preparation time: 10 min.
Cooking time: 45 min.
Serves: 6
Suggested Wines:
Sylvancr or Riesling

Melt 2 tablespoons (28 g) butter in a skillet and sauté the frogs' legs. Add salt and pepper and sprinkle with the chopped shallot.

After 5 minutes, add wine and cook for another 5 minutes.

When the frogs' legs are cooked, drain, reserving the liquid, and allow to cool. Skin and bone the frogs' legs.

Boil the cooking liquid until reduced to half its original volume. Stir in cream. Taste for seasoning, and add remaining butter. Place the frogs'-leg meat in this sauce. Add the chives and keep hot.

Prepare 6 omelettes as directed for Basic Omelette. Before folding omelettes, fill each with some sauce mixture. Serve hot.

melette Plate aux Pommes de Terre

Potato omelette

1 medium potato
1 onion, chopped
¼ cup (50 g) butter
1 recipe Basic Omelette (page 106)
1 teaspoon chopped parsley

Preparation time: 30 min.
Cooking time: 15 min.
Serves: 1

Cook the potato in salted water. Peel and slice into rounds.

Melt butter in a skillet and cook potato with onion until golden.

Pour omelette mixture over potato and cook as directed for Basic Omelette. When top is moist yet firm, place a plate over omelette and invert. Slide omelette out of plate back into skillet, and brown the other side.

Slide omelette onto a hot platter. Sprinkle with chopped parsley.

In the valleys, it is a common practice to add diced smoked bacon to the potatoes when the latter are half cooked. When the bacon has browned (it takes about 5 minutes), the mixture of bacon and potatoes is added to the omelette mixture.

This is an omelette of the mountain country, very popular at all times of the year.

SOUPS

The favorite tastes of Alsace are again evident in these soups. Here we have soups that are gutsy purées of dried beans, delicate cream soups with crayfish or frogs' legs, and specialties such as the Beer Soup and the Milk Soup. Another favorite, included in the chapter on meats, is Boiled Beef and Beef Broth with Quenelles of Marrow (page 149).

All recipes for soups serve six persons.

Potage aux Lentilles avec Saucisses de Porc

Lentil soup with pork sausages

1½ cups (300 g) lentils
1 leek
1 carrot
1 onion
1 stalk celery
½ cup (100 g) butter
1 tablespoon all-purpose flour
2½ quarts (2½ L) water or Chicken Stock (page 60)
4 ounces (100 g) smoked bacon, in 1 piece
Salt and pepper
3 smoked pork sausages

Soaking time: 12 hr.
Preparation time: 30 min.
Cooking time: 1 hr., 20 min.

Soak lentils in water to cover for 12 hours. Drain.

Chop the leek, carrot, onion, and celery into small pieces and sauté in butter. Sprinkle the flour over the vegetables; add the water or stock.

Add the lentils and the bacon to the stock. Season with salt and pepper to taste. Simmer for 90 minutes.

After 1 hour, begin simmering the sausages in water, in a separate pot, for 15 minutes.

Remove the bacon from the vegetables and dice it. Drain the sausages and cut them into small rounds, then add the rounds and the diced bacon to the soup.

Taste for seasoning and serve piping hot.

The kind of pork sausage you use does not make much difference so long as it is smoked. In the mountain villages of Alsace, pork sausages are usually made at home in December, when the family's pig is slaughtered.

Potage aux Pois Cassés

Purée of split pea soup

Soaking time: 3 hr.
Preparation time: 15 min.
Cooking time: 90 min.

1 cup (150 g) split peas
1 carrot
1 onion
1 stalk celery
¾ cup (180 g) butter
1 tablespoon all-purpose flour
Bouquet garni (thyme, parsley, celery leaves, parsnip)
2 quarts (2 L) Chicken Stock (page 60)
2 tablespoons crème fraîche or heavy cream
Salt and black pepper
8 slices white bread, diced

Soak the split peas for 3 hours in a large pot of cool water.

Cook the peas for 4 or 5 minutes in boiling water. Drain.

Dice the carrot, onion, and celery, then sauté them in ¼ cup (½ dL) of the butter. Sprinkle vegetables with the flour and add the peas and bouquet garni. Stir in the stock and cook for 1 hour.

Press soup through a strainer or food mill or whirl in a blender. Stir in the cream and ¼ cup (½ dL) of the butter. Season to taste with salt and pepper. Soup may be thinned if necessary with more stock.

Fry bread cubes in remaining butter. Serve piping hot topped with croutons.

Soups made from dried beans are very popular in Alsace. The present recipe is characteristic of both the hill country and the plain of lower Alsace.

Potage des Vendangeurs, or Potage Parmentier

Vintager's soup, or Purée of potato parmentier 

- *2 onions, sliced, and 1 onion, chopped*
- *2 leeks, sliced*
- *⅔ cup (150 g) butter*
- *1¼ pounds (500 g) potatoes, peeled and quartered or cut into sixths, depending on size*
- *2 quarts (2 L) water*
- *Salt and black pepper*
- *Dash of grated nutmeg*
- *1 cup (2 dL) crème fraîche or heavy cream*
- *Chopped parsley and chives*

Preparation time: 10 min.
Cooking time: 45 min.

Sauté the onion slices and the leeks in 1 tablespoon of butter. Add the potatoes and the water, salt, pepper, and nutmeg. Bring to a boil.

When the vegetables are cooked, drain and press them through a fine strainer or whirl in a blender or food processor and mix with cooking liquid. Stir in ½ cup (1 dL) of butter and the cream. Taste for seasoning.

Sauté the chopped onion in remaining butter until golden brown. Add to the soup just before serving. Serve soup sprinkled with parsley and chives. Soup should be served very hot.

This is the traditional soup of Alsatian grapegrowers. Usually, 2 to 4 Strasbourg or other smoked sausages per person are served with the soup. The sausages are heated in simmering water for 5 minutes before serving.

Crème aux Écrevisses de la Vallée de la Weiss

Cream of crayfish soup

Preparation time: 1 hr.
Cooking time: 1 hr., 25 min.
Suggested Wines:
Riesling or Sylvaner

30 crayfish
2 tablespoons (28 g) butter
½ cup (100 g) rice flour
4 egg yolks
1 cup (2 dL) crème fraîche or heavy cream
1 teaspoon chopped chives

Court-Bouillon:
1 bottle Sylvaner or Riesling wine
2 quarts (2 L) water
1 onion, chopped
1 carrot, chopped
½ stalk celery, finely chopped
2 cloves garlic, finely chopped
1 bay leaf
Pinch of thyme
Pinch of saffron
Salt and black pepper

First prepare the court-bouillon.

In a large saucepan, combine wine, water, onion, carrot, celery, garlic, bay leaf, thyme, saffron, salt, and pepper. Bring to a boil and simmer 5 minutes.

Place the crayfish into the hot court-bouillon and simmer gently for 7 or 8 minutes. Separate the tails and shell them. Reserve the court-bouillon and the meat from the tails.

Crush the bodies and tail shells of the crayfish and sauté them in 1 tablespoon (14 g) butter. Sprinkle with the rice flour. Add all of the court-bouillon and cook over low heat for 45 minutes to 1 hour.

Strain and place broth back in saucepan. Add a mixture of the egg yolks and cream. Stir over low heat until soup thickens; do not boil. Season with salt and pepper. Sauté crayfish tails in remaining butter.

Serve soup garnished with crayfish tails and sprinkled with chives.

Crème aux Grenouilles

Cream of frogs' legs soup

Preparation time: 1 hr.
Cooking time: 30 min.
Suggested Wines:
Riesling or Traminer

1¼ pounds (500 g) sorrel
¾ cup (150 g) butter
Salt
1 cup (2 dL) crème fraîche or heavy cream
3 shallots, chopped
24 frogs' legs
Pinch of black pepper
⅓ cup (1 dL) Sylvaner wine
1½ quarts (1½ L) consommé or beef broth or Chicken Stock (page 60)
6 egg yolks
1 tablespoon chopped chives

Clean and wash the sorrel.

Melt half the butter with a pinch of salt in a saucepan and sauté the sorrel until all the liquid has evaporated.

Add half the cream and cook for a few minutes more. Then press mixture through a strainer or food mill or whirl in a blender or food processor. Reserve the purée.

Heat the remaining butter and sauté the shallots. Add the frogs' legs, salt, and pepper. Cook for several minutes. Add the wine. Simmer until frogs' legs are cooked.

Remove the frogs' legs and skin them. Stir the cooking liquid into the consommé. Add the sorrel purée and heat.

Over very low heat or in a double boiler, whisk the egg yolks and the remaining cream, mixing continually until frothy. Gently and gradually add the hot consommé to this mixture while stirring constantly with the whisk. Heat once more, without boiling, until slightly thickened.

Taste for seasoning, then ladle the soup over the frogs' legs placed in large soup bowls. Serve sprinkled with chopped chives.

Soupe à la Bière

Beer soup

½ cup + 2 tablespoons (125 g) butter
½ cup (50 g) all-purpose flour
1½ quarts (1½ L) light beer
Salt and black pepper
2 tablespoons (15 g) confectioners' sugar
Pinch of ground cinnamon
1 cup (2 dL) crème fraîche or heavy cream
6 thin slices French bread

Preparation time: 10 min.
Cooking time: 25 min.

Heat 6 tablespoons (75 g) butter and stir in flour. Cook until mixture becomes golden brown. Gradually add the beer and season to taste with salt, pepper, and—once the beer is thoroughly mixed with the *roux*—sugar and cinnamon. Bring to a boil. Let simmer, stirring occasionally, for approximately 20 minutes.

At the last moment, stir in cream.

While the soup is simmering, use a separate pan to fry slices of French bread in remaining butter until golden brown. Place the bread in the bottom of the soup tureen and pour the soup over it. Serve piping hot.

This soup may be served before the main dish; or it may be used as the main dish itself for a simple winter meal. In the latter case, serve smoked bacon with it or Strasbourg smoked sausages with mustard.

Beer soup has been a traditional dish for 3 centuries in both upper and lower Alsace.

Pike de l'Ill in Cream Sauce (p. 131).

Soupe à l'Oignon Gratinée

Onion soup au gratin

1 pound (400 g) yellow onions
½ cup (100 g) butter
½ cup (50 g) all-purpose flour
2 quarts (2 L) beef broth
Salt and black pepper
1 10-ounce (300 g) loaf French bread
1½ cups (150 g) grated Gruyère cheese

Preparation time: 10 min.
Cooking time: 50 min.

Chop the onions finely and sauté in butter, stirring frequently. Sprinkle with the flour. Cook for 5 minutes, stirring gently.

Add the broth and season with salt and pepper. Cook for 30 minutes, stirring occasionally. Taste for seasoning.

Pour the soup into an ovenproof or an earthenware pot.

Toast several slices of French bread and float them on the surface of the soup. Sprinkle with the grated Gruyère.

Place the tureen in broiler and heat until a golden crust forms on the surface of the soup.

This soup can also be served in individual bowls.

Although Swiss in origin, this soup has been adopted in southern Alsace and in the valleys of the mountain country.

Soupe au Lait

Milk soup

Preparation time: 5 min.
Cooking time: 15 min.

8 ounces (200 g) bread
½ cup (100 g) butter
2 shallots, chopped
2 cups (5 dL) milk
2 cups (5 dL) crème fraîche or heavy cream
Salt and black pepper
1 tablespoon chopped chives
1 tablespoon chopped chervil

Cut the bread into cubes. In a large saucepan, sauté bread in 2 tablespoons (28 g) of the butter.

Add shallots and stir in the milk and cream. Season with salt and pepper.

Bring soup to a gentle boil for 5 or 10 minutes, being careful not to let the milk boil over.

Add remaining butter and sprinkle with the chives and chervil.

This is a family-style soup popular among both townspeople and farmers in the middle and upper valleys of the mountain country.

FISH AND SHELLFISH

Alsatian seafood dishes are noted for their use of *écrevisses* (crayfish). Since these are of limited availability in the United States, see the note on page 56.

All recipes are for six servings.

Ecrevisses à la Nage au Traminer

Crayfish poached in Traminer

36 medium crayfish

Court-bouillon:
1 carrot
2 onions
3 shallots
½ celeriac
1 leek, white part only
1 clove garlic
1 bottle Gewürztraminer wine
3 cups (¾ L) water
1 sprig thyme
Several sprigs parsley
Pinch of tarragon
1 teaspoon ground cumin
Salt and black pepper

Preparation time: 30 min.
Cooking time: 1 hr., 10 min.
Suggested Wines: Riesling, Gewürztraminer, or Pinot Gris

Peel, wash, and chop the vegetables.

Place vegetables in a saucepan with the wine and water. Add the herbs, spices, salt, and pepper. Simmer for 1 hour.

Meanwhile, clean the crayfish and wash them. Add to the simmering wine mixture for about 10 minutes.

Remove the crayfish and place in individual soup bowls. Spoon some of the cooking liquid over and serve.

Ecrevisses à l'Alsacienne

Alsatian crayfish

Preparation time: 30 min.
Cooking time: 45 min.
Suggested Wines:
Riesling or Pinot Gris

1 carrot
½ celeriac
1 leek, white part only
3 shallots
1 cup (200 g) butter
½ cup (1 dL) oil
2 cups (½ L) Sylvaner wine
1 cup (¼ L) Fish Stock (page 63)
1 tablespoon chopped tomato
Pinch of salt
1 mill-turn black pepper
36 medium crayfish
1 teaspoon chopped parsley
1 teaspoon chopped fresh tarragon

Dice the vegetables and the shallots and sauté for 20 minutes in a combination of ¼ cup (50 g) butter and all the oil.

Add the wine and stock. Add the chopped tomato. Season with salt and pepper. Boil for 3 minutes.

Clean the crayfish. Wash and add to the above mixture. Cook for 10 minutes, then remove the crayfish and place in a vegetable dish. Keep hot.

Boil cooking liquid until reduced by half its original volume. Remove from heat and stir in the remaining butter. Reheat slightly only if necessary since long heating breaks down the sauce.

Taste for seasoning, then pour this sauce over the crayfish.

Sprinkle with parsley and tarragon. Serve immediately.

A rich, delicious crayfish dish of rare delicacy.

Flan d'Écrevisses

Crayfish flan

1 recipe Court-Bouillon, as given for Crayfish Poached in Traminer, (page 122)
24 crayfish
1⅔ cups (6 dL) crème fraîche or heavy cream
1½ cups (4 dL) milk
Salt and black pepper
Dash of grated nutmeg
4 large eggs
8 egg yolks
1 recipe Crayfish Sauce (page 66)

Preparation time: 15 min.
Cooking time: 1 hr. (plus additional time to prepare court-bouillon)
Suggested Wine: Riesling

Prepare the court-bouillon as described on page 122.

Cook the crayfish in the court-bouillon. This can be prepared ahead of time.

Pull off the tails and reserve; they will be used in preparing the sauce. Grind the carcasses coarsely and place in a pot. Add the cream and the milk. Simmer over very low heat for about 30 minutes.

Strain, pressing out all liquid. Season liquid with salt, pepper, and nutmeg. Place mixture over heat and simmer for 15 minutes, stirring steadily.

Meanwhile beat together the whole eggs and the egg yolks in a large bowl. Blend the cream mixture into the eggs, beating continuously.

Preheat the oven to 400°F (200°C).

Pour mixture into 6 small buttered 6-ounce (1½-dL) molds or custard cups. Place the molds in a pan and fill pan with water until it reaches ⅔ of the way up the side of the molds.

Poach flans in a hot oven for about 25 to 30 minutes or until firm to the touch.

While hot, loosen edges of the flans with the tip of a knife and unmold onto serving platters. Spoon Crayfish Sauce over the flan.

This is an outstanding shellfish dish—aromatic as well as nourishing.

Ragoût de Queues d'Écrevisses

Crayfish-tail ragoût

Preparation time: 30 min.
Cooking time: 25 min.
Suggested Wines:
Sylvaner or Riesling

60 crayfish
½ cup (100 g) butter or Crayfish Butter (page 59)
2 cups (½ L) crème fraîche or heavy cream
Salt and black pepper

Court-Bouillon:
1 carrot
1 leek
1 onion
2 quarts (2 L) water
1 sprig thyme
½ bay leaf
Salt and black pepper

Prepare the court-bouillon.

Peel, wash, and thinly slice the vegetables. Cook in water with the thyme, bay leaf, salt, and black pepper for about 15 minutes.

Wash and clean the crayfish, then simmer in this liquid for about 10 minutes.

Cool the crayfish, then remove and shell the tails. Reserve the carcasses for preparing the Crayfish Butter (page 59).

Sauté the tails in the butter or Crayfish Butter until they are lightly browned. Add the cream, salt, and black pepper. Cook for about 5 minutes longer. Taste for seasoning.

Pour mixture into a buttered ovenproof dish and brown quickly in a broiler, about 2 to 3 minutes. Serve immediately.

Grenouilles au Riesling

Frogs' legs in Riesling sauce

36 frogs' legs, skinned
1 cup (200 g) butter
Salt and black pepper
2 shallots, chopped
1½ cups (3 dL) Riesling wine
1 cup (2 dL) Chicken Stock (page 60)
1 cup (2 dL) crème fraîche or heavy cream
4 egg yolks
Juice of ½ lemon
1 tablespoon chopped parsley
1 tablespoon chopped chives

Preparation time: 15 min.
Cooking time: 25 min.
Suggested Wines:
Riesling or Pinot Blanc

Sauté the frogs' legs in half the butter until they are golden brown. Add salt, pepper, shallots, wine, and stock. Cook for 10 minutes.

Remove and drain the frogs' legs. Strain the cooking liquid, skim fat, and return to heat. Cook until reduced by half.

Mix cream with egg yolks. Stir mixture quickly into hot broth. Mix until thickened.

Put the frogs' legs into sauce and stir in the remaining butter and the lemon juice. Taste for seasoning.

Sprinkle with the parsley and chives. Serve piping hot.

Truites Farcies Braisées au Riesling

Stuffed trout baked in Riesling

Preparation time: 30 min.
Cooking time: 1 hr.
Suggested Wine: Riesling

6 trout, 8 ounces (200 g) each
1 onion, thinly sliced
2 cups (½ L) Riesling wine
2 cups (½ L) crème fraîche or heavy cream
⅓ cup (75 g) butter
Salt and pepper

Stuffing:
1 medium carrot
1 stalk celery
1 leek, white part only
12 ounces (300 g) fresh mushrooms
1 large truffle
2 tablespoons (28 g) butter
2 eggs, beaten
Salt and black pepper

Clean and bone the trout, removing long spinal bone. Wash and dry well. Prepare stuffing. Cut carrot, celery, leek, mushrooms, and truffle into thin strips. Sauté in butter for 25 minutes.

Preheat the oven to 350°F (175°C). Cool the vegetables, then stir in the beaten eggs. Season with salt and pepper.

Stuff the trout with truffle mixture. Arrange stuffed trout on a buttered ovenproof dish. Sprinkle with onion. Add the wine and bake in moderate oven for 10 to 15 minutes or until cooked.

Remove the trout from the baking dish and gently pull off the skins. Arrange on a warm buttered serving platter. Keep hot.

Strain the cooking liquid and reduce to half its original volume. Stir in the cream, and simmer until reduced and thickened. Remove from heat and stir in butter. Season with salt and pepper.

Cover the trout with sauce and serve.

OPTIONAL

The dish may be decorated with a few sautéed mushroom caps, and with a few truffle slices. It may also be served with a Crayfish Sauce (page 66).

Truites au Bleu

Blue trout

6 very fresh trout, about 8 ounces (200 g) each

Court-Bouillon:
1 onion, chopped
2 carrots, chopped
½ celeriac or 1 stalk celery, chopped
1 leek, white part only, chopped
Dash of thyme
½ bay leaf
3 cups (¾ L) water
1 cup (¼ L) Alsatian white wine, preferably Sylvaner
Salt and black pepper

Garnish:
Lemon slices
5 to 6 tablespoons chopped parsley

Preparation time: 10 min.
Cooking time: 40 min.
Suggested Wines:
Sylvaner, Pinot Blanc, or Riesling

Make the court-bouillon by combining all the vegetables, herbs, and liquids. Add salt and pepper and cook for 20 to 30 minutes.

Put the trout into the hot court-bouillon and simmer for about 8 minutes. The skin will turn blue.

Serve the trout directly on a fish dish, or arrange them on a dish lined with a folded napkin. Garnish and decorate with lemon slices and chopped parsley. Serve with steamed new potatoes and melted butter or Hollandaise Sauce (page 67).

Note: For this recipe to be authentic, you should have live, fresh trout if possible. Have fish man filet the trout removing the long spine bone and the head, if desired. This dish can be made with frozen trout but the color of the skin will not turn blue.

Truites aux Amandes

Trout almondine

Preparation time: 30 min.
Cooking time: 15 min.
Suggested Wine: Riesling

6 trout, 8 ounces (200 g) each
Salt and black pepper
Flour for dredging
1 cup (250 g) butter
2 shallots, chopped
1 cup (¼ L) Riesling or Sylvaner wine
1 cup (¼ L) crème fraîche or heavy cream
1 cup (100 g) blanched and sliced almonds
1 tablespoon each chopped parsley and chopped chives

Preheat the oven to 400°F (200°C).

Clean the trout and remove the gills. If trout are frozen, then use frozen; do not thaw. Season with salt and pepper, and roll lightly in flour.

Heat ¼ cup (60 g) of the butter in a skillet and sauté the trout until lightly browned.

Butter a baking dish with ¼ cup (60 g) butter, and sprinkle with the shallots. Place the trout on the dish and sprinkle wine over them.

Bake fish in hot oven for 8 minutes, basting from time to time.

Pour the cream over trout.

Place the remaining butter in a skillet and melt. Sauté the almonds lightly until they turn golden.

Pour the butter and almonds over the trout. Sprinkle with parsley and chives.

This is one of the most tasty traditional recipes of Alsatian cuisine.

Pâté de Truite et de Brochet

Pâté of trout and pike

3 trout, 8 ounces (250 g) each
Salt and black pepper
1 cup (2 dL) Riesling wine
1 recipe Pike Mousse (page 134)
1 truffle, chopped
2 hard-cooked eggs, chopped
18 crayfish, prepared as for Alsatian Crayfish (page 123)
1 teaspoon chopped parsley
1 recipe Pie Dough (page 210)
⅓ recipe (300 g) Puff Pastry (page 212)
1 egg yolk
1 recipe Crayfish Sauce (page 66) or 1 recipe White Butter (page 58)

Marinating time: 10 min.
Preparation time: 45 min.
Cooking time: 35 min.
Suggested Wines:
Sylvaner or Riesling

Filet the trout, sprinkle with salt and pepper, and marinate 10 minutes in wine.

Mix Pike Mousse with the truffle, hard-cooked eggs, crayfish tails, and parsley.

Preheat the oven to 400° F (200° C).

Butter a 9-inch (23-cm) springform pan and line the bottom and side with the Pie Dough. Spread half the pike mixture over the dough. Place the trout filets on top. Cover with remaining pike mixture. Roll out Puff Pastry large enough to cover pan. Seal the pastry to the other dough by brushing edges with water and pressing them firmly together. Cut a 1-inch (2½-cm) round hole in the middle of the covering dough so that the steam may escape.

Brush the top of the pâté with egg yolk and bake in hot oven for 50 to 60 minutes or until richly browned.

Cool slightly, then remove sides of pan. Cut into wedges.

Serve the Crayfish Sauce or White Butter separately.

This is a scrumptuous gourmet treat.

Brochet de l'Ill à la Crème

Pike de l'Ill in cream sauce

photo page 118

1 pike, 5½ to 6 pounds (2½ to 3 kg)
½ cup (100 g) chopped shallots
Salt and black pepper
1 cup (¼ L) Riesling wine
2 cups (½ L) crème fraîche or heavy cream
Juice of ½ lemon
½ cup (100 g) butter
1 tablespoon chopped parsley

Preparation time: 30 min.
Cooking time: 30 min.
Suggested Wines:
Riesling or Sylvaner

Preheat the oven to 400° F (200° C).

Clean and wash the pike. Generously butter a baking dish and sprinkle with shallots. Place fish in pan and season with salt and pepper. Add the wine and cream.

Bake in a hot oven for 20 minutes, basting frequently.

When the pike is cooked, place on a hot serving platter.

Strain pan juices into a saucepan and season to taste with salt and pepper. Heat to just bubbling, then remove from heat and stir in lemon juice and butter.

Cover the pike with sauce and sprinkle with the chopped parsley. Serve very hot.

OPTIONAL

The pike may be garnished with 1 pound (450 g) thinly sliced mushrooms that have been sautéed in ¼ cup (50 g) butter and with a slice of lemon. Spoon mushrooms over pike before topping with the sauce.

This is a sumptuous dish with an unforgettable taste.

rochet au Pinot Noir

Pike in Pinot Noir

6 pounds (3 kg) pike, preferably 6 individual small fish
1 onion
1 carrot
½ stalk celery
1 leek
1 cup (300 g) butter
Salt and black pepper
2 cups (½ L) Pinot Noir wine
½ cup (1 dL) crème fraîche or heavy cream
1 tablespoon chopped parsley
1 tablespoon chopped chives

Preparation time: 30 min.
Cooking time: 30 to 40 min.
Suggested Wines: Pinot Noir or Riesling

Clean and wash the fish.

Peel and wash vegetables. Slice them thinly. Melt ⅓ of the butter in a heatproof roasting pan and sauté vegetables.

Place the fish on the vegetables, season with salt and pepper, and add the wine. Cover tightly.

Cook fish over low heat for 20 to 30 minutes or until pike flakes easily. The time will vary according to the size of the fish.

Note: Excessive cooking harms the fish. It is better, in this case, to undercook than to overcook.

Pour off pan juices and vegetables and boil rapidly until liquid is reduced to half its original volume. Stir in cream and remaining butter.

Arrange the fish on a serving platter and spoon some of the sauce over them. Sprinkle with chopped parsley and chives. Serve the remainder of the sauce in a separate dish.

This outstanding dish probably goes back to the eighteenth century. It originated in the valley at the foot of Mount Hohneck.

Matelote de Poissons au Riesling

Riesling fish stew

4½ pounds (2 kg) pike, sea bass, perch, trout, and eel (whole)
2 quarts (2 L) water
2 onions, chopped coarsely
2 carrots, chopped coarsely
2 leeks, chopped coarsely
1 tablespoon chopped parsley
2 stalks thyme
½ bay leaf
Pinch of tarragon
Pinch of grated nutmeg
Salt and black pepper
2 cups (½ L) Riesling wine
6 tablespoons (80 g) butter
½ cup (50 g) all-purpose flour
1 cup (¼ L) crème fraîche or heavy cream
4 egg yolks

Preparation time: 45 min.
Cooking time: 1 hr.
Suggested Wine: Riesling

Garnish:
Slices of French bread
4 tablespoons butter
¼ pound (100 g) fresh mushrooms, sliced

Clean fish and remove heads. Wash fish and cut into medium-sized pieces. Use the fish heads to prepare a stock. Put them in a large pot with the water, vegetables, herbs, and spices and add salt and pepper to taste. Simmer over low heat for about 30 minutes.

In another pot, combine the pieces of fish with about 1½ quarts (1½ L) of the fish stock and the wine and heat. Put the pieces of eel in first because eel takes longer to cook. Then add the other fishes in the following order: pike, sea bass, perch, trout. Add salt and pepper. Simmer for 15 minutes, then remove fish and keep hot.

In a saucepan, melt the butter and stir in the flour. Cook without browning for 5 minutes. Let cool, then very gradually stir in all of the liquid in which the fish were cooked. Simmer uncovered for 10 minutes.

Beat the cream with the egg yolks. Stir this mixture into the sauce quickly and mix until thickened. Do not boil.

Prepare the garnish. Sauté the bread slices in half the butter and set aside. Then sauté the mushrooms in the remaining butter.

Arrange the fish on a hot platter and cover with sauce. Decorate with bread and mushrooms. Serve with Alsatian Noodles (page 203).

Mousse de Brochet

Pike mousse

Preparation time: 10 min.
Cooking time: 20 min.

12 ounces (300 g) pike filet, cut into cubes
3 egg whites
1 cup (2 dL) crème fraîche or heavy cream
Salt and black pepper
1 recipe Crayfish Sauce (page 66)

Place pike filet and egg whites in a food processor and process until smooth.

Gradually beat in cream. Season to taste with salt and pepper.

Preheat the oven to 350° F (180° C).

Pour mousse mixture into well-buttered custard cups and place cups into pan with water coming two-thirds up the sides of the cups. Bake in a moderate oven for 20 minutes.

Loosen the edges of the cups with the tip of a knife. Unmold onto a serving dish and cover with Crayfish Sauce.

Note: This mousse is also used uncooked for stuffing various kinds of fish or—especially—the Pâté of Trout and Pike (page 130).

Filet of Sole with Noodles (p. 139), with Cabbage Salad (p. 87). (These two dishes are shown together here for the sake of illustration, and should not be served at the same meal.)

APPELLATION

Carpe à la Bière

Carp in beer

1 carp, about 4½ to 6 pounds (2 to 3 kg)
1¼ cups (150 g) chopped white onions
⅔ cup (150 g) butter
½ cup (30 g) crumbled gingerbread
½ cup (50 g) chopped celery
Salt and black pepper
Bouquet garni (celery leaves, dill, lemon rind, thyme)
2 to 3 quarts (2 to 3 L) light beer

Preparation time: 40 min.
Cooking time: 1 hr., 15 min.
Suggested Wines:
Sylvaner or Riesling

Preheat the oven to 300° F (150° C).

Clean carp. Reserve milt.

In a fish or baking pan, sauté the onions lightly in ⅓ cup (75 g) of the butter.

Sprinkle gingerbread and celery over the onions. Lay the carp on the bed of gingerbread, celery, and onions. Sprinkle with salt and pepper. Add the bouquet garni.

Cover the fish completely with beer and bake in a slow oven for 1 hour.

Meanwhile, poach the milt in boiling salted water for 5 minutes, then dice.

Remove the carp from the pan with great care and place on a hot serving platter. Decorate with the pieces of milt. Keep warm.

Strain half the pan juices into a saucepan and boil until reduced by half. Remove saucepan from heat and stir in remaining butter. Pour this sauce over the carp and serve immediately.

This is a traditional recipe of the slopes and valleys in the mountain country.

Saumon en Papillote Sauce aux Herbes

Salmon en papillote with an herb sauce

Marinating time: 1 hr.
Preparation time: 30 min.
Cooking time: 25 min.
Suggested Wine:
Riesling

4½ pounds (2 kg) fresh salmon
1 cup (2 dL) Riesling wine
1 lemon slice
Salt and black pepper
3 slices lean smoked bacon, each slice cut into 2 lengthwise strips
1 tablespoon chopped parsley
1 teaspoon dried thyme, crumbled
½ bay leaf, crumbled

Sauce:
2 shallots, chopped
¼ teaspoon tarragon
2 egg yolks
8 ounces (250 g) butter, melted
1 tablespoon crème fraîche or heavy cream
1 pinch each chopped parsley, chervil, and leek

Filet the salmon or have the fish merchant do it.

Cut the filets into 6 serving-size pieces and marinate for 1 hour in a mixture of the wine, lemon slice, salt, and pepper. Drain fish and reserve marinade.

Preheat the oven to 400° F (200° C).

Wrap each salmon piece in a thin strip of bacon, from which you have trimmed off the fat. Salt very lightly.

Grease a large sheet of parchment paper or aluminum foil with oil and place on cookie sheet. Arrange the pieces of salmon on one-half of the sheet. Sprinkle with some of the parsley, thyme, and bay leaf. Fold the other half of the sheet over the salmon and seal.

Bake in a hot oven for 15 minutes.

Over low heat, combine the reserved marinade with the shallots and tarragon and cook until reduced by half. Remove the lemon slice. Beat the egg yolks, mixing gently with a whisk. Beat in some of the hot liquid, then stir the sauce into remaining hot liquid. Cook over low heat until sauce thickens slightly, but do not boil. Gradually incorporate butter in small amounts, then beat in the cream.

Add a bit of parsley, chervil, and leek. Season to taste with salt and pepper.

Arrange the salmon, still in its paper wrapper, on a heated platter. Serve the sauce separately. Open the wrapper only when the platter is on the table, so that everyone can have the full advantage of the salmon's delicious aroma. Serve topped with sauce.

Carpe Frite

Fried carp

1 large carp about 4½ pounds (2 kg), or 2 each about 2¼ pounds (1 kg)
Salt and black pepper
2 cups (½ L) milk
⅔ cup (100 g) all-purpose flour
Fat or oil for deep-frying
Parsley sprigs
1 recipe Sauce Mayonnaise (page 72) or Rémoulade Sauce (page 71)

Preparation time: 15 min.
Cooking time: 20 min.
Suggested Wines:
Sylvaner or Riesling

Clean the carp and wash well. Split the fish in half and then cut it into medium pieces (or you can have your fish man do this for you). Season with salt and pepper.

Dip the fish pieces in milk, then roll in flour.

Heat the fat to 300–350° F (150–175° C). Fry the fish for 1 minute. Remove and drain. This will "blanche" the fish, as it is called.

Just before serving, increase the heat of the fryer to between 400 and 450°F (200 to 225°C). Put the pieces of carp into fat again and fry until they become golden, about 5 to 6 minutes.

Drain fish on absorbent paper and arrange on a hot serving platter.

Lightly fry the parsley sprigs in hot fat for 30 seconds then sprinkle over fish. Accompany with a Mayonnaise or Rémoulade Sauce.

VARIATION

Marinate the pieces of fish for 2 hours in a mixture of 2 parts vinegar with 1 part water—enough to cover. Add 1 chopped onion, a tablespoon of chopped parsley, 2 stalks of thyme, ½ bay leaf, 1 pinch of salt, and 2 mill-turns of black pepper.

Drain the fish, wipe dry, and roll in flour. Fry as directed.

This is a succulent, rich, and nourishing dish.

ilets de Soles aux Nouilles

Filet of sole with noodles

photo page 134

Preparation time: 30 min.
Cooking time: 20 min.
Suggested Wine:
Riesling

12 filets of sole, about 1¼ to 1½ pounds (500 to 600 kg)
2 shallots, chopped
1 tomato, diced
1 cup (¼ L) Sylvaner or Riesling wine
1 recipe Fish Stock (page 63)
Salt and black pepper
8 ounces (250 g) very thin noodles
1 cup (2 dL) crème fraîche or heavy cream
1 recipe Hollandaise Sauce (page 67)
6 cooked whole crayfish (optional)

Preheat the oven to 350° F (180° C).

Flatten the filets gently with the flat edge of a knife and fold each in half lengthwise. Arrange fish in a buttered baking platter and sprinkle with shallots and tomato. Cover with wine and stock. Sprinkle with salt and pepper.

Bake fish in a moderate oven for 10 minutes.

Cook the noodles in boiling salted water for 8 minutes. Drain.

Mix the noodles with half the cream. Season with salt and pepper and heat until bubbly. Place noodles and sauce on 6 ovenproof serving dishes.

Remove the filets from the oven and strain poaching liquid into a saucepan. Arrange 2 filets with some of the vegetables on each dish atop the noodles. Keep warm.

Boil the poaching liquid until reduced by half. Add the remaining cream and simmer 5 minutes longer. Gently fold in the Hollandaise Sauce. Taste for seasoning and spoon over the filets of sole.

Increase oven temperature to 400° F (200° C) or preheat the broiler.

Brown fish slightly in hot oven or place under broiler until golden brown.

Serve garnished with crayfish, if desired.

Soles au Traminer

Sole Traminer

- *6 whole sole, each weighing 8 ounces (250 g)*
- *1 cup (2 dL) Fish Stock (page 63), made from the sole fish heads*
- *8 ounces (200 g) fresh mushrooms, sliced*
- *4 small shallots, chopped*
- *1 cup (100 g) chopped parsley*
- *Salt and black pepper*
- *2 cups (½ L) Traminer wine*
- *½ cup (1 dL) crème fraîche or heavy cream*
- *1 recipe Hollandaise Sauce (page 67)*

Preparation time: 20 min.
Cooking time: 15 min.
(additional time needed to prepare stock)
Suggested Wines: Riesling or Traminer (but not too heavy)

Clean the fish and remove the heads. Use the heads to make the stock, following the directions on page 63.

Preheat the oven to 400° F (200° C).

Place the mushrooms, shallots, and parsley in a buttered baking dish. Place fish on this vegetable bed and sprinkle with salt and pepper.

Pour a mixture of the wine and stock over the fish. Cover with greased paper or foil and bake in a hot oven for about 10 minutes.

Strain the poaching liquid into a saucepan. Leave fish and vegetables on platter. Keep warm.

Boil the poaching liquid until it is reduced to about 6 tablespoons.

Stir in the cream and the Hollandaise Sauce. Pour this sauce over the fish and glaze rapidly in a very hot oven (400°F or 200°C) or place under the broiler until browned.

A subtle and unusual dish.

Morue à la Ménagère

Country-style mackerel

2½ pounds (1 kg) salted mackerel (See note)
2 quarts (2 L) water
1 cup (2 dL) milk
1¼ cups (300 g) butter
3 onions, thinly sliced
12 ounces (300 g) French bread
1 pound (400 g) potatoes
Salt and black pepper

Soaking time: 24 hr.
Preparation time: 20 min.
Cooking time: 1 hr.
Suggested Wines:
Riesling or Pinot Gris

Wash and remove salt by soaking fish in fresh water for 24 hours, changing water several times.

Cook the fish in water mixed with milk until tender and easily flaked. Drain and remove skin. Break into large chunks.

In a skillet, heat ⅓ of the butter. Sauté the onions until they are lightly browned.

Cut the bread into large cubes and brown in half the remaining butter in another skillet.

Peel the potatoes and cook in salted water until tender. Cut into thin slices.

Preheat the oven to 350° F (180° C).

In a buttered baking dish, make successive layers of onions, potatoes, croutons, and mackerel. Sprinkle each layer with salt and pepper.

Melt remaining butter and pour over fish. Bake in a moderate oven for 15 to 20 minutes. Serve very hot.

Note: This can also be made with fresh mackerel. Eliminate the soaking step at the beginning.

This is a traditional Alsatian dish which was served mostly during Lent. It is really good, but remember, don't try to reduce the amount of butter.

MEATS

Although this chapter includes some of the more familiar, also consider those special Alsatian dishes that are rarely tried in this country. Along with the very famous Choucroute are also Schifela, which combines a shoulder of pork with pickled turnips, Quenelles of Pork Liver, and Blood Sausage. These hearty meals all serve six persons unless otherwise noted.

Baeckeofe, or Beckenoffe

Meat and vegetable pie

photo page 150

1 pound (500 g) boneless lamb, preferably shoulder or neck
1 pound (500 g) boneless pork, preferably neck
1 pound (500 g) boneless beef, preferably shoulder or brisket
2 pigs' feet
3 large onions
3 leeks
3 large carrots
3 stalks celery
3½ pounds (1½ kg) potatoes
6 tablespoons (80 g) rendered goose fat or lard
Salt and black pepper
1 cup (100 g) all-purpose flour

Marinade:
2 carrots
1 onion
1 leek, white part only
1 clove garlic
1 shallot
3 stalks thyme
½ bay leaf
Salt and black pepper
1 bottle Sylvaner wine

Marinating time: 12 hr.
Preparation time: 45 min.
Cooking time: 2 hr., 30 min.
Suggested Wines:
Sylvaner or Traminer

Cut the meats and the pigs' feet into pieces of 3 to 4 ounces (80 to 100 g) each. Place into a large earthenware or glass container.

Prepare the marinade. Peel, wash, and cut into rounds the carrots, onion, leek, garlic, and shallot. Sprinkle over meats. Add the thyme, bay leaf, salt, pepper, and wine. Mix, and let the meats marinate overnight.

Peel the remaining vegetables. Cut the onions, leeks, carrots, and celery into thin slices. Peel and wash the potatoes, then cut into slices about ¼ inch (½ cm) thick. Mix with vegetables.

Drain the meats and vegetables and reserve the marinade. Remove the bay leaf.

Preheat the oven to 400° F (200° C).

Grease the inside of a 4-quart (4-L) earthenware casserole with goose fat. Make a layer of half the raw vegetables and potatoes. Follow with a layer of all the marinated meats and vegetables. Top with remaining vegetables and potatoes. Season each layer with salt and pepper as you make it.

Pour in enough of the marinade to cover. If necessary to ensure covering, add a small amount of water to the marinade.

Make a paste of the flour mixed with some water.

Cover the pot and seal all around the lid with the pastry dough. This will prevent any steam from escaping. Bake in a hot oven for 2 hours, 30 minutes. Serve in the same pot.

Baeckeofe, the name given to this dish in Alsace, is a German word meaning "baker's oven." In the old days, housewives gave this dish to the local baker to cook in his oven. It is an unusually tasty, aromatic, and nourishing dish.

Daube à l'Aigre-Doux

Daube of sweet and sour beef 

3½ pounds (1½ kg) beef bottom round, cut into long, thin strips
1 quart (1 L) Pinot Noir wine
1 onion, sliced
2 cloves garlic, crushed
1 carrot, sliced
1 sprig parsley
1 sprig tarragon
Salt and black pepper
4 lumps sugar
1 tablespoon oil
½ cup (100 g) raisins
½ cup (1 dL) Kirsch
½ cup (1 dL) crème fraîche or heavy cream

Marinating time: 4 days
Preparation time: 30 min.
Cooking time: 2 hr.
Suggested Wine: Pinot Noir

Place the meat in an earthenware bowl, along with the wine and the onion, garlic, carrot, parsley, tarragon, salt, pepper, and sugar. Cover and allow to marinate for 3 or 4 days in the refrigerator.

Remove the meat, straining and reserving the marinade. Pat meat dry with paper towels.

Heat oil in a Dutch oven and brown the meat. Add the marinade and simmer for between 1½ to 2 hours, depending on the kind of beef and the size of the strips.

Meanwhile soak the raisins in the Kirsch for 1 hour.

Add the raisins to the stew. Cook for 10 minutes more. Season to taste with salt and pepper. Place the meat on a heated serving platter. Keep warm. Mix pan juices with cream and cook until thickened. Serve sauce spooned over meat and vegetables.

This is a very old recipe of the plains which seems to have originated in the upper Rhine country.

VARIATION

You may use Pinot Blanc in place of the Pinot Noir, but then serve a Pinot Blanc with the dish.

Pièce de Boeuf au Pinot Noir

Beef with marrow in Pinot Noir
photo page 166

- *1 cup (200 g) butter*
- *1 beef filet, about 3 pounds (200 g)*
- *Salt and black pepper*
- *4 shallots*
- *1 cup (2 dL) Pinot Noir wine*
- *½ bay leaf*
- *1 sprig thyme*
- *1 cup (2 dL) Brown Veal Stock (page 61)*
- *1 tablespoon Meat Glaze (page 64)*
- *6 ounces (150 g) beef marrow (ask your butcher to remove it from the bones), cut into ½-inch (1½-cm) slices*
- *1 tablespoon of mixed chopped parsley, chervil, and chives*

Preparation time: 20 min.
Cooking time: 1 hr.
Suggested Wine: Pinot Noir

Preheat the oven to 400° F (200° C).

Melt ¼ cup (60 g) butter.

Brush beef filet with melted butter. Sprinkle with salt and pepper.

Roast meat in a hot oven for 30 to 35 minutes or until a meat thermometer registers "rare." Keep filet hot.

Peel and chop the shallots. In a saucepan heat ¼ cup (60 g) of butter. Sauté the shallots until very brown. Add the wine and, using a whisk, scrape the bottom of the pan.

Add the bay leaf, thyme, stock, and meat glaze. Boil until liquid is reduced by half. Strain and stir in remaining butter. Taste for seasoning.

Poach marrow in salted water to cover.

Pour sauce from pan over meat. Place marrow on beef. Sprinkle with the herbs.

Cut beef into thick slices and serve with the sauce and a slice of marrow. Accompany this dish with Leeks Au Gratin (page 197) or Baked Sliced Potatoes (page 201).

Emincé de Boeuf à la Strasbourgeoise

Strasbourg beef

1½ pounds (600 g) beef filet
6 ounces (150 g) fresh foi gras (See note, page 55)
3 artichoke bottoms
⅔ cup (150 g) butter
3 shallots, minced
Salt and black pepper
2 tablespoons brandy
½ cup (1 dL) Riesling wine
1 cup (2 dL) Brown Veal Stock (page 61)
24 truffle slices
½ cup (1 dL) Port wine

Preparation time: 30 min.
Cooking time: 20 min.
Suggested Wines: Pinot Noir or Riesling

Cut the beef, the foie gras, and the artichoke bottoms into small ½-inch (1½-cm) cubes.

Heat 2 tablespoons (28 g) of the butter in a skillet and brown the beef. Add the foie gras and the artichokes, and sauté for about 3 minutes. Sprinkle with the shallots, salt, and pepper.

Remove beef, foie gras, and artichokes. Pour off the excess grease. Drain beef in a strainer. Stir the brandy and the Riesling into skillet. Bring to a boil, scraping loose the brown particles and allowing the liquid to cook until it has almost evaporated. Add the stock.

Simmer the truffle slices in Port for 10 minutes. Drain.

Place the meat, foie gras, and artichokes into the sauce and stir in the remaining butter. Taste for seasoning.

Place meat mixture on a heated platter and garnish with the slices of truffle. Pour wine juices over meat and serve.

Boeuf Bouilli et Bouillon de Boeuf aux Quenelles de Moelle

Boiled beef and beef broth with quenelles of marrow

2 white turnips
2 carrots
½ green cabbage
2 leeks
2 onions
1 stalk celery
3 sprigs parsley
3 cloves garlic
3½ pounds (1½ kg) boneless beef, preferably shoulder or ribs or brisket
1 oxtail, cut into 2-inch (5-cm) pieces
Several beef bones, with marrow
Salt and black pepper
1 bay leaf
½ cup (50 g) chopped chives
1 recipe Horseradish Sauce (page 70)

Preparation time: 30 min.
Cooking time: 3 hr.
Suggested Wines: Pinot Noir or Riesling

Quenelles:
12 ounces (300 g) beef marrow (from the bones used in the broth)
½ cup (50 g) dry bread crumbs
2 tablespoons (30 g) Cream of Wheat
3 egg yolks
Salt and black pepper
Dash of grated nutmeg

First prepare the bouillon. Peel, wash, and dice all the vegetables and garlic.

Put the beef, oxtail, and bones into a pot. Add water to cover and bring to a boil. Spoon off the foam. Add the vegetables, and skim foam once more. Add salt, pepper, and bay leaf.

Continue to skim foam during cooking so as to obtain a clear broth. Cook for 3 hours adding water to keep up level of liquid. Strain bouillon. Keep meats and vegetables hot.

Prepare the quenelles. Remove the marrow from the bones used in the bouillon. Press through a strainer into a bowl. Add the bread crumbs, cream of wheat, and egg yolks. Add salt, pepper, and nutmeg. Mix well.

Make small ¾-inch (2-cm) ovals of this mixture and cook in the bouillon for 10 minutes.

Add the chives. Serve bouillon and quenelles in a tureen. The meats are served on a heated platter, surrounded by the vegetables. Meats are enhanced with Horseradish Sauce.

This dish goes well with a green salad, red cabbage, braised celery, Pickled Plums (page 78). It is a recipe for what is actually an old Alsatian stew dating back to the Middle Ages. It is a traditional family dish.

Médaillons de Veau aux Fines Herbes

Medallions of veal with herbs

12 veal medallions, cut ½ inch (1½ cm) thick
Salt and black pepper
½ cup (50 g) all-purpose flour
1 cup (200 g) butter
1 cup (2 dL) Sylvaner wine
1 cup (2 dL) crème fraîche or heavy cream
1 tablespoon Dijon mustard
1 tablespoon mixed chopped parsley, tarragon, chervil, and chives

Preparation time: 15 min.
Cooking time: 20 min.
Suggested Wines:
Sylvaner or Riesling

Dry meat well, then dust with salt, pepper, and flour. Sauté veal in half the butter until brown on both sides and cooked. Arrange slices on a hot serving platter and keep hot.

Drain the butter from the skillet. Add the wine and cook for 5 minutes, scraping up the particles from the pan. Add the cream and simmer until the mixture has thickened. Stir in the mustard. Taste for seasoning.

Strain the sauce, then stir in the remaining butter.

Spoon the sauce over the veal and sprinkle generously with the herbs.

Serve this dish with Spaetzle (page 204) or Alsatian Noodles (page 203).

Meat and Vegetable Pie (p. 144).

ambon en Croûte

Ham en croute

Preparation time: 30 min.
Cooking time: 2 to 3 hr.
Serves: 15 to 20
Suggested Wines:
Sylvaner or Riesling

1 small smoked (precooked) ham, about 10 pounds (4½ kg)
1 bottle Sylvaner wine
2 onions, chopped
2 carrots, chopped
1 leek, chopped
1 sprig thyme
½ bay leaf
1 recipe Basic Bread Dough (page 206) or 2 recipes Pie Dough (page 210)
2 egg yolks, beaten

Place the ham in a large pot. Pour in the wine and additional water to cover. Add the vegetables along with the thyme and bay leaf.

Cook the ham in simmering water, allowing 10 minutes for each pound of ham. Remove the pot from heat and allow ham to cool in the cooking liquid.

Preheat oven to 350° F (180° C).

Remove the ham from the liquid and trim off the fat. Dry with paper towels.

Roll out the Bread Dough to a thickness of ⅛ inch (⅕ cm) on a floured surface and wrap the ham in the dough. Seal the edges by brushing with water and pressing with your fingers.

Make a round hole at the top of the ham. (If using Bread Dough, do not allow dough to rise.) Brush the dough with the egg yolks. Place on a greased baking pan.

Bake in a moderate oven for 1 hour or until crusty and brown.

Serve hot on a heated platter, accompanied by cooked spinach, Potatoes au Gratin (page 198), or a well-seasoned salad.

Poitrine de Veau Farcie

Stuffed breast of veal

1 veal breast, about 6 pounds (2¾ kg), cut with a pocket
1 tablespoon oil
¼ cup (50 g) butter, melted
1 carrot, diced
1 onion, diced
½ cup (1 dL) Sylvaner or Riesling wine
½ cup (1 dL) water or Brown Veal Stock (page 61)

Stuffing:
2 cups (150 g) fresh white bread crumbs
½ cup (1 dL) milk
2 onions, chopped
¼ cup (50 g) butter
8 ounces (250 g) ground pork, preferably from the neck
2 large eggs
1 tablespoon chopped parsley
Salt and black pepper

Preparation time: 1 hr.
Cooking time: 1 hr., 45 min.
Suggested Wines: Sylvaner or Riesling (according to what you use in the recipe)

Prepare the stuffing first. Soak the bread crumbs in the milk.

Cook the onions in butter for about 5 minutes.

Squeeze the bread crumbs dry with your hands, then mix with the pork. Add the eggs, sautéed onions, parsley, salt, and pepper. Mix well. Fill the breast of veal with this dressing and sew the opening closed.

Preheat the oven to 350° F (180° C).

Salt and pepper the exterior of the breast.

Pour the oil and butter into a roasting pan. Use onion and carrot to line the bottom of the pan. Place the breast on this bed of vegetables.

Place the pan into a moderate oven and roast. When the veal has browned—in about 30 to 40 minutes—add the wine and water or stock. Cover and roast gently for about 1 to 1½ hours, or until veal is tender. Timing depends on tenderness of veal. Baste often during cooking.

Remove the veal and cut into thick slices. Arrange on a hot serving platter.

Skim the grease from the cooking liquid and pour the liquid with the vegetables over the veal.

This dish may be served hot, with Spaetzle (page 204), or cold, with a green salad (lettuce or escarole).

The recipe has been a selection of the Prosper Montagné Gastronomic Club.

Estomac de Porc Farci

Stuffed stomach of pork

- *1 pork stomach*
- *2 handfuls rock salt*
- *2 cups (½ L) red wine vinegar*
- *2½ pounds (1 kg) potatoes, peeled and cubed*
- *½ cup (100 g) butter*
- *3 onions, chopped*
- *1 cup (100 g) chopped shallots*
- *12 ounces (300 g) pork filet*
- *1½ pounds (600 g) boneless pork shoulder*
- *½ cup (50 g) chopped parsley*
- *2 large eggs, beaten*
- *Salt and black pepper*
- *1 tablespoon Alsatian Four Spices (page 73)*
- *1 cup (2 dL) Brown Veal Stock (page 61)*

Soaking time: 2 days
Preparation time: 1 hr.
Cooking time: 3 hr., 30 min.
Suggested Wines: Riesling or Pinot Noir

Soak the pork stomach for 2 days in a mixture of rock salt and vinegar. Wash well in a sufficient quantity of water and remove the skin by scraping with a knife.

Parboil potatoes for 5 minutes in boiling salted water.

In a skillet, melt 2 tablespoons (28 g) of the butter and cook the onions and shallots until wilted. Add the potatoes and sauté for 10 minutes.

Cut the pork filet into ½-inch (1½-cm) cubes and brown in 2 tablespoons (28 g) of the butter.

Grind the pork shoulder coarsely and mix with the cubes of pork filet, parsley, eggs, and seasonings. Mix thoroughly. Add the cooked potatoes and onions, again mixing thoroughly.

Fill the stomach with this stuffing and sew openings closed. Cook for 2 hours in a pot of simmering water. From time to time during cooking, insert a thin needle into the stomach. When no liquid runs out through the hole made by the needle, the dressing is cooked. At that point, remove the stomach from the water and allow to drain.

Preheat the oven to 350° F (180° C).

Melt remaining butter in a heatproof roasting pan and put the stomach into the pan. Turn until stomach is coated with butter.

Roast stomach for about 45 minutes, then remove from oven and pour in the stock.

Cut the stomach into slices and arrange on a hot serving platter.

Heat the mixture of butter and broth—the roasting liquid—until bubbly. Serve with meat.

This recipe originated in the farm communities of the upper valleys. Typically, it is a late-autumn dish, since pigs are slaughtered in the pre-Christmas season.

Palette Salée et Fumée

Braised smoked shoulder of pork

1 smoked pork shoulder
½ cup (1 dL) water
1 carrot, chopped
1 onion, chopped
1 leek, chopped
½ celeriac, chopped
2⅓ cups (5 dL) Sylvaner wine
½ bay leaf

Steeping time: 6 hr.
Preparation time: 30 min.
Cooking time: 1 hr., 30 min.
Suggested Wines:
Sylvaner or Pinot Blanc

Put the pork into the water with the vegetables, wine, and bay leaf. Add more water if necessary until meat is covered.

Bring to a boil, lower heat, and simmer covered for approximately 90 minutes. Remove bay leaf.

Serve hot, on a heated platter, with potato salad.

Palette de Porc Salée aux Petits Légumes

Shoulder of pork with vegetables

1 leek, white part only, chopped
2 carrots, cut julienne style
½ celeriac, cut julienne style
12 small white onions
½ cup (100 g) butter
1 smoked pork shoulder
1 cup (2 dL) Riesling wine
1½ cups (3 dL) Brown Veal Stock (page 61)

Preparation time: 30 min.
Cooking time: 1 hr., 30 min.
Suggested Wines: Sylvaner or Riesling

Preheat the oven to 350° F (180° C).

Sauté leek, carrots, celeriac, and onions for 5 minutes in butter. Spread the vegetable mixture in a heatproof roasting pan. Place the pork shoulder atop this bed of vegetables. Add the wine and the stock.

Roast in a moderate oven for about 1 hour, 15 minutes, basting frequently.

Remove pork from the oven and cut into thin slices. Arrange the slices on a hot serving platter and surround with the vegetables.

Boil the cooking liquid until reduced to half its volume and spoon the remainder over the meat and vegetables.

Serve hot, with sautéed potatoes and a green salad; or, in the fall, with a corn salad.

This is a very tasty dish which seems to have originated along the lower Rhine in the eighteenth century.

Foie de Porc au Vinaigre

Pork liver au vinaigre

1½ pounds (600 g) pork liver
Salt and black pepper
1 cup (200 g) butter
1 tablespoon oil
12 ounces (300 g) fresh mushrooms, chopped
3 shallots, chopped
½ cup (1 dL) white wine vinegar
½ cup (1 dL) Sylvaner wine
1 cup (2 dL) Brown Veal Stock (page 61)
1 tablespoon chopped parsley and chives

Preparation time: 15 min.
Cooking time: 10 min.
Suggested Wine:
Sylvaner

Cut the liver into small pieces about ¾ inch (2 cm) long and ⅛ inch (½ cm) wide. Season with salt and pepper.

Sauté the liver in a mixture of half the butter and all the oil until cooked but not dry. Drain the liver and keep hot on a serving platter.

In a saucepan, sauté mushrooms and shallots lightly in ¼ cup (60 g) butter until golden, then place atop the pieces of liver.

Pour the vinegar and the wine into the saucepan and boil until only 2 tablespoons of liquid are left. Add the stock and, if necessary, continue cooking until slightly thickened.

Stir in remaining butter and taste for seasoning.

Pour sauce over liver and sprinkle with the parsley and chives.

Quenelles de Foie de Porc, or Lawerknepfle

Quenelles of pork liver

photo page 54

1 onion, chopped
2 cloves garlic, chopped
¼ cup (50 g) butter
8 ounces (250 g) fatty pork
8 ounces (250 g) pork liver
¾ cup (80 g) all-purpose flour
4 large eggs, lightly beaten
Salt and black pepper

Garnish:
2 onions, chopped
½ cup (100 g) butter
1 tablespoon chopped parsley

Preparation time: 30 min.
Chilling time: 4 to 5 hr.
Cooking time: 20 min.
Suggested Wine:
Sylvaner

Sauté onion and garlic lightly in butter.

Grind the pork and liver coarsely.

Add the onion, garlic, flour, and eggs to the chopped meat. Season with salt and pepper and mix thoroughly. Chill several hours. Shape mixture into 1-inch (2½-cm) ovals.

Bring salted water to a boil in a large pot. Cook the quenelles for 10 minutes in simmering water. They are cooked when they rise to the surface.

Remove dumplings from the water with a slotted spoon. Arrange on a hot serving platter.

Sauté onions in butter until golden, then sprinkle over quenelles. Top with parsley.

These quenelles go very well with, among other dishes, Alsatian Choucroute (page 160) or sautéed potatoes and a green salad.

Tripes au Riesling

Tripe in Riesling

Preparation time: 20 min.
Cooking time: 1 hr., 45 min.
Suggested Wines:
Riesling or Sylvaner

2½ pounds (1 kg) tripe (sold pre-cooked)
1 tablespoon oil
¾ cup (200 g) butter
2 large onions, chopped
3 cloves garlic, crushed
⅓ cup (50 g) all-purpose flour
1 cup (2 dL) Riesling wine
Salt and black pepper
Dash of grated nutmeg
1 tablespoon curry powder
1 cup (2 dL) Chicken Stock (page 60)
½ cup (1 dL) crème fraîche or heavy cream
1 tablespoon mixed chopped parsley and chives

Cut the tripe into julienne-style strips and sauté in a saucepan with the oil and ¼ cup (60 g) of the butter.

Add the onions and the garlic. Sprinkle with the flour and stir in the wine, salt, pepper, nutmeg, curry powder, and stock.

Simmer, covered, for 60 to 90 minutes, or until tripe is tender.

Stir in the cream and the remaining butter. Taste for seasoning.

Serve the tripe in a hot bowl, sprinkled with the parsley-and-chive mixture.

This is a very old recipe.

Choucroute Garnie à l'Alsacienne

Alsatian choucroute
photo page 54

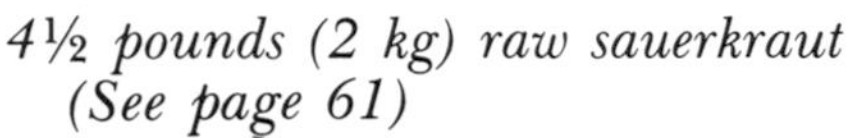

4½ pounds (2 kg) raw sauerkraut *(See page 61)*
2 smoked ham hocks
2½ pounds (1 kg) salt pork, or ½ smoked pork shoulder
12 ounces (300 g) smoked bacon, in 1 piece
12 ounces (300 g) salt bacon, in 1 piece
⅔ cup (150 g) lard
2 onions, chopped
2 cups (½ L) Sylvaner or Riesling wine
1 cup (¼ L) water
Salt and black pepper
3 cloves
6 juniper berries
1 bay leaf
3 cloves garlic
6 frankfurters (kosher kind) or Strasbourg sausage
3 smoked sausages or Colmar sausage
6 slices pork liver
8 ounces (200 g) bratwurst
1 ring blood sausage

Preparation time: 1 hr.
Cooking time: 2 hr.
Suggested Wines:
Riesling or Sylvaner (depending on which you've used in the recipe)

Wash the sauerkraut several times in a large amount of water. Drain well.

If meats are heavily salted, then wash or soak them before cooking.

Preheat the oven to 350° F (180° C).

In a heatproof roasting pan, melt half the lard and add the onions. Sauté until wilted, then add the wine and water.

Add the ham hocks, salt pork or smoked shoulder, smoked bacon, and salt bacon. Place the sauerkraut on top of these meats. Salt very lightly and sprinkle with black pepper.

Tie in a piece of cheesecloth the cloves, juniper berries, bay leaf and garlic. Add spice bag to pan.

Cover and cook in a moderate oven for 1 hour, 30 minutes.

In a saucepan, in simmering water, separately parboil the frankfurters, smoked sausages, and liver slices each for about 10 minutes.

Melt remaining lard in a skillet and brown the bratwurst and blood sausage. Cut blood sausage into 6 pieces.

When the sauerkraut is cooked, taste for seasoning. Remove cheesecloth bag.

Place sauerkraut in a large hot bowl or deep platter. Arrange the various meats and sausages over the sauerkraut. Serve the liver in a separate dish. Also in a separate dish, serve some boiled potatoes.

Note: This recipe calls for a large number of ingredients. Several meats, for example, are cooked with the sauerkraut. Obviously—and especially when you are cooking just for your family—you don't have to use all of them. You must in any case retain the bacon.

This is no doubt the best known of all Alsatian dishes. It is often mentioned in the literature of past centuries.

We know not only that it has always been popular as a family dish, but also that it often graced the tables of princes and bishops.

The origins of sauerkraut are lost in the dim reaches of time. The name itself, is old German: *sûrkrût,* meaning "sour cabbage." The Alsatian plain is ideal for growing the cabbage used in making sauerkraut. Essentially, the cultivation of this cabbage is limited to 3 areas of the lower Rhine, to the southeast of Strasbourg: Geispolsheim, Blaesheim, and Krautergersheim; and to 5 areas of the upper Rhine: Riedwihr, Illhaeusern, Holtzwihr, Bischwihr, and Wickerschwihr.

Sauerkraut may either be bought in stores in Alsace or made at home. The procedure is as follows: Remove any damaged leaves of a head of cabbage and remove the stem and core. Place the green leaves of the cabbage at the bottom of a small wooden barrel or stoneware pot. On top of these, place shredded cabbage leaves in layers, each layer alternating with a layer of rock salt mixed with juniper berries. On top, place a piece of cloth and, over the cloth, a lid—but a lid smaller than the diameter of the barrel or pot. Weigh the lid with a heavy rock so that it presses down on the cabbage. By the next day, the lid will be submerged in brine.

It requires 3 weeks of steeping before the cabbage becomes sauerkraut. The sauerkraut is then used as needed, with water being added to that which remains in the barrel so that it remains covered by liquid at all times.

If old sauerkraut is being used, it is soaked for 30 minutes in cold, clear water before being cooked.

chifela

Shoulder of pork with pickled turnips 

2 onions
⅔ cup (150 g) rendered goose fat or lard
4½ pounds (2 kg) salt turnips (available in specialty stores)
1 smoked boneless pork shoulder, about 1½ pounds (600 g)
12 ounces (300 g) smoked bacon, in 1 piece
12 ounces (300 g) salt bacon, in 1 piece
2 cloves garlic, chopped
2 cloves
½ bay leaf
2 cups (½ L) Sylvaner wine
2 cups (½ L) water
12 ounces (300 g) pork sausage links
¼ cup (50 g) butter

Preparation time: 1 hr.
Cooking time: 2 hr., 30 minutes
Suggested Wines: Sylvaner or Riesling

Preheat the oven to 350° F (175° C).

Peel and slice the onions thinly. Sauté lightly in a heatproof roasting pan with the goose fat.

Wash the turnips. Drain well and press dry with your hands. Spread half the turnips over the onions in the pan. Place the pork shoulder on the turnips, and then the smoked bacon followed by the salt bacon.

In a small square of cheesecloth, place the garlic, cloves, and bay leaf. Tie the end of the cloth to form a bag and put the spice bag into the pan. Cover with the rest of the turnips. Add the wine and water. Cover and bring to boil over medium heat. Then place in moderate oven for approximately 2 hours. Check the meat and the bacon occasionally during cooking and remove them as soon as they are sufficiently cooked. Avoid overcooking. Remove spice bag. Drain vegetables.

Cook the pork sausage in butter for about 10 minutes, turning often or until brown and cooked. Carve the meats into thick slices.

Arrange the turnips on a hot serving platter and over them spread the slices of meat, bacon, and sausage. Serving hot with either baked or boiled potatoes. This is a selection of the Prosper Montagné Gastronomic Club.

Boudin

Blood sausage

Preparation time: 1 hr.
Cooking time: 1 hr.
Suggested Wines: Pinot Noir or Sylvaner

5 large onions, chopped finely
3 leeks, chopped
½ cup (100 g) lard
1 tablespoon (7 g) all-purpose flour
4 small hard rolls
2⅓ cups (5 dL) crème fraîche or heavy cream
2⅓ cups (5 dL) milk
3 quarts (3 L) pig's blood (available from a pork butcher)
Salt and black pepper
Pinch of Alsatian Four Spices (page 73)
Sausage casings in 10-inch (25-cm) lengths

Garnish:
2 onions, thinly sliced or 2 apples, peeled, cored, and quartered
2 tablespoons (28 g) butter

Cook the onions and leeks in half the lard for 20 minutes. When cooked, sprinkle with the flour and mix well.

Soak the rolls in a mixture of the cream and milk for 20 minutes. Squeeze rolls dry.

Grind the onions, leeks, and bread together in a food processor or meat grinder set at medium.

In a bowl, mix crumb mixture with the blood. Season with salt, pepper, and the spices.

Fill individual lengths of casings with this mixture. Tie both ends.

Place the sausages in cold water and heat. The sausages should cook for about 30 minutes in simmering—not boiling—water. Test sausages by sticking a pin into them; if no liquid comes out, the sausages are cooked. Drain sausages and pat dry.

Brown the sausages in a skillet in remaining lard for 10 minutes.

Prepare garnish by sautéing either onions or apples in butter.

Place sausages on a hot platter and garnish with onions or apples.

POULTRY

All recipes serve six persons.

olailles aux Écrevisses

Chicken with crayfish

Preparation time: 30 min.
Cooking time: 1 hr.
Suggested Wines:
Riesling or Sylvaner

24 medium crayfish
2 very small chickens, about 2 pounds (900 g) each, or 2 game hens
Salt and black pepper
¾ cup (200 g) butter
3 shallots, chopped
1⅓ cups (3 dL) Riesling wine
Pinch of saffron
1⅓ cups (3 dL) crème fraîche or heavy cream
4 egg yolks
1 small truffle, sliced (optional)

Court-Bouillon:
1 quart (1 L) water
2 carrots, sliced
2 leeks, white part only, sliced
1 onion, sliced
1 stalk celery, sliced
Bouquet garni (thyme, marjoram, tarragon, parsley, rosemary)

Make the court-bouillon by cooking water with the carrots, leeks, onion, celery, and bouquet garni for 5 minutes.

Add crayfish to court-bouillon and simmer 8 to 10 minutes. Let cool.

Shell the crayfish. Reserve the meat from the tails and crush the carcasses into very small pieces.

Truss the chickens. Season chickens inside and out with salt and pepper. Melt ½ cup (125 g) of the butter in a large cast-iron pot or Dutch oven. Place the chickens into the pot and cook in the butter without browning. Add the shallots and the wine.

Add to the pot the crushed crayfish carcasses and the saffron. Cover and simmer for about 30 to 35 minutes.

Remove the cooked chickens and cut into serving-size pieces. Arrange the pieces on a platter and keep hot.

Beef with Marrow in Pinot Noir (p. 147), served with Baked Sliced Potatoes (p. 201) and Leeks au Gratin (p. 197).

Strain the cooking liquid into a saucepan and stir in 1 cup (2 dL) of the cream. Bring to a boil for just a few seconds.

Meanwhile, beat egg yolks with remaining cream.

Remove pot from heat and stir in the egg-cream mixture. Replace pot again over heat and stir until thickened. Do not boil. Season to taste with salt and pepper.

Heat the crayfish tails in remaining butter and spoon them over the pieces of chicken. Spoon sauce over chicken.

At your option, garnish with slices of truffle.

Volailles Sautées à la Vigneronne

Grape growers' chicken in wine sauce

2 small chickens, 2½ pounds (1.3 kg) each
Salt and black pepper
1 cup (250 g) butter
8 cloves garlic, finely chopped
4 shallots, finely chopped
½ cup (1 dL) white wine vinegar
½ cup (1 dL) Riesling wine
1 tablespoon tomato paste
½ cup (1 dL) Brown Veal Stock (page 61) or Chicken Stock (page 60)
1 tablespoon chopped parsley

Preparation time: 20 min.
Cooking time: 1 hr., 10 min.
Suggested Wines:
Riesling or Sylvaner

Quarter the chickens and season the pieces with salt and pepper.

Melt ¾ cup (170 g) of the butter in a skillet. Brown the pieces of chicken on both sides. Remove from the skillet and place in a Dutch oven.

Drain the butter from the skillet and add the garlic and the shallots. Immediately stir in vinegar and wine.

Stir in the tomato paste and cook until reduced to half its volume. Add the stock, reheat, and pour into a small bowl.

Place chicken back in skillet and pour in cooking liquid. Cover and simmer for 25 to 30 minutes, or until chicken is tender.

Arrange the chicken on a hot serving platter. Keep hot.

Skim the grease from the cooking liquid and stir in the remaining butter. Taste for seasoning.

Pour the sauce over the chicken and sprinkle with chopped parsley. The sauce should be slightly sour, so add a touch of additional vinegar if needed.

Poulardes au Riesling

Chicken in Riesling

2 small chickens, about 2½ pounds (1¼ kg) each
Salt and black pepper
¾ cup (280 g) butter
1 onion, quartered
1 clove garlic, chopped
2 cups (½ L) Riesling wine
12 ounces (300 g) fresh mushrooms, sliced thinly
Juice of ½ lemon
2 cups (½ L) crème fraîche or heavy cream

Preparation time: 45 min.
Cooking time: 45 min.
Suggested Wine:
Riesling

Quarter the chickens and season with salt and pepper.

In a skillet, brown the chicken pieces lightly in ¼ cup (60 g) of the butter. Add the onion and garlic and pour in the wine.

Sauté the mushrooms in another skillet with ¼ cup (60 g) of the butter and the lemon juice. Drain mushrooms and reserve. Keep hot.

Pour the mixture of butter and lemon juice over the pieces of chicken and simmer, covered, for 30 to 35 minutes.

When the chickens are cooked, place them on a hot serving platter and spread the mushrooms over them. Keep warm.

Boil the pan juices until reduced to half the volume. Stir the cream into the pan juices and let cook for 5 minutes or until thickened. Stir in the remaining butter.

Taste for seasoning, then strain the sauce and spoon over the pieces of chicken.

oussins de la Wantzenau

Wantzenau roast game hens 

6 small game hens, 1 pound (450 g) each
Salt and black pepper
6 sprigs tarragon, plus 2 or 3 sprigs chopped
⅔ cup (150 g) butter
½ cup (1 dL) Riesling wine
½ cup (1 dL) crème fraîche or heavy cream

Preparation time: 20 min.
Cooking time: 30 min.
Suggested Wines:
Riesling or Sylvaner

Preheat the oven to 350° F (180° C).

Season game hens inside and out with salt and pepper. Place a sprig of tarragon inside each game hen.

Melt ½ cup (110 g) butter. Brush some over game hens. Place in a roaster and put in moderate oven for 40 to 45 minutes, or until tender. Brush with butter frequently.

Place game hens on a platter and keep hot.

Pour off the fatty drippings from the roaster and discard. Add the wine and heat on top of range. Reduce liquid to half its volume, scraping up all brown particles.

Stir in the cream, then cook until thickened. Season with salt and pepper.

Strain sauce into a small saucepan, then stir in remaining butter. Heat and taste for seasoning.

Spoon the sauce over the game hens and sprinkle with additional chopped tarragon.

Generally game hens are simply roasted and served crisp, with a salad. This somewhat more elaborate recipe is an excellent one from the municipality of Wantzenau, near Strasbourg.

igeonneaux au Blanc de Volaille

Squab with chicken white meat

6 squab
1 small chicken, about 2½ pounds (1 kg)
2 quarts (2 L) water
2 carrots, diced
2 turnips, diced
3 leeks, sliced
1 celery stalk, chopped
Bouquet garni (thyme, rosemary, celery leaves, parsley)
8 ounces (200 g) fresh mushrooms
⅔ cup (150 g) butter
Juice of 1 lemon
Salt and black pepper
½ cup (1 dL) crème fraîche or heavy cream
1 cup (2 dL) Riesling wine
½ cup (50 g) chopped parsley

Preparation time: 1 hr.
Cooking time: 2 hr.
Suggested Wines:
Riesling or Sylvaner

Thaw squab, if frozen. Remove giblets and reserve livers. Tie legs together and turn wings under. Chop livers and set aside.

Place the chicken in a saucepan and add water, carrots, turnips, leeks, celery, and bouquet garni. Bring to a boil and cook for 45 minutes.

Let the chicken cool in the broth. When the chicken is cool, remove it from the pot and reserve the broth.

Remove skin and bones of white meat of the chicken. Cut into small cubes.

Preheat the oven to 325° F (160° C).

Sauté the mushrooms in 2 tablespoons (30 g) butter mixed with the lemon juice, for 5 minutes. Cool and cut into small cubes.

In a small skillet, sauté the chicken cubes and mushrooms in 2 tablespoons (30 g) butter, but without allowing the chicken to brown. Add salt and pepper, then stir in the cream.

Season the squab inside and out with salt and pepper, then fill their cavities with a mixture of 2 tablespoons (60 g) softened butter and the reserved livers.

Heat 2 tablespoons (60 g) butter in a roasting pan. Place the squab in the pan and roast in a slow oven for about 15 minutes, basting frequently.

Remove the squab from the pan and keep them hot. Drain off the butter from the pan and pour in the wine. Place on top of range. Cook until reduced by half.

Add 1 cup (2 dL) of the reserved chicken broth and cook for 10 minutes. Stir in the remaining butter. Taste for seasoning.

Remove chicken-and-mushroom mixture from squab. Place some of the mixture in the centers of 6 warmed plates.

Cut the squab into quarters and arrange the pieces fan-shaped on the plates. Spoon the sauce over them and sprinkle with the parsley.

Oie Farcie

Stuffed goose

Preparation time: 1 hr.
Cooking time: 3 hr.
Suggested Wines: Pinot Noir or Riesling

1 young goose, 5½ to 6½ pounds (2⅕ to 3 kg)
Salt and black pepper
½ cup (1 dL) water or Brown Veal Stock (page 61)

Stuffing:
3 large onions
½ cup (100 g) butter
2 chicken livers
Salt and black pepper
⅓ cup (¾ dL) brandy
8 ounces (250 g) bread
1 cup (2 dL) milk
12 ounces (300 g) fresh pork filet, chopped coarsely
2 large eggs, lightly beaten

Thaw goose, if frozen. Remove giblets and reserve liver for stuffing.

Prepare the stuffing. Chop the onions and sauté lightly in half the butter.

Cook goose and chicken livers until firm in remaining butter. Add salt and pepper. Warm brandy in a cup. Then flambé livers with brandy.

Soak the bread in the milk, then squeeze out the moisture. Pass the pork, livers, onions, and bread through a meat grinder or food processor for a medium grind. Combine all these ingredients in a bowl and mix thoroughly. Add eggs, salt, and pepper. Preheat the oven to 350° F (180° C).

Season the interior of the goose with salt and pepper, then fill the cavity with the stuffing and sew closed. Salt and pepper the exterior of bird.

Grease the inside of a large roasting pan. Place goose in pan and roast slowly in a moderate oven for 2 to 2½ hours, basting frequently, until a leg can be moved easily. Prick skin under wings and on back to allow fat to drain off. When goose is cooked, drain off grease in the pan and add water or stock to the cooking liquid.

Make an *au jus* by boiling the liquid on the top of the range until reduced by at least half. Scrape up all brown particles sticking to bottom. Serve the goose very hot, along with Red Cabbage with Chestnuts (page 194).

GAME

Alsatian cuisine is rich with the taste of venison, partridge, pheasant, and hare. All recipes are for six portions.

Selle de Chevreuil Saint-Hubert

Saddle of venison Saint Hubert

1 saddle of venison, about 6 pounds (2½ kg)
4 ounces (100 g) fat bacon
1 tablespoon oil
⅔ cup (150 g) butter

Marinade:
1 cup (2 dL) Sylvaner wine
1 tablespoon oil
Juice of ½ lemon
1 sprig thyme
½ bay leaf
6 juniper berries

Sauce:
¼ cup (½ dL) brandy
1 cup (2 dL) Sylvaner wine
1 cup (2 dL) Game Stock (page 62) or Brown Veal Stock (page 61)
½ cup (1 dL) crème fraîche or heavy cream
Salt and black pepper

Garnish (optional):
½ pound (225 g) button mushrooms
4 tablespoons (60 g) butter
1 tablespoon mixed chopped herbs (parsley, chives, thyme, rosemary)

Marinating time: 12 hr.
Preparation time: 30 min.
Cooking time: 1 hr.
Suggested Wines: Pinot Noir or a heavier red Burgundy or Bordeaux

Clean thoroughly the saddle of venison.

Cut the bacon into thin strips.

Make narrow cuts in the venison and insert 1 bacon strip into each of the cuts.

Combine the marinade ingredients and marinate venison overnight in an earthenware dish. Turn meat in marinade several times.

Preheat oven to 400° F (200° C).

Remove the venison and wipe with a cloth. Strain marinade and set aside.

Brush meat with the oil and half of the butter, then roast for about 20 minutes, or until internal temperature registers 130° F (55° C). You want the venison to remain rather rare. Turn oven down to 300° F (150 ° C) and let stand for 15 to 20 minutes in oven. Set aside and keep warm.

Drain the grease from the roasting pan and discard. Place pan on top of range. Pour in the brandy, wine, reserved marinade, and the stock. Bring to a boil, scraping up all brown particles, and boil until reduced to half its volume. Stir in the cream and the remaining butter. Season with salt and pepper.

Carve the venison and arrange the pieces on a hot serving platter. Spoon some of the sauce over the meat. Serve the rest of the sauce in a boat.

Prepare garnish by sautéing button mushrooms in butter and sprinkling with herbs, or serve with Sweet and Sour Huckleberries (page 77), Spaetzle (page 204), Chestnut Purée (page 196), or Purée of Celeriac and Potatoes (page 195).

This is one of the great recipes originating in the valley of the upper Rhine.

Noisettes de Chevreuil

Noisettes of venison
photo page 182

Marinating time: 12 hr.
Preparation time: 1 hr.
Cooking time: 30 min.
Suggested Wines: Pinot Noir or a heavy red Burgundy or Bordeaux

1 saddle of venison, about 6 pounds (2½ kg)
Salt and black pepper
All-purpose flour for dredging
⅔ cup (150 g) butter
¼ cup (½ dL) brandy
½ cup (1 dL) Pinot Noir wine
1 cup (2 dL) venison stock, made from saddle bones or Brown Veal Stock (page 61)
½ cup (1 dL) crème fraîche or heavy cream

Marinade:
1 sprig thyme
½ bay leaf
6 juniper berries, crushed
1 cup (2 dL) Pinot Noir wine

Garnish:
½ pound (225 g) button mushrooms
4 tablespoons (60 g) butter
1 tablespoon mixed chopped herbs (parsley, chives, thyme, rosemary)

Bone the saddle of venison and make a stock with the bones, following the directions on page 62.

Trim the filets and make small round cutlets of each. Marinate the cutlets overnight in a mixture of thyme, bay leaf, juniper berries, and wine.

Remove the cutlets from the marinade. Strain and reserve marinade. Dry cutlets on paper towels.

Season meat with salt and pepper and coat with flour lightly. Sauté in ½ cup (110 g) of butter, being careful to keep venison from becoming too well cooked—you want it pink inside.

Arrange cutlets on a hot serving platter and keep warm.

Drain the butter from the skillet and pour in the brandy, wine, and the reserved marinade. Add the stock and bring to a boil. Cook until reduced by half.

Stir in the cream and the remaining butter, and simmer until thickened. Season to taste.

Quickly sauté the mushrooms in butter, then sprinkle with herbs.

Spoon the sauce over the cutlets and serve hot.

With the cutlets, serve Sweet and Sour Huckleberries (page 77), button mushrooms, Spaetzle (page 204), Chestnut Purée (page 196), or Purée of Celeriac and Potatoes (page 195).

Ragoût de Chevreuil

Ragout of venison

Marinating time: 12 hr.
Preparation time: 1 hr.
Cooking time: 2 hr.
Suggested Wines: Pinot Noir or a heavy red Bordeaux

4½ pounds (2 kg) boneless venison, cut from the shoulder, neck, or breast
2 tablespoons oil
½ cup (50 g) all-purpose flour
6 shallots, chopped
4 cloves garlic, chopped
3 sprigs thyme
½ bay leaf
1 cup (2 dL) Brown Veal Stock (page 61)
Salt and black pepper

Marinade:
1 onion
1 carrot
6 cloves garlic
6 shallots
1 cup (2 dL) red wine
1 cup (2 dL) Sylvaner wine
3 sprigs thyme
½ bay leaf
Salt and black pepper

Garnish:
5 ounces (150 g) lean smoked bacon
12 ounces (300 g) button mushrooms
⅔ cup (150 g) butter
1 tablespoon chopped parsley

Cut the venison into 2-inch (5-cm) cubes.

Prepare the marinade. Peel and chop the onion, carrot, garlic, and shallots. Place in an earthenware bowl, along with the meat, red and white wines, thyme, and bay leaf. Season the pieces of venison with salt and pepper. Marinate overnight.

Preheat the oven to 400° F (200° C).

Drain the venison. Strain and reserve the marinade.

In a Dutch oven, brown the venison in oil for 10 minutes, then sprinkle with flour. Stir well and place the pan in a hot oven for 5 minutes—long enough for the flour to brown lightly.

Remove meat from the oven and add the shallots and garlic. Stir well and add the thyme and bay leaf.

Pour in the marinade and then the stock. Season with salt and pepper and simmer over low heat for approximately 90 minutes, or until venison is tender.

Meanwhile cut the bacon into thin strips and fry until crisp. Set aside.

In a skillet, lightly sauté the mushrooms in half the butter. Set aside.

Remove the pieces of venison and arrange in a hot bowl.

Strain the sauce, stir in remaining butter, and taste for seasoning. Pour over the meat.

Garnish with the bacon and mushrooms, and sprinkle with parsley.

Cotelettes de Marcassin

Stuffed wild boar chops

Preparation time: 30 min.
Cooking time: 20 min.
Suggested Wines: Pinot Noir or Riesling

6 chops from a young wild boar
Salt and black pepper
⅔ cup (150 g) butter
1 caul (fatty covering) or 6 bacon slices
1 recipe Pickled Plums (page 78)
1 cup (2 dL) Black Pepper Sauce (page 68)

Stuffing:
4 ounces (100 g) fresh mushrooms
1 shallot, chopped
¼ cup (50 g) butter
4 ounces (100 g) boneless pork, cut from the neck, chopped coarsely
4 ounces (100 g) fresh foie gras (See note, page 55), or regular goose liver
1 teaspoon Spiced Salt (page 73)
1 large egg, lightly beaten
1 tablespoon brandy

First prepare the stuffing.

Sauté the mushrooms and shallot in butter for 5 minutes.

In a meat grinder or food processor, finely grind the pork, foie gras, sautéed mushrooms and shallot. Add the Spiced Salt, egg, and brandy. Combine thoroughly.

Preheat the oven to 350° F (180° C).

Season the chops with salt and pepper. Sauté in half the butter 1 minute on each side.

Put chops on a platter. Divide the stuffing among the chops and place some on top of each chop. Wrap each chop in a piece of the caul.

Place the chops side by side in a shallow roasting pan and dot tops with remaining butter. Bake in a moderate oven for 30 to 35 minutes.

Place the chops on a serving platter. Serve the Pickled Plums and the Black Pepper Sauce in separate dishes.

This can also be served with Baked Potatoes à la Suzette (page 202) or with puréed potatoes.

Lapin au Pinot Noir

Rabbit in Pinot Noir

Preparation time: 20 min.
Cooking time: 1 hr.
Suggested Wine: Pinot Noir

1 rabbit, about 3½ to 4½ pounds (1½ to 2 kg)
Salt and black pepper
2 tablespoons oil
1 cup (250 g) butter
6 shallots, chopped
6 cloves garlic, chopped
1 cup (2 dL) Pinot Noir wine
1 cup (2 dL) Brown Veal Stock (page 61)
1 tablespoon mixed chopped parsley and chopped chives
1 cup (50 g) sliced fresh mushrooms

Cut the rabbit into serving-size pieces, as you would for a stew. Season with salt and pepper.

Brown the rabbit in oil in an enameled cast-iron pot or a copper saucepan. When the pieces are browned on all sides, drain off the oil and add ½ cup (100 g) butter. Cover and simmer for 45 minutes.

Arrange the rabbit on a serving platter and keep warm. Drain excess fat from cooking pan.

In the same pot or saucepan, sauté the shallots and garlic in the pan drippings until golden brown.

Add the wine and boil until reduced by half.

Add the stock and stir in ¼ cup (60 g) butter. Taste for seasoning.

Pour the sauce over the rabbit, and sprinkle with the mixture of herbs.

Sauté the mushrooms in the remaining butter and serve separately.

Civet de Lièvre à l'Alsacienne

Alsatian jugged hare

1 hare, about 6 pounds (2½ kg)
Salt and black pepper
8 ounces (200 g) lean smoked bacon, in 1 piece
¾ cup (200 g) butter
⅓ cup (50 g) all-purpose flour
½ cup (1 dL) Brown Veal Stock (page 61)
3 sprigs thyme
½ bay leaf

Marinade:
2 onions, chopped
2 carrots, chopped
5 cloves garlic, chopped
8 shallots, chopped
2 sprigs thyme
½ bay leaf
1 quart (1 L) dry red wine
Salt and black pepper

Marinating time: 12 hr.
Preparation time: 1 hr.
Cooking time: 1 hr., 45 minutes
Suggested Wine: Pinot Noir

Noisettes of Venison (p. 176), served with Spaetzle (p. 204).

Skin the hare and clean, reserving the blood, lungs, and liver. Carefully remove the green gall from the liver. Chop liver and set aside.

Cut the hare into serving-size pieces and season with salt and black pepper. Place into a glass or earthenware dish.

Prepare the marinade. To the dish, add the onions, carrots, garlic, shallots, thyme, bay leaf, wine, salt, and pepper. Marinate in refrigerator overnight.

Drain hare. Strain and reserve marinade liquid.

Dice the bacon. Cook for 5 minutes in boiling water to cover and drain.

In a Dutch oven, brown bacon in half the butter and set aside. Remove with a slotted spoon and reserve.

Brown the hare and the vegetables from marinade in the same butter. Cook for about 10 minutes.

Preheat the oven to 400° F (200° C).

Place hare back in pot with vegetables and sprinkle the flour over the mixture. Brown in a hot oven for about 10 minutes.

Remove pot from oven and reduce oven heat to 350° F (180° C). Stir in the reserved marinade and the stock. Add the thyme and bay leaf. Cover and cook in moderate oven for 1 hour to 1 hour, 15 minutes.

Remove the hare and put into a large saucepan. Cover and keep hot over low heat.

Skim the fat from the pan juices. Stir the reserved liver, the blood, and the remaining butter into the sauce. Heat without boiling and taste for seasoning.

Arrange the hare in a hot serving bowl.

Press the sauce through a strainer or food mill and pour over the hare. Sprinkle with bacon cubes.

Serve very hot, with Alsatian Noodles (page 203).

Rables de Lièvres à la Crème

Hare backs in cream

Marinating time: 12 hr.
Preparation time: 30 min.
Cooking time: 30 min.
Suggested Wines:
Sylvaner or Riesling

2 or 3 hare backs, about 6 pounds (2½ kg)

Marinade:
1 tablespoon oil
½ cup (1 dL) Sylvaner wine
Juice of ½ lemon
2 sprigs thyme
½ bay leaf

Sauce:
Salt and black pepper
1 tablespoon oil
½ cup (100 g) butter
½ cup (1 dL) Sylvaner wine
1 cup (2 dL) crème fraîche or heavy cream
Juice of ½ lemon

Trim the fat and tendons from the hare (or ask your butcher to do so). Marinate overnight in a mixture of oil, wine, lemon juice, thyme, and bay leaf.

Preheat the oven to 400° F (200° C).

Remove the meat and sponge dry with a cloth. Season with salt and pepper. Brush with oil mixed with half the butter.

Roast meat in a hot oven for 15 minutes, basting often. Remove the backs and let stand at low heat while you prepare the sauce.

Drain the grease from the roasting pan and discard. Pour in the wine. Place pan on top of range and bring to a boil. Reduce by half then stir in the cream and cook again until thickened. Gradually stir in the remaining butter with a whisk. Taste for seasoning, add the lemon juice.

Place the hare on a hot serving platter and cover with sauce. Serve with Alsatian Noodles (page 203) or a Purée of Celeriac and Potatoes (page 195).

VARIATION

Just before serving, stir in 1 tablespoon of Dijon mustard.

aisans à l'Alsacienne

Alsatian pheasant

Preparation time: 20 min.
Cooking time: 30 min.
Suggested Wines: Pinot Noir or Riesling

2 pounds (1 kg) uncooked sauerkraut
12 ounces (300 g) bacon, smoked or lightly salted
½ bay leaf
3 sprigs thyme
1 cup (2 dL) white wine, preferably Sylvaner or Riesling
1 cup (2 dL) water
2 young pheasant
Salt and black pepper
1 cup (200 g) butter
1 slice bacon
1 cup (2 dL) Brown Veal Stock (page 61) or broth
1 pound (400 g) smoked sausage links
1 tablespoon rendered goose fat or lard

Cook the sauerkraut and bacon as in the recipe for Alsatian Choucroute (page 160), using the bay leaf, thyme, white wine and water.

Preheat the oven to 350° F (180° C).

Thaw pheasant, if frozen, and remove giblets. Season partridges inside and out with salt and black pepper and place ¼ cup (50 g) butter into cavity of each.

Truss and make small cuts into breasts. Cut thin strips of the bacon and press into cuts made in each bird.

Melt remaining butter in a heatproof or cast-iron roasting pan and place pheasant in it. Roast in a moderate oven for 25 to 30 minutes, basting frequently.

When done, remove the pheasant and drain the grease from the pan and discard. Pour in the stock and place pan on top of range. Boil liquid until reduced by half. Taste for seasoning.

Brown the sausages in the goose fat or lard.

Carve pheasant.

Spread the sauerkraut on an earthenware platter. Over the sauerkraut arrange the bacon and the sausages, then the pheasant. Serve the *au jus* separately.

This sumptuous dish is traditionally served in the fall.

Faisans au Foie Gras et aux Truffles

Pheasant with foie gras and truffles

2 young pheasant
1 pound (400 g) fresh foie gras (See note, page 55)
6 ounces (180 g) truffles
½ cup (1 dL) brandy
Salt and black pepper
1 slice bacon, sliced in strips
½ cup (100 g) butter, melted
1⅓ cups (3 dL) Gewürztraminer wine
2¼ cups (½ L) Game Stock (page 62) or Brown Veal Stock (page 61)
½ cup (50 g) flour, mixed with ¼ cup (½ dL) water

Preparation time: 45 min.
Cooking time: 55 min.
Suggested Wines:
Riesling or Traminer

Thaw pheasant, if frozen, and remove giblets.

Cut the foie gras and the truffles into large cubes. Marinate in brandy for 10 minutes.

Preheat the oven to 400° F (200° C).

Season the pheasant inside and out with salt and pepper, then stuff them with the mixture of foie gras and truffles. Sew or skewer opening closed.

Truss the birds and make several cuts with a knife into the breasts. Into each cut, press a thin strip of bacon. Brush with butter and roast in hot oven for about 30 minutes.

Remove the birds, untruss, and place in an earthenware casserole. Reduce oven temperature to 350° F (180° C).

Pour the wine into the roasting pan and place pan on top of range. Reduce liquid by half, scraping up all brown particles. Stir in the stock and cook again until reduced by half. Taste for seasoning. Strain and pour over the birds.

Place the lid on the earthenware pot. Seal with the mixture of flour and water. Place in moderate oven for about 20 minutes.

Serve pheasant in the pot. Do not unseal the lid until everyone is around the table.

This is a very rich but succulent dish. It is one of the highlights of Alsatian cooking and dates from the nineteenth century.

Faisans Sauce Crème aux Champignons

Pheasant in cream sauce with mushrooms

2 young pheasant
Salt and black pepper
1½ pounds (700 g) button mushrooms
¾ cup (200 g) butter
1 slice bacon, cut into thin strips
1 tablespoon oil
1 cup (2 dL) Riesling wine
1 cup (2 dL) Brown Veal Stock (page 61) or broth
½ cup (1 dL) crème fraîche or heavy cream
1 tablespoon chopped chervil

Preparation time: 1 hr., 30 min.
Cooking time: 1 hr.
Suggested Wines: Pinot Noir or Riesling

Thaw pheasant, if frozen. Discard giblets. Sprinkle inside and out with salt and pepper.

Sauté mushrooms in ¼ cup (50 g) of butter. Set aside.

Preheat the oven to 350° F (180° C).

Make several cuts in the breast of each bird and insert a thin strip of bacon into each cut. Truss.

Melt ¼ cup (50 g) butter with oil in a pot or roasting pan, and roast pheasant for 35 to 40 minutes. Baste frequently. Remove the pheasant and keep hot.

Drain the grease from the pan and discard. Pour in the wine and place pan on top of range. Cook until half the liquid boils away. Add the stock and cook until again reduced by half. Add the cream and bring to a boil. Strain and stir in remaining butter.

Carve the pheasant and arrange the pieces on a serving platter. Surround with the sautéed mushrooms. Add some of the sauce and sprinkle with the chervil. Serve the rest of the sauce separately.

Suprêmes de Faisans Sauce Crème

Breast of pheasant with cream sauce

3 young pheasant
Salt and black pepper
2 cups (½ L) crème fraîche or heavy cream
2 large eggs, lightly beaten
2 cups (300 g) dry bread crumbs
¾ cup (200 g) butter
1 pound (454 g) button mushrooms

Sauce:
2 tablespoons oil
1 onion, chopped
1 carrot, chopped
1 cup (2 dL) Sylvaner wine
1 cup (2 dL) Brown Veal Stock (page 61) or broth
¼ cup (50 g) butter

Marinating time: 6 hr.
Preparation time: 40 min.
Cooking time: 45 min.
Suggested Wines:
Sylvaner or Riesling

Thaw pheasant, if frozen. Remove giblets.

Remove the breasts (the white meat) of each pheasant. Split, bone, and remove the skin. Salt and pepper the breasts and marinate in cream for from 3 to 6 hours in the refrigerator.

Prepare the base for the sauce. Chop up the breast carcasses and the remaining pheasant parts and brown in oil, along with the onion and carrot, over low heat.

When the browning is done, drain off the grease and discard. Stir in the wine and stock. Boil, scraping up all the particles from the bottom of the pan, until liquid is reduced to half its volume. Season with salt and pepper, then strain. Set aside.

Remove breasts from the cream and reserve 1 cup (¼ L) of cream for the sauce. Coat the breasts first with the eggs and then with the bread crumbs.

Melt half the butter in a skillet and cook pheasant over medium heat, allowing about 5 minutes for each side.

Place the breasts on a hot serving platter and keep warm.

Sauté the mushrooms in the remaining butter and keep warm.

Bring stock base to a boil in a small saucepan and then stir in the reserved cream. Cook until thickened. Stir in butter for sauce and taste for seasoning.

Serve sauce separately from meat.

Perdreaux aux Raisins

Young partridge with grapes

6 young partridge
Salt and black pepper
6 grape leaves
6 slices bacon
½ cup (100 g) soft butter
1 cup (2 dL) Chicken Stock (page 60) or Brown Veal Stock (page 61)
1 large bunch of white grapes, preferably slightly sweet
6 slices firm white bread
2 livers from chicken or other fowl
2 tablespoons brandy
4 ounces (100 g) fresh foie gras (See note, page 55) or regular goose liver

Preparation time: 30 min.
Cooking time: 35 min.
Suggested Wines:
Riesling or Sylvaner

Preheat the oven to 400° F (200° C).

Thaw partridge, if frozen. Remove giblets. Season partridge inside and out with salt and black pepper.

Wash the grape leaves thoroughly; rinse well with water if leaves were packed in brine. Place a leaf on the breast of each bird. Cover breast with a piece of the bacon and fasten with string.

Place the partridge in a heatproof roasting pan, and spread thickly with ¼ cup (60 g) of butter. Roast on all sides in a hot oven for about 20 minutes (the birds should be slightly rare), basting frequently. Remove the birds from the pan and keep hot.

Pour off fatty drippings and reserve drippings for browning.

Pour the stock into the roasting pan. Place pan on top of range and boil, scraping all brown particles. Taste for seasoning.

Gently remove the skins and seeds of the grapes, trying to keep the grapes as intact as possible. Heat the grapes in 1 tablespoon (14 g) of butter. (Allow at least 6 grapes per bird.)

Cut the crusts off the slices of bread and brown slices in the reserved pan drippings.

Place remaining butter in a pan and heat in moderate oven (350° F or 175° C) for 5 minutes. Arrange the partridge in the pan. Surround the birds with the grapes. Put back into the oven to heat to piping hot, about 10 minutes.

Lightly sauté the livers and foie gras in 1 tablespoon (14 g) of butter, retaining their pink color. Season with salt and pepper.

Heat the brandy in a small cup and flambé livers with brandy. Press liver mixture through a strainer, then taste for seasoning.

Spread liver purée on the slices of bread.

Serve partridge with grapes. Serve pan juices separately, along with the liver-spread crusts.

Potatoes au Gratin à la Fernand Point (page 198) go well with this dish, along with a salad of Bibb or romaine.

VEGETABLES AND STARCHES

ll recipes serve six persons, as side dishes.

Asperges d'Alsace aux Trois Sauces

Alsatian asparagus with three sauces

Preparation time: 45 min.
Cooking time: 20 min.

3½ pounds (1½ kg) fresh asparagus
1 cup (200 g) Hollandaise Sauce (page 67)
1 cup (2 dL) Sauce Mayonnaise (page 72)

Vinaigrette:
4 tablespoons oil
2 tablespoons white wine vinegar
1 tablespoon mixed chopped parsley, chives, and leek
Salt and black pepper

Trim tough ends from asparagus. Peel thinly and wash the asparagus.

Tie asparagus in 6 bunches and cook in boiling salted water for about 10 to 20 minutes so that they remain somewhat firm. The cooking time depends on thickness of asparagus.

Drain and serve hot on a napkin. Remove strings.

Prepare a vinaigrette by beating together the oil, vinegar, herbs, salt, and pepper.

Serve asparagus with separate bowls of Hollandaise, Mayonnaise, and vinaigrette.

Note: Alsatian asparatus is renowned for its taste. It is grown in the sandy soil of Hoerdt, fro Lampertheim on the lower Rhine to Horbourg, Andolsheim, and Village-Neuf on the upper Rhine.

Alsatians love asparagus in the spring, and it is not unusual to be served as much as a 2-pound (1 kg) portion.

For asparagus to be really good, it should be served on the same day that it is gathered.

Feuilleté d'Asperges au Riesling et aux Fines Herbes

Asparagus in puff pastry with wine and herbs

Preparation time: 45 min.
Cooking time: 30 min.

4½ pounds (2 kg) cooked asparagus
1 pound (500 g) Puff Pastry (¼ recipe) (page 212)
1 large egg, well beaten
1 cup (2 dL) Riesling wine
1 cup (2 dL) crème fraîche or heavy cream
¼ cup (50 g) butter
Salt and black pepper
1 tablespoon mixed chopped tarragon and chives

Preheat the oven to 400° F (200° C).

Roll out the pastry to a thickness of ⅛ inch (½ cm) and cut into 6 4 × 8-inch (10 × 20-cm) pieces.

Place the pastry pieces on a floured cookie sheet. Brush the dough with beaten egg and bake for 5 minutes in hot oven. Cool and cut each piece into 2 layers. Keep hot.

Pour the wine into a saucepan and boil until reduced to half its volume.

Add ½ cup (1 dL) of cooking water from the asparagus and reduce by one-third.

Stir in the cream and cook for a few seconds. Stir in the butter, salt, pepper, and herbs.

Place a bottom layer of pastry on each of 6 plates. Top with some asparagus, and spoon the sauce over the asparagus. Cover with the second piece of pastry. Serve piping hot.

Chou Rouge aux Marrons

Red cabbage with chestnuts

1 head red cabbage
2 pounds (1 kg) chestnuts
2 onions, sliced thinly
3 tablespoons rendered goose fat
1 cup (2 dL) Sylvaner wine
1 cup (2 dL) water
1 clove
½ bay leaf
Salt and black pepper
Juice of ½ lemon
4 green cooking apples

Preparation time: 45 min.
Cooking time: 1 hr., 35 min.

Trim, wash, and core the cabbage. Cut into long, thin strips.

Score chestnuts with a knife, cutting an *x* on the flat side. Cover chestnuts with water and simmer 15 minutes.

Peel chestnuts and remove brown inner skin.

Sauté onions for 5 minutes in the goose fat.

Add the cabbage and pour in the wine and water. Add the clove, bay leaf, salt, pepper, and lemon juice. Simmer, covered, for 30 minutes.

Add the chestnuts to the pan. Cover and simmer for 45 minutes more.

Peel, core, and cube the apples. Add to cabbage and cook for another 15 minutes. Remove clove and bay leaf.

Serve hot.

This goes beautifully with all meat or game dishes.

Purée de Céleri

Purée of celeriac and potatoes

2 celeriac
2 large (200 g) potatoes
Large pinch of coarse salt
½ cup (100 g) butter
½ cup (2 dL) crème fraîche or heavy cream
Dash of grated nutmeg
Salt and black pepper

Preparation time: 15 min.
Cooking time: 30 min.

Peel the celeriac and the potatoes and cut each into small pieces.

Cook vegetables for 30 minutes in boiling salted water.

Preheat the oven to 300° F (150° C).

Drain vegetables and allow to dry for 3 or 4 minutes in a pan in slow oven.

Press celeriac and potatoes through a fine sieve or food mill or purée in a blender or food processor.

Beat the butter and the cream into this purée. Add nutmeg and season to taste.

Rehcat. Scrvc very hot on a hot serving platter.

This is an excellent companion dish for all meats.

Purée de Marrons

Chestnut purée

Preparation time: 1 hr.
Cooking time: 30 min.

4½ pounds (2 kg) chestnuts
½ celeriac
Salt
2 quarts (2 L) bouillon or water
¾ cup (200 g) butter
1 cup (2 dL) crème fraîche or heavy cream
2 cups (½ L) milk (optional)
Pinch of granulated sugar

Score the chestnuts with an *x* on the flat side. Cover chestnuts with water and cook for 15 minutes.

Peel the chestnuts. Remove brown inner skin.

Peel and dice the celeriac.

Place celeriac in a pot with chestnuts and bouillon or water to cover. Cover and cook at a gentle boil for 30 minutes. Drain well.

Press vegetables through a sieve or food mill.

Mix butter and cream into the purée, and, if necessary, dilute with milk until the consistency is fluffy like mashed potatoes. Season with salt and add a little sugar.

Serve hot with game and fowl dishes.

Gratin de Poireaux

Leeks au gratin
photo page 166

10 large leeks
½ cup (100 g) butter
½ cup (1 dL) milk
½ cup (1 dL) crème fraîche or heavy cream
Salt and black pepper
Dash of grated nutmeg
1 cup (200 g) Hollandaise Sauce (page 67)

Preparation time: 15 min.
Cooking time: 50 min.

Trim and chop the leeks, both white and 1 inch (2½ cm) of the green part. Wash well to remove all sand.

Cook leeks in boiling salted water for 15 to 20 minutes, letting them remain somewhat crisp. Remove from heat, run cold water over them, and drain.

In a skillet, cook the leeks in butter over low heat for 5 minutes, without allowing them to brown.

Stir in the milk and cream. Season with salt, pepper, and nutmeg, and cook over low heat for about 10 minutes more or until mixture is thick.

Preheat the oven to 400° F (200° C), or preheat broiler.

Pour the leeks into a buttered pan and spoon Hollandaise Sauce over them. Brown for 3 minutes in a hot oven or broil until golden brown. Serve very hot.

This is an excellent dish to accompany meats, game, and fowl.

Galettes de Pommes de Terre

Potato galettes

Preparation time: 20 min.	
Cooking time: 15 min.	

2½ pounds (1 kg) potatoes
4 large eggs, lightly beaten
2 onions, chopped
1 tablespoon mixed chopped parsley and chives
Salt and black pepper
Dash of grated nutmeg
Oil for frying

Peel the potatoes, then grate them on a medium-fine grater. Place immediately into a bowl of cold water to prevent browning.

Drain potatoes in a colander for several minutes, pressing out all liquid.

Put the potatoes in a bowl. Stir in the eggs, onions, parsley and chives, salt, pepper, and nutmeg. Mix well.

Using a spoon, make small cakes of the potato mixture about ½ inch (1½ cm) thick.

Heat the oil ¼ inch (¾ cm) deep in a skillet and brown pancakes slowly on both sides. Add more oil as needed.

Serve hot with a fresh green salad.

Gratin de Pommes de Terre Fernand Point

Potatoes au gratin à la Fernand Point

Preparation time: 15 min.
Cooking time: 1 hr.

1 large egg
1 cup (2 dL) crème fraîche or heavy cream
1 cup (2 dL) milk
1 clove garlic
6 tablespoons (80 g) butter
1 pound (400 g) potatoes
Salt and black pepper
Pinch of grated nutmeg

Kougelhopf I (p. 216); Alsatian Huckleberry Tart II (p. 243); Cheese Tart (p. 240); Alsatian Apple Tart (p. 245).

reheat the oven to 350° F (180° C).

Break the egg into a bowl. Beat, mixing in the cream and milk.

Rub a shallow 9-inch (22.5-cm) square enameled cast-iron pan (or one of ovenproof glass) with the garlic. Butter the pan generously with half of the butter.

Peel, wash, dry, and cut the potatoes into very thin slices. Season with salt and pepper, and nutmeg.

Make a thick layer—about ½ inch (1 cm)—of potatoes in the pan. Pour in the egg mixture; it should just cover the potatoes. Dot with the remaining butter.

Bake in a moderate oven for about 1 hour, or until golden brown. Serve very hot.

This is not an old Alsatian recipe, but I wanted to include it in homage to a great chef, Fernand Point, who was also my teacher.

Pommes de Terre au Four

Alsatian baked potatoes 

6 large potatoes, preferably Idaho or Russet

Preparation time: 5 min.
Cooking time: 1 hr.

Preheat the oven to 400° F (200° C).

Wash the potatoes, but do not peel them. Put them on a tray in a hot oven for about 40 minutes to 1 hour, or until easily pierced.

Remove from oven. Hold each potato with a cloth and, in the top of each, cut a lid. Fluff potatoes with a fork.

Serve with butter or heavy cream.

This rather rustic dish is from the lower Rhine countryside. It is served with meat and game dishes of all kinds, and also enjoyed during the winter at supper, with salt, black pepper, and a bit of mustard.

ommes Farcies au Beurre

Potatoes stuffed with butter 

Preparation time: 10 min.
Cooking time: 25 min.

6 almost completely baked Idaho potatoes
⅔ cup (150 g) butter
½ cup (1 dL) crème fraîche or heavy cream
1 tablespoon mixed chopped parsley, chervil, chives
1 teaspoon salt
½ teaspoon black pepper

Preheat the oven to 400° F (200° C).

Just before potatoes are done, remove them from the oven, cut the lid in the top of each, and, with a spoon, remove a piece of potato about the size of a large egg yolk.

Mash potato pulp.

Mix butter with cream, herbs, salt, and pepper.

Fill the hole in each potato with the butter mixture. Cover with mashed potato. Replace the lid on each potato and place back in hot oven for 3 to 5 minutes.

Serve very hot.

This makes an especially savory and aromatic dish, since the cream and butter penetrate the whole potato.

In some villages, it is traditional to eat these stuffed potatoes with small smoked sausage links (2 per person) which have been browned in butter for about 10 minutes.

Pommes Paysanne

Baked sliced potatoes
photo page 166

⅔ cup (150 g) butter
1½ pounds (500 g) potatoes
Salt and black pepper

Preparation time: 10 min.
Cooking time: 25 min.

Preheat the oven to 400° F (200° C).

Generously grease a 15 × 10 × 1-inch (37.5 × 25 × 2.5-cm) baking pan with some of the butter.

Peel and wash the potatoes. Cut into paper-thin rounds. Season with salt and black pepper.

Place potatoes in a thin layer in pan. Melt remaining butter and drizzle over potatoes.

Bake in a hot oven for 20 to 25 minutes or until brown and crisp. From time to time, press down on the potatoes with a spatula in order to flatten them.

Serve very hot.

These go with any meat, fowl, or game dish.

Pommes de Terre Suzette

Baked potatoes à la Suzette

6 Idaho potatoes
⅔ cup (150 g) butter
½ cup (100 g) diced cooked ham
1 tablespoon mixed chopped parsley and chives
Pinch of salt
2 mill-turns black pepper
Dash of grated nutmeg
½ cup (50 g) dry bread crumbs

Preparation time: 15 min.
Cooking time: 1 hr., 5 min.

Preheat the oven to 400° F (200° C).

Wash the potatoes thoroughly but do not peel.

Bake potatoes on an ungreased tray in a hot oven for about 40 to 45 minutes, or until easily pierced.

Remove potatoes from oven and allow to cool somewhat. Cut each potato in half lengthwise. Scoop out the inside with a small spoon, being very careful not to damage the skin.

Reduce oven temperature to 350° F (180° C).

Press the potato pulp through a sieve, potato ricer or food mill.

Mix ½ cup (110 g) of butter into the purée. Stir in the ham and the herbs. Season with salt, pepper, and nutmeg.

Use this mixture to stuff the potato skins.

Melt the remaining butter and mix with the crumbs. Sprinkle over the potatoes.

Brown stuffed potatoes slowly for 20 minutes in a moderate oven.

Serve piping hot, 2 halves for each person.

This goes beautifully with meats and game.

ouilles à l'Alsacienne

Alsatian noodles

8 large eggs
1 teaspoon salt
1 teaspoon wine vinegar
4 cups (500 g) all-purpose flour
2 quarts (2 L) water
½ cup (110 g) butter, melted

Resting time: 1 hr., 20 min.
Preparation time: 20 min.
Cooking time: 8 min.

Beat the eggs in a large bowl. Add the salt and vinegar, then gradually stir in the flour until a sticky, stiff dough forms.

Knead dough for 5 minutes on a floured board until smooth and elastic. Wrap in a white cloth and let stand 1 hour. (Dough can also be mixed and kneaded in a food processor.)

Divide the dough into pieces about the size of a 3-inch (8-cm) egg. Roll out each piece to an ⅛-inch (½ cm) thickncss on a floured surface.

Cut dough into ¼-inch (¾-cm)-wide strips to make noodles. Spread out noodles and dry 20 minutes. Reserve a handful of the noodles for browning.

Bring water to a boil. Put the noodles into the water and lower the heat. Cook for 8 minutes.

Drain and place the noodles on a hot serving platter. Sprinkle with ¼ cup (50 g) melted butter and stir.

Brown the reserved raw noodles in remaining melted butter, then use these as a garnish for buttered noodles.

Fresh noodles are traditional in Alsace and they are still made at home.

Spaetzle, or Wasserstriwle

photo page 182

4 large eggs
Salt
Dash of grated nutmeg
½ cup (1 dL) water
2 cups (250 g) all-purpose flour
1 tablespoon (7½ g) semolina or cornstarch
1 tablespoon oil
½ cup (100 g) butter

Resting time: 1 hr.
Preparation time: 1 hr., 15 min.
Cooking time: 15 min.

Beat the eggs in a large bowl until smooth. Add the salt, nutmeg, and water. Gradually beat in the flour and the semolina until you have a soft dough. Let stand for 1 hour.

Bring salted water to a boil in a large pot. Add the oil.

Into a spaetzle strainer (or any kind of strainer or colander with large holes) held over the boiling water, place the dough and press down lightly so as to force the dough through the holes and into the boiling water.

As soon as the spaetzle rise to the surface, they are done. Remove from the water and put into a pot of cold water. Drain. Melt butter in a skillet and sauté spaetzle in butter until piping hot.

Spaetzle are firmer than ordinary noodles and they are usually served with meat or game dishes.

BREADS, ROLLS, AND PASTRY DOUGHS

Refer to the recipes in this chapter whenever these ingredients are needed for major dishes. In each instance, the approximate yield of the recipe is given, so that you may adjust the quantities accordingly for your own purposes.

Also, since many recipes use these doughs in various stages of preparation, we advise you to check the final recipe before proceeding with these recipes.

âte à Pain Paysan

Basic bread dough

2 envelopes (20 g) active dry yeast or baker's yeast
½ cup (1 dL) warm water
6 cups (750 g) unsifted all-purpose flour
2 teaspoons (15 g) salt
2 cups (½ L) water

Preparation time: 15 min.
Rising time: 2 hr.
Baking time: 40 min.
Yield: 4 *baguettes* (long thin loaves), 2 *pain ordinaire* (larger, wider), or 1 large round loaf

Mix yeast, warm water, and ½ cup (50 g) flour until smooth and yeast is dissolved. Let rise in a warm place until doubled in volume.

Pour the remaining flour and the salt into a bowl and make a crater in the center. Add water and yeast mixture and mix into a stiff dough.

Knead the dough on a floured surface until it is smooth and elastic, about 10 minutes.

Grease a bowl and place dough in it, turning to coat top with grease. Cover and let rise in a warm place until doubled in bulk, about 1 hour.

Punch down the dough and knead again briefly. Shape the dough in one of the following ways:

To form *baguettes,* cut dough into 4 pieces. Roll each piece into an oblong 6 × 16 inches (15 × 40 cm). Roll up tightly lengthwise and taper the ends. Place loaves seam-side down on a greased cookie sheet or in a baguette bread pan and slash diagonally 4 times.

To form *pain ordinaire,* cut the dough into 2 pieces and roll each piece into an oblong 12 × 16 inches (30 × 40 cm). Roll up tightly lengthwise and taper ends. Place rolls seam-side down on greased cookie sheets or in a suitable bread pan and slash diagonally 4 times.

To form a large round loaf, shape the whole piece of dough into a large round ball and place ball on a greased cookie sheet or in a cloth-lined *banneton* (basket). Cut a cross in the top.

Let the dough rise again until the loaves are approximately twice their original size.

When ready, preheat the oven to 425° F (220° C). Brush loaves with water and bake until done (15 to 20 minutes for *baguettes,* 20 to 25 for *pain ordinaire,* and 40 to 45 minutes for round loaf). Loaf should sound hollow when tapped.

Pâte à Brioche

Brioche dough

4 cups (500 g) all-purpose flour
1 teaspoon (10 g) salt
¼ cup (60 g) granulated sugar
1 envelope (20 g) active dry yeast or baker's yeast
⅓ cup (¾ dL) warm milk
5 large eggs
1 cup (250 g) butter
1 egg yolk beaten with 2 tablespoons water

Preparation time: 20 min.
Rising time: 5 hr.
Baking time: as directed in individual recipes
Yield: 1 loaf, or 1 egg braid, or 12 individual brioche

Place the flour in a bowl. Mix with salt and sugar and make a crater in the middle.

Blend the yeast with the milk until yeast is dissolved. Add the yeast mixture and eggs to the flour. Stir until it forms a sticky dough.

On a floured surface, knead the dough until it is smooth and elastic.

Soften the butter and knead it into the dough, adding a small amount at a time. Continue to knead and work until you have a firm, homogeneous dough.

Place the dough in a greased bowl and turn to coat. Cover and let dough rise in refrigerator for 5 hours.

Shape the dough as desired or use to cover casseroles or meats en croute. Before baking, brush with beaten egg yolk mixture.

TO PREPARE INDIVIDUAL BRIOCHE

Butter the brioche molds or muffin pans. Cut dough into 12 pieces, then cut ¼ of the dough off each piece. Shape the large pieces into smooth balls and place into the pans. Shape the small pieces into pear-shaped ovals. Snip a small cross on top of the large balls and press the point of the small oval down into the cut.

Refrigerate the dough overnight, covered with plastic wrap. Let the dough warm to room temperature for 15 minutes, then brush with beaten yolk and bake in a moderate oven (350° F or 180° C) for 20 to 22 minutes, or until richly browned.

Pâte Levée

Sweet yeast dough

- *2 envelopes (30 g) active dry yeast or baker's yeast*
- *1½ cups (3½ dL) lukewarm milk*
- *6 cups (750 g) unsifted all-purpose flour*
- *1½ teaspoons (15 g) salt*
- *4 large eggs, beaten*
- *⅓ cup (125 g) granulated sugar*
- *½ cup (125 g) butter, softened*
- *2 egg yolks beaten with 2 tablespoons water*

Preparation time: 15 min.
Rising time: 8 to 12 hr.
Baking time: 15 to 20 min.
Yield: 25 rolls, 2 ounces (50 g) each

In a small bowl, mix the yeast with half the milk until dissolved.

Place the flour and salt in a bowl and make a crater. Into the crater put the remaining milk, eggs, sugar, and yeast mixture. Mix thoroughly until a soft sticky dough forms.

On a floured surface, knead the butter into the dough, and continue to knead until the dough no longer sticks to your fingers.

Place dough into a greased bowl and turn to coat. Cover the bowl and refrigerate overnight.

Knead the dough again so that it loses some of its volume, then let stand for 30 minutes more.

Shape the dough into bread rolls, croissants, or other desired form. Place on a greased sheet and let rise until doubled.

Preheat the oven to 350° F (180° C).

Just before baking, brush rolls with the egg yolk mixture. Bake in a moderate oven for 15 to 20 minutes.

Pains au Lait, or Milchweka

Milk rolls

Preparation time: 20 min.
Rising time: 40 min.
Baking time: 20 to 25 min.
Yield: about 25 rolls, 2 ounces (50 g) each

6 cups (750 g) all-purpose flour
2 tablespoons (30 g) granulated sugar
1½ teaspoons (20 g) salt
2 envelopes (30 g) active dry yeast or baker's yeast
1 cup (2 dL) milk
½ cup (125 g) butter, softened
2 egg yolks beaten with 2 tablespoons water

Mix flour, sugar, and salt in a bowl.

Blend yeast with milk.

Make a crater in the flour and add yeast mixture and butter. Blend until you have a soft dough.

Knead dough on a floured surface until smooth and elastic. Cut the dough into 25 pieces and shape the pieces into smooth balls.

Place dough pieces on greased cookie sheets and let rise until doubled in bulk, about 35 to 40 minutes.

Preheat the oven to 400° F (200° C).

Brush rolls with egg yolk mixture and bake in hot oven for 20 to 25 minutes.

In some Alsatian communities, milk rolls are distributed among school children on Bastille Day, Armistice Day, and the Feast of St. Nicholas.

Pâte Brisée

Pie and tart dough

2 cups (250 g) all-purpose flour
½ teaspoon (5 g) salt
½ cup (125 g) butter, in small pieces
1 egg yolk
⅓ cup (¾ dL) water

Preparation time: 15 min.
Resting time: 2 hr.
Baking time: 10 min.
Yield: 1 10-inch (25-cm) crust or 8 individual 3-inch (8-cm) tart shells

Mix flour with salt.

Cut the butter into the flour until the mixture is of particles like small peas. Add the egg yolk and water. Mix well with a fork.

Knead the dough a few times until it forms a smooth ball. Wrap in wax paper and chill until ready to use, at least 2 hours.

Preheat the oven to 400° F (200° C).

Roll out the dough on a floured surface to the desired size, making the dough about ¼ inch (¾ cm) thick and 2 inches (5 cm) wider than the bottom of the tart or flan pan.

Line baking pan with dough and prick the bottom with a fork. Line shell with cheesecloth and fill it with dried beans or rice.

Bake crust in a hot oven until lightly browned—about 10 to 12 minutes for larger tart crusts and less time for smaller, individual ones. If crust is to be used for a quiche, then bake only 7 to 8 minutes.

Cool crust before filling.

Pâte Sucrée

Sweet tart dough

1½ cups (250 g) unsifted all-purpose flour
⅓ cup (100 g) granulated sugar
½ teaspoon salt
½ cup (125 g) butter, broken into small pieces
1 egg, beaten
1 tablespoon cold water

Resting time: 2 hr.
Preparation time: 15 min.
Yield: 1 9-inch (23-cm) crust or 6 individual 3-inch (8-cm) tart shells

Mix flour, sugar, and salt in a bowl. Cut in butter until particles are very fine.

Add the egg and the water. Mix well.

Knead the dough a few times until you have a smooth ball of dough. Cover with a cloth and chill for 2 hours.

The dough is ready to use. Follow directions given for Pâte Brisée regarding the rolling out and prebaking of the crust.

Note: This dough may be flavored with vanilla or almond extracts, grated orange or lemon rind, or with spices.

Pâte Feuilletée

Puff pastry dough

4 cups (500 g) all-purpose flour
1 teaspoon (10 g) salt
1½ cups (2½ to 3 dL) water
1 pound (450 to 500 g) butter

Preparation time: 25 min.
Resting time: 3 hr., 40 min.
Baking time: as directed in individual recipes
Yield: 2 pounds (1 kg) dough

Mix together the flour and salt. Gradually add the water, working it into the flour. Knead only a few times until it forms a smooth ball. Wrap and chill for 20 minutes.

Knead the butter with your hands, dipping them from time to time in cold water so as to not warm the butter, until it is smooth and waxy. Pat out an 8-inch (20-cm) square on wax paper. Chill butter for 20 minutes.

Roll out the dough on a floured surface, making a 10-inch (25-cm) square. Place the butter diagonally on top of the dough. Fold the dough in thirds, like a business letter. Rest the dough for 10 minutes.

Roll out the dough on a floured surface into an oblong 8 × 10 inches (20 × 45 cm) with an even thickness of about ½ inch (1 cm). Fold the dough in thirds and turn the open edge to the right.

Roll out the dough again to an 8 × 18-inch (20 × 45-cm) oblong and fold into thirds again. Turn the open edge again to the right. Chill, covered, for 1 hour.

Repeat this turning process 2 more times, always turning the open edge to the right. After each turn, chill the dough.

Dough is now ready to be used, following directions in individual recipes.

Note: The dough and butter must be the same consistency. Roll the dough on a floured surface to prevent sticking, but brush off excess flour when folding. Do not press on the edges of the dough or butter will squeeze out. The dough keeps best in the freezer, but thaw in the wrapping in the refrigerator. It is better to make the full amount of the recipe and store excess in the refrigerator than to try for a smaller quantity.

DESSERTS AND PASTRIES

Pastries are one of the most brilliant jewels of Alsatian cuisine. If anyone requires proof of that, all that is needed is to inspect the counters of any bakery shop in Strasbourg or Colmar, or any other village in the province.

Since portions vary somewhat, the serving quantity or yield of each recipe is noted.

Cakes

egi

Plum and fig roll

photo page 214

7 ounces (200 g) pitted prunes
7 ounces (200 g) dried figs
½ cup (100 g) raisins
½ cup (75 g) shelled walnuts
¼ cup (½ dL) plum eau-de-vie or brandy
Pinch of ground aniseed
1 teaspoon ground cinnamon
¼ cup (50 g) granulated sugar

Dough:
1 egg yolk beaten with 1 tablespoon water
2 cups (160 g) confectioners' sugar mixed with ¼ cup (½ dL) milk
4½ cups (500 g) unsifted all-purpose flour
1 envelope (10 g) active dry yeast or baker's yeast
1 cup (2 dL) lukewarm milk
⅓ cup (75 g) granulated sugar
2 egg yolks
½ cup (100 g) butter, softened

Preparation time: 45 min.
Macerating time: 12 hr.
Rising time: 1 hr., 45 min.
Baking time: 25 min.
Yield: 2

Pear Loaf (p. 219); Plum and Fig Roll (p. 214).

Soak the prunes for 1 hour in hot water. Soak the figs and the raisins in hot water for 30 minutes. Drain.

Cut the figs and prunes into small cubes. Combine with raisins, mixing thoroughly.

Chop the walnuts coarsely and mix with the fruits. Pour the *eau-de-vie* over the mixture. Sprinkle with the aniseed, cinnamon, and sugar. Mix thoroughly and let stand overnight at room temperature.

For the dough, make a crater in the flour. Dissolve the yeast in milk and add to the flour, along with the sugar, egg yolks, and butter. Stir until a stiff dough forms. Turn out dough on a floured surface and knead for 10 minutes, or until smooth and elastic. Let rise, covered, in a warm place until doubled in bulk, about 1 hour.

When the dough has risen, knead again. Roll out half of the dough to form a rectangle of about 12 × 16 inches (30 × 40 cm). On the dough, spread a layer—not too thick—of half the fruit mixture. Roll like a jelly roll, starting at the narrower side. Do the same with the other half of the dough and remaining fruit.

Place rolls seam-side down on 2 greased cookie sheets. Let rise in a warm place for 45 minutes.

Preheat the oven to 350° F (180° C).

Brush rolls with egg yolk mixture. Bake in a moderate oven for 25 to 30 minutes, or until richly browned.

Remove rolls from oven and spoon confectioners'-sugar mixture over top. Serve warm.

This delicious pastry is traditional in Alsace during the holiday season. It is a specialty of the Lapoutroie Corridor.

Kougelhopf I

photo page 198

1 recipe Sweet Yeast Dough (page 208)
1 cup (150 g) raisins
2 tablespoons Kirsch or water (optional)
16 to 20 (75 g) whole blanched almonds

Preparation time: 45 min.
Macerating time: 30 min.
Baking time: 1 hr.
Yield: 1 large cake

Prepare Sweet Yeast Dough according to recipe directions but do not chill. Let dough rise covered in a warm place until doubled in bulk. Punch down and knead again until smooth and elastic. Let rise again, covered, in a warm place until doubled in bulk.

Soak raisins in Kirsch or water, if desired, for 30 minutes. Drain.

Punch down the dough again. Knead in raisins.

Heavily butter a 3-quart (3-L) *kougelhopf* mold or Bundt pan and line the grooves on the bottom with almonds. Place the dough into the mold and let rise to the top.

Preheat the oven to 350° F (180° C).

Bake cake in a moderate oven for about 1 hour, or until richly browned. If the cake seems to be browning too quickly, cover the top of the mold with a piece of paper.

Cool, invert, and serve.

Kougelhopf is traditionally served at breakfast, but it may also be served as a dessert. In the latter case, sprinkle with Kirsch or rum and top with Chantilly cream; or serve it with Caramel Sauce (page 269).

Since 1972, every June there is a Kougelhopf festival at Ribeauvillé. But Alsatians bake and eat this scrumptous pastry everywhere—and in unbelievable quantities, at home as well as in restaurants.

Kougelhopf II

½ cup (50 g) sultana raisins
2 tablespoons Kirsch or Mirabelle plum brandy
4½ cups (500 g) unsifted all-purpose flour
2 envelopes (20 g) active dry yeast or baker's yeast
½ cup (1 dL) lukewarm water
3 large eggs, beaten
1 cup (125 g) confectioners' sugar
1 teaspoon salt
½ cup (1 dL) lukewarm milk
½ cup (125 g) butter, softened
½ cup (50 g) slivered almonds
1 cup (125 g) confectioners' sugar mixed with 2 tablespoons milk

Preparation time: 30 min.
Rising time: 2 hr., 30 min.
Baking time: 1 hr.
Yield: 1 medium cake

Wash and drain the raisins and soak in brandy. Drain.

Put the flour in a large bowl and make a crater in the center. Dissolve the yeast in warm water and pour into the crater.

Add the eggs, sugar, salt, and milk. Mix thoroughly and beat the dough for about 15 minutes.

Beat in the butter and then knead dough on a floured surface until it no longer sticks to your hand. Knead in the raisins.

Place dough in a greased bowl and turn to coat. Cover and let stand for 1 hour in a warm place until double in bulk.

Knead the dough again and let rise again in a warm place until double in bulk.

Knead dough again.

Heavily butter a 2-quart (2-L) *kougelhopf* mold or Bundt pan and sprinkle the walls with the almonds. Place the dough into the mold and let rise until it reaches the top.

Preheat the oven to 350° F (180° C).

Bake cake in a moderate oven for 1 hour.

Unmold the cake and, when it has cooled, spoon confectioners'-sugar mixture over top.

The Kougelhopf conquered France long ago. It is no stranger to other European countries, and it has been spotted in Japan and the United States as well.

Gâteau Fourré aux Amandes

Cinnamon and almond pinwheels

1 recipe Kougelhopf II (page 217)
½ cup (125 g) butter, softened
1 cup (125 g) confectioners' sugar
2 large eggs
7 ounces (200 g) finely chopped almonds
2 teaspoons ground cinnamon
2 cups (250 g) confectioners' sugar mixed with ¼ cup (½ dL) Kirsch

Preparation time: 30 min.
Rising time: 2 hr.
Baking time: 1 hr.
Yield: 18

Prepare dough with raisins as directed in recipe. Cover the bowl with a towel and let rise in a cool place until doubled in bulk.

In a bowl, mix the butter, sugar, eggs, almonds, and cinnamon. Combine thoroughly so that you have a very smooth, well-blended mixture.

Flour a work surface and roll out the dough into a rectangle 9 × 18 inches (23 × 45 cm) about ½ inch (1 cm) thick. Spread a layer of the butter-and-egg mixture on the entire surface of the dough. Roll the dough, starting at the 18-inch (45-cm) side, like a jelly roll and seal closed.

Butter a 9 × 13 × 2-inch (23 × 33 × 4-cm) baking pan generously.

Cut the roll into slices 1 inch (2½ cm) thick (18 slices), and arrange the slices cut side-up in the pan. The slices should be pressed against one another.

Let cakes stand in warm place until doubled in size, about 1 hour.

Preheat the oven to 350° F (180° C).

Bake cakes in a moderate oven for 1 hour.

Remove cakes from sheet and drizzle confectioners'-sugar glaze over top.

Beerawecka or Pain de Poires

Pear loaf
photo page 214

½ recipe (500 g) Sweet Yeast Dough (page 208)
10 ounces (300 g) dried pears
7 ounces (200 g) pitted prunes
6 ounces (150 g) dried figs
4 ounces (100 g) shelled walnuts
4 ounces (100 g) shelled hazelnuts
4 ounces (100 g) seedless golden raisins
¼ teaspoon ground cloves
2 teaspoons ground cinnamon
Grated rind of ½ lemon
2 ounces (50 g) mixed chopped candied fruits
½ cup (1 dL) pear eau-de-vie or brandy
2 egg yolks beaten with 2 tablespoons water

Preparation time: 40 min.
Macerating time: 2 hr., 30 min.
Rising time: 9 hr.
Baking time: 40 min.
Yield: 2

Prepare Sweet Yeast Dough and let rise once.

Soak the dried pears in hot water for about 30 minutes. Drain.

Cut the pears, prunes, and figs into small pieces. Chop the walnuts and hazelnuts, and combine with the fruit in a large bowl. Add the raisins, cloves, cinnamon, lemon rind, candied fruits, and *eau-de-vie*. Mix thoroughly. Let stand for at least 2 hours.

Flatten the dough on a floured surface. Sprinkle fruit over top. Fold dough over fruit and knead until fruit is blended into dough.

Cut the dough into 2 pieces and shape each piece into a long narrow loaf about 12 inches (30 cm) long.

Place on a greased cookie sheet. Brush the tops of the loaves with egg-yolk mixture and let stand for 1 hour in a warm place until slightly risen.

Preheat the oven to 400° F (200° C).

Bake for 40 minutes in a hot oven or until richly browned.

Formerly, Beerawecka was "New Year's bread" or holiday bread. It was served, along with a glass of Kirsch, to family and friends who came to wish one a Happy New Year.

Galette aux Amandes

Almond cake

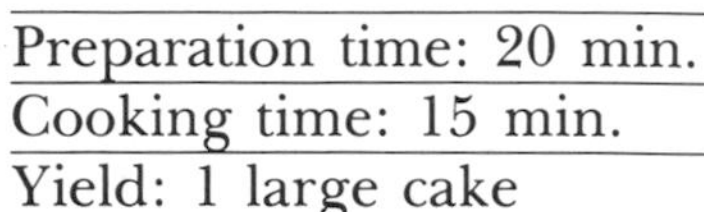

Preparation time: 20 min.
Cooking time: 15 min.
Yield: 1 large cake

1 pound (500 g) confectioners' sugar
6 large eggs
12 ounces (350 g) chopped blanched almonds
1 teaspoon ground cinnamon
¼ teaspoon grated nutmeg
Grated rind of ½ lemon
1 envelope (15 g) active dry yeast
4 cups (500 g) unsifted all-purpose flour

Preheat the oven to 350° F (180° C).

Pour the sugar into a bowl. Break the eggs over the sugar and beat well until thick and lemon colored.

Stir in the almonds, cinnamon, nutmeg, and lemon rind. Add the yeast. Gradually stir in the flour until all ingredients are well blended.

Spread the dough in a buttered 9 × 13-inch (12 × 33-cm) pan to an even thickness. Bake in a moderate oven for about 15 to 20 minutes, or until puffed and brown.

Remove cake from oven and immediately cut into finger slices. Cool in pan.

This almond cake will keep for 8 to 10 days in an airtight container.

Gâteau Saupoudré, or Streuselkuchen

Cinnamon coffee cake

3 cups (350 g) unsifted all-purpose flour
2 tablespoons (30 g) granulated sugar
1 teaspoon salt
1 envelope (15 g) active dry yeast or baker's yeast
⅔ cup (1½ dL) lukewarm milk
1 large egg
½ cup (125 g) butter, softened
1 egg yolk, beaten
Granulated sugar

Preparation time: 50 min.
Rising time: 45 min.
Baking time: 30 min.
Yield: 1 9-inch (23-cm) cake

Streusel topping:
½ cup (100 g) butter
1 cup (120 g) all-purpose flour
⅓ cup (70 g) granulated sugar
½ teaspoon ground cinnamon

Place the flour in a bowl. Mix with the sugar and salt. Make a crater in the center.

Dissolve the yeast in the milk. Put the yeast mixture and egg into the crater and mix with the flour.

Knead dough on a floured surface.

Add butter to the dough and knead again, mixing thoroughly. The dough should not be too firm.

Prepare streusel topping. Melt the butter and stir in the flour. Add the sugar and cinnamon and stir until bubbly.

Remove saucepan from heat and let cool. Scrape mixture out of pan and, with a knife, chop into very small pieces.

Roll out the yeast dough to a thickness of about 1 inch (3 cm) and use it to line a buttered 9-inch (23-cm) square baking pan.

Brush the surface of the dough with egg yolk and sprinkle with the small pieces of streusel topping. Let dough rise in a warm place for 30 to 45 minutes, or until doubled in bulk.

Preheat the oven to 350° F (180° C).

Bake cake in a moderate oven for 30 minutes. Let cool in pan, then sprinkle with sugar before serving. Cut into squares to serve.

This cake is usually served at breakfast.

This dough may be prepared the day before and stored in a cool place. (If this is done, allow more time for rising before baking.)

Savarin au Rhum

Rum savarin
photo page 262

Preparation time: 30 min.
Rising time: 2 hr.
Cooking time: 5 min.
Baking time: 35 min.
Yield: 1 9-inch (23-cm) ring

1 envelope (10 g) active dry yeast or baker's yeast
1 cup (2 dL) lukewarm milk
2¼ cups (250 g) unsifted all-purpose flour
3 large eggs
½ cup (100 g) butter, softened
1 tablespoon granulated sugar
¼ teaspoon salt
Whipped cream or mixed macerated fruits

Rum syrup:
1¼ cups (250 g) granulated sugar
1¾ cups (4 dL) water
½ cup (1 dL) dark rum

Dissolve the yeast in the warm milk.

Put the flour in a bowl and make a crater in the middle. Into the crater put the eggs and the dissolved yeast. Mix well and beat for 3 minutes.

Cover the bowl and let stand in a warm place. It should double in volume in about an hour.

Knead the butter, along with the sugar and salt, into the dough. Knead the dough until very smooth and elastic.

Generously butter a 1½-quart (1½-L) ring mold and put in the dough. Let stand in a warm place until dough rises to the top of the pan.

Preheat the oven to 350° F (180° C).

Bake savarin in a moderate oven for 30 to 35 minutes, or until golden brown. Unmold and cool.

While savarin cools, prepare syrup. Boil sugar and water for 5 minutes. Cool and stir in rum.

Place savarin on a platter and spoon syrup over slowly to allow syrup to be absorbed into cake.

Serve decorated with whipped cream or center filled with mixed fruits.

This cake owes its existence to the old Alsatian habit of pouring rum or Kirsch syrup over a Kougelhopf.

Biscuit aux Noisettes

Hazelnut cake

6 large eggs, separated
1 cup (200 g) superfine sugar
2 cups (200 g) shelled hazelnuts
¾ cup (80 g) unsifted all-purpose flour
Grated rind of ½ lemon
1 tablespoon Kirsch
Several roasted whole hazelnuts for decoration

Preparation time: 25 min.
Cooking time: 1 hr.
Yield: 1 9-inch (23-cm) cake

Preheat the oven to 325° F (170° C).

Beat the egg yolks with the sugar until thick and lemon colored.

Grate the hazelnuts finely in a blender, Mouli mill, or food processor and gently stir into the egg mixture, along with the flour, lemon rind, and Kirsch.

Beat the egg whites until stiff and fold gently into the batter.

Pour batter into a greased and floured 9-inch (23-cm) springform baking pan. Bake in a moderate oven for 1 hour.

Let cake cool in pan. Unmold. Sprinkle with superfine sugar and decorate with the whole roasted hazelnuts. Cut into wedges to serve.

âteau au Chocolat

Chocolate cake

6 large eggs, separated
2 cups (250 g) confectioners' sugar
1 cup (125 g) finely grated unblanched almonds
1 cup (250 g) butter, softened
8 ounces (250 g) semisweet chocolate, melted
1 cup (100 g) unsifted all-purpose flour
Fruit preserves, chocolate frosting, or whipped cream

Preparation time: 30 min.
Cooking time: 45 min.
Yield: 9-inch (23-cm) cake

Preheat the oven to 325° F (170° C).

Beat the egg yolks and sugar together for about 10 minutes until thick and lemon colored.

Fold in the almonds, butter, and melted chocolate. Gradually stir in the flour.

Beat the egg whites until stiff and fold gently into the batter.

Pour the batter into a lightly buttered and floured 9-inch (23-cm) springform pan. Bake for 45 minutes in a moderate oven.

Let the cake cool before removing from pan. Spread top with your favorite fruit preserves, chocolate frosting, or sweetened whipped cream.

Fritters, Crêpes, Omelettes, Soufflés

Beignets de Carnaval, or Fastnachtskiechla

Beer fritters
photo page 262

2¼ cups (250 g) unsifted all-purpose flour
½ teaspoon salt
4 large eggs, beaten
½ cup (100 g) granulated sugar
½ cup (100 g) butter, softened
½ cup (1 dL) beer
Oil for deep-frying
Confectioners' sugar mixed with ground cinnamon

Preparation time: 30 min.
Resting time: 1 hr.
Cooking time: 25 min.
Yield: 24, depending on size

Pour the flour and salt into a bowl and make a crater. Into the crater put the eggs, sugar, butter and beer. Mix well with a wooden spoon, then turn out of bowl onto a heavily floured surface. Knead until mixture is a firm dough. Let stand, covered, for 1 hour.

Roll out the dough on a floured surface to a thickness of about ¼ inch (½ cm). Use a cutter or a knife to cut the dough into any shapes you wish: squares, rectangles, crescents, hearts, etc.

Heat the oil to 375° F (190° C).

Fry the fritters in hot oil for about 3 to 4 minutes turning to brown on both sides. Remove when they are the proper shade of golden brown.

Drain on absorbent paper and sprinkle with a mixture of confectioners' sugar and cinnamon.

These may be served as dessert; but they are also delicious at breakfast or for between-meal snacks.

Beignets Fourrés de Carnaval

Apricot fritters
photo page 262

1 envelope (10 g) active dry yeast
½ cup (1 dL) lukewarm milk
2¼ cups (250 g) unsifted all-purpose flour
Pinch of salt
2 tablespoons granulated sugar
4 egg yolks, lightly beaten
3 tablespoons butter, softened
½ cup (1 dL) crème fraîche or heavy cream
1 tablespoon rum
Apricot (or currant) preserves
Oil for deep-frying
Granulated or confectioners' sugar

Preparation time: 30 min.
Rising time: 1 hr., 30 min.
Cooking time: 25 min.
Yield: 24

Dissolve the yeast in the warm milk.

Place the flour, salt, and sugar into a bowl. Add the egg yolks, butter, cream, yeast mixture, and rum. Beat until well blended, then knead on a floured surface until dough no longer sticks to your fingers.

Cover dough with a cloth and let stand in a warm place until double in bulk, about 45 minutes to 1 hour.

Punch down and knead again.

On a floured surface, roll out the dough to a thickness of ½ inch (1 cm). Cut into 48 rounds about 2 to 2½ inches (5 to 6 cm) in diameter. Brush the edges of 24 of the rounds with a bit of water. Spoon a small amount of apricot (or currant) preserves into the center of each round, then cover with remaining rounds. Seal the edges with your fingers.

Place the fritters on a floured cloth and let stand in a warm place for 30 minutes or until double in bulk.

Heat the oil to 375° F (190° C).

Fry fritters in hot oil until brown on both sides. The cooking time is about 10 minutes. Drain and sprinkle the fritters with granulated or confectioners' sugar.

This is a traditional treat throughout Alsace before Mardi Gras.

Beignets aux Pommes

Apple fritters
photo page 262

Preparation time: 15 min.
Resting time: 2 hr.
Cooking time: 25 min.
Yield: 24

2¼ cups (250 g) unsifted all-purpose flour
Pinch of salt
1 tablespoon granulated sugar
⅔ cup (1½ dL) beer
1 cup (2 dL) warm water
2 egg yolks
2 tablespoons butter, melted
2 egg whites, stiffly beaten
Oil for deep-frying
½ cup (100 g) superfine sugar mixed with 1 teaspoon ground cinnamon

Filling:
6 apples (Granny Smith, Rome Beauty, Pippin)
½ cup (100 g) granulated sugar
½ cup (1 dL) Kirsch

Combine flour, salt, sugar, beer, water, yolks, and butter. Beat until smooth. Let stand for 2 hours. When ready to use, fold in the egg whites.

Prepare the filling. Use a corer to remove the cores of the apples. Peel the apples and cut them into rounds about ¼-inch (¾-cm) thick. Sprinkle with the sugar, then with the Kirsch. Cover and let stand for 20 minutes. Drain apples and dry on paper towels.

Heat the oil to 375° F (190° C).

Dip the apple rounds into the batter and plunge immediately into hot oil. Fry until brown on both sides, about 5 to 6 minutes. Drain on absorbent paper.

Sprinkle with the mixture of sugar and cinnamon.

Serve on a heated platter.

Beignets Soufflés

Egg fritters

1 cup (2½ dL) water
½ cup (50 g) butter
2 teaspoons granulated sugar
Pinch of salt
1 cup (125 g) unsifted all-purpose flour
4 large eggs
Oil for deep-frying
Granulated sugar

Preparation time: 20 min.
Cooking time: 25 min.
Yield: about 24

In a saucepan, combine the water, butter, sugar, and salt and bring to a boil. Gradually stir in the flour, mixing well. Continue cooking until the dough no longer sticks to the pan and it forms a ball.

Remove from heat and, while the dough is still hot, beat in the eggs one by one. Mix the batter until well blended after each egg is added. (Use food processor for better results.—ed.)

Heat oil to 375° F (190° C). Use a teaspoon to drop a small amount of the batter into the hot fat. Fry until puffed and golden brown, about 5 to 6 minutes. Drain on absorbent paper, and sprinkle fritters with sugar.

Soufflé à la Mirabelle

Plum soufflé

8 ounces (200 g) Mirabelle plums (or very small Italian prune plums)
1 cup (2 dL) water
Generous ½ cup (100 g) granulated sugar
4 egg yolks
1 cup (2 dL) milk
6 egg whites
¼ cup (½ dL) Mirabelle eau-de-vie or brandy
6 Petit Beurre biscuits, crumbled fine
Superfine sugar

Preparation time: 20 min.
Cooking time: 10 min.
Baking time: 25 min.
Serves: 6

Remove the pits from the plums and parboil for 5 minutes in a syrup made from the water and ¼ cup (50 g) sugar. Set aside.

Beat the egg yolks with the remaining sugar.

Heat the milk to boiling, then gradually add the egg-yolk-and-sugar mixture. Heat again, stirring constantly, until the mixture thickens and coats a spoon. Do not allow to boil.

Strain the mixture through a fine sieve, then pour into a bowl. Cover and cool to room temperature.

Preheat the oven to 350° F (180° C).

Beat the egg whites until very stiff.

Add 2 tablespoons of the *eau-de-vie* to the egg-yolk-and-sugar mixture and then very gently fold the egg whites in.

Butter and sugar a 1½-quart (1½-L) soufflé dish.

Make a layer of the biscuit crumbs at the bottom of the dish.

Drain the plums and place on top of the biscuits. Sprinkle with remaining *eau-de-vie.*

Pour in the soufflé batter until the mold is three-fourths full. Bake in a moderate oven for 20 to 25 minutes, or until puffed and brown.

Sprinkle soufflé with a little sugar and serve immediately.

Note: If you wish a high rising soufflé, use a 1-quart (1-L) soufflé dish and make a 3-inch (7½-cm) high collar of foil around outer edge. Grease or butter lightly and sprinkle with sugar. Prepare soufflé as above. After baking, remove collar and serve soufflé at once.

At your option, serve this soufflé with a fruit salad aromatized with Mirabelle *eau-de-vie.*

Soufflé au Kirsch

Kirsch soufflé

photo page 230

This soufflé is made exactly as is the Plum Soufflé (page 228), except that the plum *eau-de-vie* is replaced by Kirsch, and the plums, by cherries.

Basic Recipe for Crêpes

2 cups (200 g) unsifted all-purpose flour
Pinch of salt
¾ cup (80 g) confectioners' sugar
8 large eggs, lightly beaten
2 cups (½ L) lukewarm milk
⅓ cup (70 g) butter, melted
3 tablespoons Kirsch or raspberry eau-de-vie

Preparation time: 30 min.
Resting time: 2 hr.
Yield: 32 crêpes

Combine the flour, salt, and sugar in a bowl. Add the eggs and beat well until you have a smooth, thick batter.

Beat the milk into the egg mixture. Stir in the melted butter. Let stand for 2 hours before use.

Just before cooking, stir in Kirsch or raspberry *eau-de-vie.*

Using a small ladle (¼-cup measure or ½ dL), spoon the batter into a lightly buttered 7-inch (15-cm) crêpe pan. Rotate pan until entire bottom is covered. Cook and turn so both sides are golden.

Stack crêpes as they are made. Wrap and refrigerate or freeze until needed.

Crêpes aux Cerises Gratinées

Cherry crêpes au gratin

12 crêpes, made from Basic Recipe (page 230)
¾ pound (300 g) pitted ripe cherries
½ cup (1 dL) Sylvaner wine
1 cup (200 g) granulated sugar
1 teaspoon ground cinnamon
2 large eggs
1 cup (2 dL) milk
½ cup (100 g) crumbled macaroons
6 tablespoons (80 g) butter, melted

Preparation time: 20 min.
Baking time: 20 min.
Serves: 6

Kirsch Soufflé (p. 229); Fruit Salad (p. 253); Gewürztraminer Sherbet (p. 264).

DE
70 cl

Preheat the oven to 350° F (180° C).

Keep crêpes hot.

Parboil the cherries for 5 to 8 minutes in a mixture of the wine, ½ cup (100 g) sugar, and cinnamon.

Place 5 of the cooked cherries on each crêpe. Fold each crêpe in four and place side by side in a buttered and sugared 9 × 13-inch (23 × 33-cm) pan or into 6 individual casseroles.

Beat the eggs and remaining sugar together. Gradually add the milk and mix until smooth.

Cover the crêpes with this mixture and sprinkle with the crushed macaroons. Top with the melted butter. Bake in a moderate oven for 15 to 20 minutes, or until puffed and brown.

This recipe appears to have originated in upper Alsace. It is especially popular during the cherry season in the valleys of Sainte-Marie-aux-Mines, Lapoutroie, and Munster.

Crêpes aux Pommes Fruits

Apple crêpes

½ Basic Recipe for Crêpes (page 230)
2 apples (Golden Delicious)
½ cup (100 g) butter
Granulated sugar mixed with ground cinnamon

Preparation time: 20 min.
Cooking time: 20 min.
Serves: 6

Make the batter using only 2 eggs.

Peel and core the apples and slice thinly. Sauté in half the butter until wilted, keeping the slices moderately firm. Let cool, then mix into the crêpe batter.

Melt a little of the remaining butter in a crêpe pan. Spoon the batter into the pan and cook like ordinary crêpes. (See Basic Recipe for Crêpes, page 230).

Preheat the oven to 300° F (150° C).

Place the cooked crêpes side by side on buttered and sugared cookie sheets. Just before serving, put crêpes in the oven briefly to reheat.

Serve crêpes sprinkled with a mixture of sugar and cinnamon.

Crêpes aux Framboises

Raspberry crêpes

18 crêpes made from Basic Recipe (page 230)
1 cup (250 g) butter, softened
¾ cup (80 g) toasted chopped almonds
½ cup (1 dL) crème fraîche or heavy cream
6 tablespoons raspberry eau-de-vie
8 ounces (200 g) fresh raspberries

Preparation time: 30 min.
Baking time: 15 min.
Serves: 6

Preheat the oven to 300° F (150° C).

Keep crêpes hot.

Mix the butter, almonds, cream, and half the *eau-de-vie.* Beat well until fluffy and well blended.

Spread about 1 heaping tablespoon of the raspberry butter on each of the crêpes.

Fold the crêpes in four and place in overlapping rows in a 7 × 12-inch (18 × 30-cm) buttered and sugared baking pan. Scatter fresh raspberries around the crêpes.

Heat crêpes for 10 minutes in a warm oven. Warm remaining *eau-de-vie* in a small cup and pour over crêpes and set aflame.

You may, if you wish, serve these crêpes with Raspberry Sauce (page 270).

Crêpes Soufflées au Kirsch

Kirsch soufflé crêpes

12 crêpes made from Basic Recipe (page 230)
1 cup (200 g) chopped canned or frozen fruit
1 cup (2 dL) Kirsch
1½ cups (3 dL) Pastry Cream (page 267)
5 egg whites

Preparation time: 20 min.
Macerating time: 10 min.
Baking time: 15 min.
Serves: 6

Preheat the oven to 350° F (180° C).

Keep crêpes hot.

Mix fruit with half the Kirsch. Macerate 10 minutes.

Drain, reserving liquid, and mix fruit with the Pastry Cream.

Beat egg whites until very stiff and gently fold them into the cream. Spoon some of this mixture onto each crêpe and fold in half. Place the crêpes, in overlapping rows, into a 1½-quart (1½-L) shallow baking dish or 6 individual casseroles, which has been buttered and sprinkled with confectioners' sugar.

Bake crêpes in a moderate oven for 12 to 15 minutes, until the crêpes have puffed out and become lightly browned.

Pour reserved liquid drained from fruit and remaining Kirsch into a small cup and heat. Pour over crêpes and set aflame. Serve after flames die.

Omelette Soufflée au Kirsch

Puffy Kirsch omelette 

8 large eggs
½ cup (100 g) granulated sugar
1 cup (2 dL) Kirsch
⅔ cup (150 g) butter
Superfine sugar

Preparation time: 20 min.
Cooking time: 10 min.
Serves: 6

Preheat the oven to 350° F (180° C).

Separate the eggs and reserve the whites. Beat the yolks with the sugar. Stir in half the Kirsch.

Beat the egg whites until stiff and fold gently into the yolk-and-sugar mixture.

Melt 2 tablespoons of butter (28 g) in a 10-inch (25-cm) omelette pan or skillet. Pour in the egg mixture and cook without stirring until golden brown on the bottom. Briefly place in broiler and broil until surface is dry.

Heavily butter and sugar a 7 × 12-inch (18 × 30-cm) baking dish.

Fold the omelette in half and place in the baking dish. Bake in a moderate oven for 5 minutes.

Remove crêpes from oven and sprinkle lightly with superfine sugar. Heat remaining Kirsch and pour over omelette. Set aflame.

This spectacular dessert is a favorite in upper Alsace.

Charlottes and Puddings

harlotte aux Marrons

Chestnut charlotte

5 ounces (125 g) ladyfingers or champagne wafers
½ cup (1 dL) rum
1½ pounds (750 g) fresh chestnuts
1 quart (1 L) milk
1 teaspoon vanilla extract
⅔ cup (150 g) butter, softened
1¼ cups (150 g) confectioners' sugar
1¼ cups (2½ dL) heavy cream, whipped
1 recipe English Cream (page 268)

Preparation time: 30 min.
Cooking time: 15 min.
Chilling time: 3 hr.

Dip the ladyfingers quickly in the rum and use them to line a lightly buttered 1-quart (1-L) charlotte mold.

Score chestnuts with an *x* on the flat side. Place in boiling water and simmer for 5 minutes. Shell and remove brown inner skin.

Cook chestnuts in the milk with the vanilla until easily pierced and tender. Drain. Grind chestnuts to a purée in a food processor or blender.

Mix the chestnut purée with the butter and sugar. Fold in whipped cream.

Fill the charlotte mold with this mixture and chill for 3 hours in the refrigerator.

Unmold and serve with English Cream.

Charlotte aux Poires

Pear charlotte

Preparation time: 1 hr.
Cooking time: 15 min.
Chilling time: 6 hr.
Serves: 6

4 pears
1 quart (1 L) water
2 cups (400 g) granulated sugar
1 teaspoon vanilla extract
3 egg yolks
2 envelopes unflavored gelatin soaked in 2 tablespoons water
2 cups (½ L) pear eau-de-vie
24 ladyfingers or champagne wafers
1 cup (2 dL) crème fraîche or heavy cream
4 egg whites
½ cup (1 dL) apricot preserves
Caramel Sauce (page 269) or Raspberry Sauce (page 270)

Peel the pears and cut in half. Remove cores.

Cook water, sugar, and vanilla until a clear syrup forms. Add the pears and simmer until tender but still firm. Cool pears in syrup, then drain and reserve pears and liquid. Slice pears.

Mix the egg yolks with 1 cup (2 dL) pear syrup and cook over medium heat (but without allowing the mixture to boil) until the liquid has the consistency of a thick cream.

Remove pot from heat and stir in the soaked gelatin. Stir in half the pear *eau-de-vie*. Cool, but do not put in the refrigerator.

While the mixture is cooling, cut the ladyfingers in half and line the bottom and sides of an 8-inch (20-cm) buttered mold with the ladyfingers. Over the ladyfingers, sprinkle the remaining pear *eau-de-vie*.

Whip the cream until stiff.

Beat the egg whites until stiff.

Gently fold the cream, then the egg whites, into the cooled gelatin mixture. Fill the mold with this mixture and chill in the refrigerator for 6 hours.

To serve, unmold the charlotte, decorate the top with the drained pears. Heat the apricot preserves and spoon over the pears.

Serve a Caramel Sauce or a Raspberry Sauce separately.

harlotte Chaude aux Pommes Flambée au Rhum

Apple charlotte flambéed with rum

Preparation time: 15 min.
Cooking time: 40 min.
Serves: 6

6 apples (Granny Smith, Rome Beauty, Pippin)
½ cup (100 g) butter
⅔ cup (150 g) granulated sugar
½ cup (60 g) raisins
½ cup (60 g) toasted chopped hazelnuts
1 loaf (454 g) firm white bread
Superfine sugar
⅓ cup (¾ dL) rum

Preheat the oven to 400° F (200° C).

Peel, core, and thinly slice the apples.

Cook apples in a saucepan with the butter and the sugar. When cooked, add the raisins and hazelnuts.

Cut the bread into slices ½ inch (1 cm) thick and trim off the crusts. Line the bottom and sides of a generously buttered 1-quart (1-L) charlotte mold with these slices. Fill the mold with layers of remaining bread and the mixture of apples, raisins, and hazelnuts.

Place the mold in a pan of water and bake in a hot oven for 30 minutes.

Unmold charlotte onto a hot plate. Sprinkle with sugar. Heat rum in a small cup and pour over charlotte. Set aflame. Serve.

Pudding de la Saint-Martin

Saint Martin's chocolate pudding

8 ounces (250 g) semisweet chocolate
8 ounces (250 g) butter, melted
2 cups (250 g) confectioners' sugar
4 egg yolks
20 to 25 ladyfingers or champagne wafers
Whipped cream
1 recipe English Cream (page 268)

Preparation time: 30 min.
Cooking time: 15 min.
Chilling time: 6 hr.
Serves: 6

Melt chocolate over very low heat or in a double boiler.

Using a whisk, combine the butter, sugar, and egg yolks. Add the chocolate and mix thoroughly.

Line the bottom and sides of a 1-quart (1-L) charlotte mold with wax paper or parchment paper. At the bottom of the mold, make a layer of ladyfingers, then a layer of the chocolate mixture. Continue alternating layers of ladyfingers and chocolate mixture until the mold is full. The top layer should be a ladyfinger layer.

Chill the mold for several hours.

Unmold the pudding. Remove the parchment paper and decorate with rosettes of whipped cream. Serve the English Cream separately.

This pudding dates from the seventeenth century. It was a traditional dish served in monasteries and clerical households on the feast of Saint Martin.

Pudding de Semoule

Semolina pudding

Preparation time: 15 min.
Cooking time: 1 hr., 20 min.
Serves: 6

2¼ cups (5 dL) milk
½ cup (125 g) granulated sugar
½ cup (125 g) semolina or Cream of Wheat
½ cup (125 g) butter
4 large eggs, separated
1 recipe English Cream (page 268)

Caramel:
⅔ cup (150 g) granulated sugar
2 tablespoons water

To prepare the caramel for mold, combine the sugar and water in a saucepan and boil until golden brown. Pour caramel into a 1-quart (1-L) mold and rotate to cover bottom.

Combine the milk and sugar and bring to a boil. When boiling, sprinkle in the semolina. Stir well and cook over low heat for 3 to 5 minutes. Remove from heat and stir in the butter and egg yolks. Cool to lukewarm.

Prchcat thc ovcn to 350° F (180° C).

Beat the egg whites until stiff. Fold egg whites into the semolina mixture.

Pour the semolina mixture into the mold. Place the mold into a pan with water halfway up the sides and bake in a moderate oven for 1 hour.

Allow pudding to cool. Unmold and spoon English Cream over each serving.

Tarts

Tarte au Fromage Blanc

Cheese tart
photo page 198

- *1 recipe (300 g) Pie Dough (page 210)*
- *½ cup (100 g) raisins*
- *2 tablespoons Kirsch*
- *12 ounces (300 g) cream cheese*
- *3 tablespoons crème fraîche or heavy cream*
- *4 large eggs, separated*
- *1¼ cups (150 g) confectioners' sugar*
- *1 teaspoon vanilla extract*
- *Grated rind of ½ lemon*

Preparation time: 30 min.
Baking time: 45 min.
Chilling time: 4 to 6 hr.
Yield: 1 10-inch (25-cm) cake

Prepare dough according to recipe, but do not shape or prebake dough.

With the dough, line the bottom and halfway up the sides of a 10-inch (25-cm) springform pan.

Soak the raisins in the Kirsch.

Preheat the oven to 325° F (170° C).

In a bowl, beat the cream cheese with the cream. Add the egg yolks, sugar, vanilla, and lemon rind. Mix thoroughly until very smooth.

Beat the egg whites until stiff and gently fold into the batter.

Pour the batter into the lined pan. Sprinkle the Kirsch-soaked raisins over the top. Bake in a moderate oven for 40 to 45 minutes, or until slightly puffed and very brown.

Cool tart and then chill for several hours before cutting.

This is a favorite summer dessert. It is a dish typical of the cuisine of the Vosgues Valley.

arte de Linz

Linzer torte

Preparation time: 35 min.
Resting time: 1 hr.
Baking time: 20 min.
Yield: 1 9-inch (22½-cm) cake

2 large eggs
1 cup (100 g) confectioners' sugar
½ cup (100 g) butter, softened
Grated rind of 1 lemon
2¼ cups (250 g) unsifted all-purpose flour
⅔ cup (70 g) finely ground hazelnuts or almonds
1 teaspoon ground cinnamon
1 cup (350 g) seedless raspberry preserves
1 egg yolk, beaten

In a bowl and using a whisk, combine the eggs, sugar, butter, and lemon rind until well blended. Stir in the flour, nuts, and cinnamon. Mix well.

Knead the dough on a floured surface until you have a smooth, firm ball. Let stand 1 hour at room temperature.

Preheat the oven to 400° F (200° C).

Take three-fourths of the dough and pat it out on the bottom of a 9-inch (22½-cm) springform pan to ½-inch (1½-cm) thickness.

Roll out the rest of the dough to ¼-inch (¾-cm) thickness and cut it into strips about ½ inch (1½ cm) wide.

Spread the dough in the pan with preserves. Place some of the dough strips over the preserves in the form of a lattice. Surround the edge of the dough with the remaining strips.

Brush the strips with egg yolk and bake torte for 20 minutes in a hot oven, or until richly browned.

Cool torte thoroughly before cutting into wedges.

Tarte aux Myrtilles à l'Alsacienne I

Alsatian huckleberry tart I

1 recipe (300 g) Pie Dough (page 210)
5 ladyfingers
1 pound (500 g) fresh huckleberries or blueberries (about 1 quart), or 1½ cups (500 g) jam or preserves (but then use only half the sugar)
½ cup (100 g) crème fraîche or heavy cream
2 large eggs
½ cup (100 g) granulated sugar

Preparation time: 15 min.
Baking time: 35 min.
Yield: 1 10-inch (25-cm) tart

Preheat the oven to 400° F (200° C).

Roll the dough out on a floured surface. Line the bottom and sides of a 10-inch (25-cm) tart pan.

Crumble the ladyfingers and sprinkle over the dough. Spread the fruit or jam evenly over the crumbs.

Bake tart in a hot oven for about 20 minutes.

While baking, beat together the cream and eggs, then add the sugar.

Remove the tart from the oven. Reduce oven heat to 350° F (180° C).

Pour the cream mixture over tart and bake for another 15 minutes in a moderate oven.

Let tart cool before serving. Remove sides and cut into wedges.

Huckelberry Tart is a characteristic dish of the Vosgues Valley.

arte aux Myrtilles à l'Alsacienne II

Alsatian huckleberry tart II

photo page 198

1¾ cups (200 g) unsifted all-purpose flour
1 tablespoon confectioners' sugar
Pinch of salt
½ cup (100 g) butter, softened
1 egg yolk
¼ cup (½ dL) water
2 tablespoons dry bread crumbs
1 quart (500 g) fresh huckleberries, or blueberries, washed and drained well
Granulated sugar

Preparation time: 25 min.
Resting time: 30 min.
Baking time: 35 min.
Yield: 1 10-inch (25-cm) tart

Topping:
2 large eggs
½ cup (100 g) crème fraîche or heavy cream
½ cup (100 g) confectioners' sugar

Place the flour, sugar, and salt in a bowl. Mix and add the butter. Work with your fingers until the particles are very fine.

Make a crater in the flour and put in the egg yolk and water. Mix these ingredients into the flour until a ball of dough is formed.

Knead dough a few times on a floured surface until it is a smooth ball. Chill for 30 minutes.

Preheat the oven to 400° F (200° C).

Roll out the dough and use it to line a buttered 10-inch (25-cm) tart pan. Take care to press the dough firmly against the sides of the pan.

Sprinkle bottom of tart shell with the bread crumbs, which will absorb some of the liquid from the fruit. Then pour in the huckleberries.

Bake tart in a hot oven for 20 minutes.

Meanwhile, beat eggs, cream, and confectioners' sugar in a bowl.

Remove the tart from the oven and pour the topping slowly over the huckleberries. Be careful that the pan does not overflow.

Continue to bake for another 15 minutes, then remove tart from oven and sprinkle with confectioners' sugar.

Wait at least 10 minutes before removing sides of pan. Serve warm.

Tarte aux Poires sur Marmelade de Pommes

Pear and apple tart

Preparation time: 15 min.
Baking time: 30 min.
Yield: 1 10-inch (25-cm) tart

1 recipe (400 g) Sweet Tart Dough (page 211)
2 large cooking apples
½ cup (1 dL) water
½ cup (100 g) granulated sugar
1¼ pounds (500 g) pears, ripe but not soft
¼ cup (85 g) apricot jam
½ cup (50 g) toasted slivered almonds

Peel, core, and quarter the apples. Cook in a mixture of water and sugar until apples are very mushy and liquid is absorbed. Press through a sieve. Cool.

Preheat the oven to 400° F (200° C).

Line the bottom and sides of a 10-inch (25-cm) tart pan with the dough. Spread the apple purée over the bottom of the shell.

Peel, core, and thinly slice the pears. Arrange in a pretty pattern over the apple purée.

Bake in a hot oven for 30 minutes.

Remove from oven and put on a rack to cool.

Heat the apricot jam until bubbly and spoon over pears. Sprinkle with the almonds.

Remove sides of pan and cut tart into wedges.

arte aux Pommes à l'Alsacienne

Alsatian apple tart

photo page 198

Preparation time: 30 min.
Baking time: 45 min.
Yield: 1 11-inch (28-cm) tart

2¼ pounds (1 kg) cooking apples, approximately 5 apples
1 recipe (300 g) Pie Dough (page 210)
1⅓ cups (150 g) confectioners' sugar
2 large eggs
1 cup (¼ L) milk
½ cup (1 dL) crème fraîche or heavy cream
Ground cinnamon

Preheat the oven to 400° F (200° C).

Peel the apples and cut in half. Remove core. Place apple halves cut-side down on a work surface and cut straight down into ¼-inch (¾-cm) thick slices. Keep the slices together.

Roll out the dough and use it to line a buttered 11-inch (28-cm) tart pan. Place 9 of the apple halves, slices together, in the shell. Use the tenth half, separated, to fill in empty spaces.

Sprinkle with ⅓ cup (70 g) of the sugar.

Bake in a hot oven for 25 to 30 minutes.

In a small bowl, beat the eggs with the remaining sugar, then add the milk and cream.

Pour cream mixture over the apples and put tart back into hot oven for another 10 to 15 minutes, or until custard is set.

When tart is cooked, sprinkle lightly with the cinnamon. Remove sides and serve warm.

This is a classic of Alsatian cuisine.

Tart aux Pommes Chaudes

Hot apple tart

½ recipe (400 g) Puff Pastry Dough (page 212)
4 Pippin or other small cooking apples, peeled, cored, and cut in thin slices
2 tablespoons confectioners' sugar
¼ cup (85 g) apricot jam mixed with 2 tablespoons water
½ cup (50 g) toasted slivered almonds

Preparation time: 30 min.
Cooking time: 10 min.
Baking time: 30 min.
Yield: 1 10-inch (25-cm) cake

Frangipane:
1⅓ cups (3 dL) milk
6 tablespoons (40 g) all-purpose flour
¼ cup (50 g) granulated sugar
Pinch of salt
1 large egg
2 egg yolks
2 tablespoons (30 g) butter
6 crisp almond macaroons, finely crumbled
1 teaspoon vanilla extract

Make the frangipane. Bring milk to a boil. Using a tin-lined copper pan, or one of stainless steel, mix together the flour, sugar, salt, egg, and egg yolks. Mix with a whisk, then, still using your whisk, beat the boiling milk into the mixture and mix thoroughly.

Heat, stirring constantly, until thick. Pour into a bowl.

Stir the butter, macaroon crumbs, and vanilla into the cream. Cover to prevent a skin from forming.

Preheat the oven to 400° F (200° C).

Roll out the Puff Pastry Dough into a 10 × 14-inch (25 × 35-cm) oblong. Line a buttered 9 × 13-inch (23 × 33-cm) pan with the dough. Fold the edges over slightly to make a border. Prick the bottom heavily with the tines of a fork.

Spread the frangipane evenly over the dough. Place the apple slices in rows over the cream and sprinkle with the confectioners' sugar.

Bake in a hot oven for 25 to 30 minutes.

Remove the tart from the oven. Heat apricot jam and water and spoon over apples. Sprinkle with the slivered almonds. Serve hot.

Tarte à la Rhubarbe

Rhubarb tart

1 pound (500 g) rhubarb stalks
⅔ cup (150 g) superfine sugar
1 recipe (400 g) Pie Dough (page 210)
2 large eggs
1 cup (¼ L) crème fraîche or heavy cream

Preparation time: 20 min.
Macerating time: 20 min.
Baking time: 40 min.
Yield: 1 10-inch (25-cm) tart

Peel the rhubarb and cut into thin, julienne-style strips. Put the strips into a bowl and sweeten with 2 tablespoons of sugar. Let stand 20 to 30 minutes.

Preheat the oven to 400° F (200° C).

Roll out dough on a floured surface to a 12-inch (30-cm) round. Line the bottom and sides of a buttered 10-inch (25-cm) tart pan.

Drain the rhubarb and spread over the dough.

Bake tart in hot oven for 20 minutes.

Beat the eggs in a bowl. Add the cream and the remaining sugar and pour the mixture over the rhubarb.

Bake tart for 15 to 20 minutes more.

Remove sides of pan and serve (warm, preferably).

Tarte aux Quetsches I

Purple-plum tart I

1 envelope (10 g) active dry yeast or baker's yeast
½ cup (1 dL) lukewarm milk
2¼ cups (250 g) unsifted all-purpose flour
½ teaspoon salt
3 tablespoons granulated sugar
1 large egg
½ cup (100 g) butter, softened
24 purple plums, about 3 pounds (1½ kg)
½ cup (100 g) confectioners' sugar
Granulated sugar mixed with ground cinnamon

Preparation time: 30 min.
Rising time: 1 hr., 30 min.
Baking time: 30 min.
Yield: 1 10-inch (25-cm) tart

In a bowl, dissolve the yeast in milk.

Mix the flour, salt, and sugar in a bowl. Make a crater and pour in the yeast mixture, egg, and butter. Mix, then beat until smooth.

Turn dough out of bowl and continue kneading on a floured surface until the dough no longer sticks to your fingers. Place into a bowl, cover, and let stand in a warm place until doubled in bulk.

Knead again so that it will lose some of its volume. Roll out dough on a floured surface to an 11-inch (27½-cm) round.

Line a buttered 10-inch (25-cm) tart pan with the dough.

Remove the pits from the plums and place the plum halves, cut-side up, side by side on the dough.

Let dough rise for 30 minutes.

Preheat the oven to 400° F (200° C).

Sprinkle tart with confectioners' sugar and bake in a hot oven for 25 to 30 minutes, or until puffed and brown around the edges.

Remove tart from oven when cooked and wait 10 minutes before unmolding. Sprinkle with the sugar mixed with cinnamon. Serve warm.

The Purple-Plum Tart is a traditional Alsatian dish.

arte aux Quetsches II

Purple-plum tart II 

1 recipe (400 g) Pie Dough (page 210)
24 purple plums, about 3 pounds (1½ kg)
1 cup (100 g) confectioners' sugar
Granulated sugar mixed with ground cinnamon

Preparation time: 10 min.
Baking time: 30 min.
Yield: 1 10 × 12-inch (25 × 30-cm) tart

Preheat the oven to 400° F (200° C).

Roll out dough to a 12 × 14-inch (30 × 35-cm) oblong on a floured surface. Place on a greased cookie sheet. Turn up the edges to form a border, making a rectangle 10 × 12 inches (25 × 30 cm).

Remove the pits from the plums. Quarter the plums and place in rows on the dough. Sprinkle with confectioners' sugar.

Bake in a hot oven for 25 to 30 minutes.

Remove tart from the oven and let cool on a rack. Sprinkle with the sugar mixed with cinnamon. Cut into squares to serve.

arte aux Mirabelles

Mirabelle plum tart 

Follow directions for the Purple-Plum Tart (page 248 or 249).

Instead of purple plums, use yellow plums. A Puff Pastry is best when used with these plums.

Tarte aux Raisins

Grape tart

1 recipe (400 g) Sweet Tart Dough (page 211)
1 cup (2 dL) Frangipane, from Hot Apple Tart recipe (page 246)
2¼ pounds (1 kg) seedless green grapes
4 egg whites
½ cup (100 g) confectioners' sugar
2 tablespoons chopped toasted almonds
Granulated sugar

Preparation time: 20 min.
Baking time: 30 min.
Yield: 1 10-inch (25-cm) tart

Preheat the oven to 350° F (180° C).

Roll out the dough on a floured surface to a 12-inch (30-cm) round. Line the bottom and sides of a buttered 10-inch (25-cm) tart pan with the dough. Perforate the bottom with a fork. Line with cheesecloth and beans or rice and bake in a moderate oven for 20 minutes or until completely baked. Remove cheesecloth.

Let tart crust cool.

Preheat the oven to 400° F (200° C).

Spread bottom with the Frangipane and arrange the grapes on top.

Beat the egg whites until stiff. Add sugar, 1 tablespoon at a time, until whites are stiff and glossy. Fold in the almonds.

Cover the grapes with the meringue, swirling the top.

Bake in a hot oven for 10 minutes or until golden brown. Keep close watch to ensure that it does not get too brown.

Remove tart from oven and cool on a rack. Sprinkle with the sugar.

Fruits

Entremets d'Abricots à l'Alsacienne

Alsatian apricots

2 pounds (800 g) firm ripe apricots
½ cup (1 dL) water
2 cups (250 g) confectioners' sugar
⅓ cup (¾ dL) Kirsch

Preparation time: 30 min.
Cooking time: 30 min.
Cooling time: 5 to 6 hr.
Serves: 6

Preheat the oven to 325° F (160° C).

Choose a ceramic, stoneware, or glass dish which can be used both on the range and in the oven.

Wash the apricots carefully and dry them. Cut in half and remove the pits. Arrange the halves on the bottom of the heatproof dish in a single layer, with the flat sides facing up. Add the water and sprinkle with 1½ cups (175 g) of sugar.

Cover the dish with a sheet of aluminum foil and bake in a slow oven for about 20 minutes. The apricots are properly cooked when no liquid is left in the bottom of the dish.

Remove from oven and sprinkle with remaining sugar. Pour the Kirsch into the bottom of the dish, but without wetting the tops of the apricots.

Place the apricots in the broiler for 10 minutes and broil until tops are caramelized.

Chill for 5 or 6 hours, then serve.

Gratin de Framboises

Raspberries baked in cream

2 cups (½ L) Pastry Cream (page 267)
½ cup crème fraîche or heavy cream
¼ cup (½ dL) raspberry eau-de-vie
12 ounces (300 g) fresh raspberries
2 cups (200 g) toasted slivered almonds
Confectioners' sugar

Preparation time: 10 min.
Baking time: 15 min.
Serves: 6

Preheat the oven to 400° F (200° C).

Mix the Pastry Cream with the cream and *eau-de-vie*.

Generously butter 6 small ¾-cup (2½-dL) custard cups and divide half the cream mixture among them.

Place some raspberries and almonds on top of each. Cover with the remaining cream and sprinkle with confectioners' sugar.

Bake in a hot oven for about 10 to 15 minutes, or until the tops are browned. Serve either warm or chilled.

Salade de Fruits

Fruit salad
photo page 230

Preparation time: 20 min.
Macerating time: 2 hr.
Serves: 6

2 regular or blood oranges
1 small fresh pineapple, or 1 can (20 ounces or ½ kg) pineapple chunks
1 bunch red grapes
1 bunch seedless green grapes
⅔ cup (150 g) superfine sugar
Juice of lemon
2 tablespoons Kirsch

Peel the oranges and cut into sections.

Peel the pineapple and cut in half lengthwise. Remove the center core, which is tough, and cut flesh into small chunks.

Seed the grapes.

Place all of the above into a salad bowl. Sprinkle with the sugar, lemon juice, and Kirsch. Mix gently. Let stand in a cool place for 2 hours before serving.

Pâté de Coings

Quince jelly candies

Fresh quince
Granulated sugar

Preparation time: 10 min.
Cooking time: 1 hr., 30 min.
Setting time: 12 hr.
Yield: depends on number of quinces used

Cut the fruit into pieces, without peeling, and put them into a copper (not lined with tin) or stainless steel pan. Cook, covered, in a small quantity of water—just enough water to keep the fruit from sticking—until quince are mushy.

Press pulp through a sieve or food mill. Measure and add 1 cup granulated sugar (200 g) for each cup of pulp.

Put this purée back into the copper pot and cook away the moisture, stirring constantly. It is done when you can clearly see the bottom of the pot in the wake of your spoon.

Sprinkle a cookie sheet with granulated sugar and spread the purée on it to a thickness of ¾ inch (2 cm). Sprinkle top with additional sugar. Let cool at least overnight.

Cut the paste into pieces—squares, rectangles, and so on—and roll again in sugar. Put the candies on a rack.

To store, make layers of the candies in an airtight container, separating each layer with wax paper.

The quince grows in abundance in Alsace, and it has always been a very popular fruit.

Cookies

Macarons

Almond macaroons

2 cups (250 g) blanched almonds
2 cups (500 g) superfine sugar
6 egg whites

Preparation time: 30 min.
Baking time: 20 min.
Yield: 3 dozen

Preheat the oven to 350° F (180° C).

Grind the almonds with half the sugar in a blender or food processor.

Place the resulting powder in a bowl. Stir in the rest of the sugar and 3 of the egg whites. Beat with a spoon until very white.

Beat remaining egg whites until quite stiff. Gently fold into the egg-and-sugar mixture.

Cover a cookie sheet with foil or parchment. Place the almond mixture in a pastry bag with a large star tip and press out rosettes, 1 inch (2½ cm) apart.

Bake in a moderate oven for 15 to 20 minutes, or until golden brown and crackled on top.

Remove from baking sheet and serve as soon as cool.

Madeleines

3 large eggs
1 cup (200 g) granulated sugar
Juice of 1 lemon
2 cups (250 g) all-purpose flour
1 cup (200 g) butter, melted

Preparation time: 30 min.
Baking time: 10 min.
Yield: 36

Preheat the oven to 350° F (180° C).

Mix eggs, sugar, and lemon juice. Beat with an electric mixer until tripled in volume. Fold in flour and butter.

Butter the madeleine molds and sprinkle with flour. Spoon in the batter.

Bake in a moderate oven for 10 minutes, or until golden brown. In practice, and depending on the size of the molds you are using, cooking time may vary from 10 to 20 minutes.

Dents de Loup, or Wolfszahn

Egg and brandy cookies 

2 egg yolks
¾ cup (175 g) butter, melted
1 cup (200 g) granulated sugar
3 large eggs, beaten
2 cups (250 g) unsifted all-purpose flour
2 tablespoons eau-de-vie or brandy
Juice of ½ lemon
2 teaspoons active dry yeast
½ cup (1 dL) crème fraîche or heavy cream

Preparation time: 20 min.
Baking time: 15 min.
Yield: 3 dozen

Preheat the oven to 300° F (150° C).

Beat the egg yolks, butter, and sugar in a bowl. When the sugar has dissolved completely and the mixture is fluffy, stir in the whole eggs.

Add the flour, *eau-de-vie*, lemon juice, and yeast. Mix thoroughly. Stir in the cream.

Butter, and flour lightly, 1 or more cookie sheets. Use a small spoon to drop the batter onto the sheet. The top of each cookie should end in a sharp point.

Bake in a slow oven for about 15 minutes.

These cookies, known as Wolf's Teeth, are very popular all along the Rhine and seem to have originated in upper Alsace.

Petits Fours de Noël

Cinnamon Christmas cookies

Preparation time: 30 min.
Resting time: 6 hr.
Baking time: 15 min.
Yield: 8 dozen

4 cups (500 g) unsifted all-purpose flour
1 teaspoon baking powder (editor's addition)
2 cups (250 g) confectioners' sugar
1 teaspoon ground cinnamon
Grated rind of 1 lemon
1½ cups (250 g) butter, softened
3 to 4 large eggs
1 egg yolk beaten with 1 tablespoon water

Place the flour, baking powder, sugar, cinnamon, and lemon rind into a bowl. Mix. Make a crater in the center. Into the crater, place the butter and 3 whole eggs. Mix well until you have a firm dough. If the dough seems too dry, add a fourth egg.

Cover and let stand a half-day in a cool place.

Preheat the oven to 350° F (180° C).

Roll out the dough on a floured surface to a thickness of ¼ inch (½ cm). Cut cookies in the form of stars, crescents, people, and other shapes.

Butter a cookie sheet generously and place the cookies on it. Brush the tops of the cookies with egg-yolk mixture.

Bake in a moderate oven for 15 minutes, or until lightly browned.

These cookies are traditionally given as gifts, and are eaten in December, during the Christmas season. They can also be served with a Caramel Sauce (page 269).

Petits Gâteaux à l'Anis, or Anis Bretla

Anise cookies

4 large eggs
1 pound (400 g) confectioners' sugar
4¼ cups (500 g) all-purpose flour
2 tablespoons aniseed

Preparation time: 40 min.
Resting time: 12 hr.
Baking time: 15 to 20 min.
Yield: 8 dozen

Beat together the eggs and sugar in a bowl. The sugar must dissolve completely, which takes at least 20 minutes. Mixture will be very thick like a mousse.

Fold in the flour and the aniseed.

Fit a pastry bag with a ½-inch (1½-cm) diameter round pastry tip. Fill bag with this mixture.

Generously butter and flour several cookie sheets. Make small rounds of the dough about the size of a walnut and place on sheets. Let stand for 12 hours in a warm place.

Preheat the oven to 350° F (180° C).

Bake for 15 to 20 minutes in a moderate oven, or until golden. Take care not to let the undersides of the cookies burn.

Schenkelés

photo page 262

1 cup (125 g) finely ground blanched almonds (done in blender or food processor)
2 cups (250 g) confectioners' sugar
4 large eggs
½ cup (125 g) butter, melted and warm
2 tablespoons brandy
4 cups (450 g) unsifted all-purpose flour
Peanut oil for deep-frying
¾ cup (175 g) granulated sugar mixed with ½ teaspoon cinnamon

Preparation time: 30 min.
Cooking time: 4 to 6 min.
Yield: 4 dozen

Combine the almonds and sugar. Add the eggs, butter, and brandy. Beat until you have a smooth mixture.

Gradually stir in the flour until a stiff dough forms. Knead on a floured surface until smooth and the dough no longer sticks to your fingers.

Roll out dough to ½-inch (1½-cm) thickness on a floured surface and cut into strips about the size and thickness of a finger.

Heat the oil to 375° F (190° C) in a fryer and cook strips 4 to 6 minutes. Remove when golden brown and drain on absorbent paper.

Arrange Schenkelés on a platter and sprinkle with the mixture of sugar and cinnamon. Serve cold.

This is an excellent dessert, but it may also be served with tea, or as a snack.

Like the Cinnamon Christmas cookies (page 258), this confection is traditional at Christmastime and at Mardi Gras.

Ice Creams and Sherbets

Glace Vanille

Vanilla ice cream

1¾ cups (4 dL) milk
1 vanilla bean, split lengthwise
1 cup (2 dL) crème fraîche or heavy cream
8 egg yolks
1 cup (200 g) granulated sugar

Preparation time: 10 min.
Cooking time: 20 min.
(plus additional time to process and chill)
Yield: 1 quart

Heat the milk and vanilla bean in a copper or stainless steel pot. When the milk comes to a boil, add the cream and bring to a boil once more. Let the vanilla flavor permeate the mixture for several minutes. Cool to lukewarm. Remove vanilla bean.

Beat the egg yolks and sugar together until fluffy. Stir in the milk and cream, mixing well. Cook over low heat, stirring with a wooden spoon.

When the cream is slightly thickened and begins to coat the spoon, remove from heat and pour through a fine strainer into a bowl. Stir to hasten cooling. Cool and then chill.

Pour cream mixture into an ice-cream freezer and process as directed on the machine.

Pack ice cream in ice or place in freezer to harden and keep until needed.

Petits Choux Fourrés à la Glace Vanille

Vanilla ice cream cakes

1 recipe Egg Fritters (page 228)
1 recipe Vanilla Ice Cream (page 261)
1⅓ cups (3 dL) heavy cream, whipped with 2 tablespoons granulated sugar
1 cup (2 dL) Chocolate Sauce (page 270) mixed with ¼ cup (½ dL) Kirsch

Preparation time: 20 min.
Baking time: 30 min.
(plus additional time to chill)
Serves: 6

Prepare Egg Fritter dough but do not fry.

Preheat the oven to 350° F (180° C).

Spoon dough into 30 small mounds on a buttered cookie sheet. Bake in a moderate oven for 30 minutes. Let cool.

Cut a thin slice from top of each fritter and pull out doughy strands. Fill with ice cream, then replace top. Place in freezer.

When ready to serve, place 5 puffs on each serving plate. Pile whipped cream on top and spoon Chocolate Sauce over cream.

Note: This dessert can also be topped with spun sugar for a really festive occasion.

A dessert sampler: Beer Fritters (p. 225); Schenkelés (p. 260); Apple Fritters (p. 227); Apricot Fritters (p. 226); Rum Savarin (p. 222).

orbet aux Fraises

Strawberry sherbet

2 cups (400 g) granulated sugar
1½ cups (3 dL) water
2 quarts (800 g) fresh strawberries
¼ cup (½ dL) lemon juice
1 cup (2 dL) orange juice

Preparation time: 20 min. (plus additional time to process and chill)
Yield: 1½ quarts

Boil the sugar in the water for 2 minutes. Let the syrup cool.

Remove the stems from the strawberries. Crush the berries slightly and purée in a blender or food processor.

Mix strawberries with the syrup. Add the lemon juice and orange juice.

Pour liquid into an ice-cream freezer and process according to directions.

Note: this can also be frozen in a container until mushy. Remove and beat with an electric mixer until fluffy. Cover and freeze until hard.

Sorbet au Marc de Gewürztraminer

Gewürztraminer sherbet
photo page 230

1½ cups (3 dL) water
2 cups (400 g) granulated sugar
½ cup (1 dL) skins of Gewürztraminer grapes after last pressing (optional; see note)
1 cup (2 dL) Gewürztraminer wine
1 bunch white grapes, stemmed, or Brandied Grapes (page 279)

Preparation time: 20 min. (plus additional time to process and chill)
Yield: 3 cups

Combine the water and the sugar and skins and cook for 2 minutes. Let cool.

Stir the wine into the syrup. Strain, pressing out all liquid, if you are using grape skins. Cool and chill.

Pour this mixture into your ice-cream freezer and process as directed. When sherbet begins to thicken, add the grape skins. Continue processing until sherbet is hard.

If freezing in a container, place sherbet in freezer until mushy, then beat with an electric mixer until fluffy. Cover and freeze until hard.

Serve the sherbet in glasses or silver cups, decorated with fresh grapes or Brandied grapes.

Note: It will be almost impossible to obtain actual Gewürztraminer grapes, so substitute a slightly sweet white grape, or use concord grapes (which will make the sherbet pink instead).

Soufflé Glacé au Kirsch

Frozen Kirsch soufflé

½ cup (100 g) pitted dark sweet cherries
½ cup (1 dL) Kirsch
¾ cup (1½ dL) water
⅔ cup (150 g) granulated sugar
6 egg yolks
2¼ cups (5 dL) crème fraîche or heavy cream, whipped
Cocoa powder

Preparation time: 30 min.
Macerating time: 5 min.
Chilling time: 3 hr.
Serves: 6

Attach a strip of foil or parchment around 6 ½-cup (1-dL) molds, about 1½ inches (4 cm) higher than the sides.

Cut the cherries into small cubes and steep in 2 tablespoons of the Kirsch.

Make the syrup by boiling the water and sugar for 5 minutes.

Place egg yolks in top of a double boiler. With an electric mixer, beat the hot syrup into the yolks in a thin stream. Place this mixture over simmering water and cook over low heat, beating constantly until smooth and thick.

Remove pot from heat and continue to beat until completely cool. Fold in the remaining Kirsch, cherries, and cream.

Divide this mixture among the molds. Chill in freezer for at least 3 hours.

To serve, remove the foil. The frozen soufflé will look like a hot soufflé. Sprinkle lightly with cocoa and serve on a platter decorated with a paper doily.

If you wish, serve this with a hot Chocolate Sauce (page 270).

This is a dessert for celebrations and special occasions. It is especially appropriate in summer.

Vacherin Glacé aux Fraises

Frozen strawberry meringue

Preparation time: 1 hr.
Cooking time: 1 hr., 30 min.
Serves: 6

2½ cups (5 dL) crème fraîche or heavy cream
⅓ cup (75 g) superfine sugar
2½ cups (5 dL) Vanilla Ice Cream (page 261)
2½ cups (5 dL) Strawberry Sherbet (page 263)
Whipped Cream
1 pint wild strawberries (in season) or fresh cultivated strawberries, washed and de-stemmed

Meringue:
6 egg whites
2 cups (250 g) superfine sugar

Note: It is advisable to make the ice cream and sherbet the day before.

Preheat the oven to 250° F (100° C).

To prepare meringues, beat 6 egg whites until very stiff and gradually add sugar, 2 tablespoons at a time, until very stiff and glossy.

On a buttered and lightly floured cookie sheet, mark 3 circles, each about 6½ inches (16 cm) in diameter. Spread meringue on circles, making 3 rounds.

Bake in a slow oven for 1 to 1½ hours, or until meringues are dry and crisp to the touch.

Cool and remove from cookie sheets.

Whip the cream with the sugar.

Place 1 meringue round on a serving platter. Spread the ice cream over the meringue with a spoon. Place the second meringue round atop the ice cream. Spread the sherbet over the second meringue round and cover with the third meringue.

Frost the sides and top with whipped cream. Place in freezer until ready to serve. Serve topped with fresh strawberries.

Creams and Sauces

Crème Patissière

Pastry cream

6 egg yolks
¾ cup (200 g) granulated sugar
6 tablespoons (40 g) all-purpose flour
2⅓ cups (5 dL) milk
1 teaspoon vanilla extract

Preparation time: 10 min.
Cooking time: 10 min.
Yield: 3 cups (6 dL)

In a bowl, mix the egg yolks with the sugar and flour.

Bring milk to a boil. Gradually stir boiling milk into the sugar mixture. Put milk-and-sugar mixture into a saucepan and place over low heat. Stir constantly until it thickens; do not boil.

Pour cream into a bowl to cool.

Stir in vanilla, cover, and cool.

Stir again and chill until ready to use.

Crème Anglaise

English cream

1½ cups (3 dL) milk
1¼ cups (150 g) confectioners' sugar
6 egg yolks
1 teaspoon vanilla extract

Preparation time: 10 min.
Cooking time: 10 min.
Yield: 2 cups

Heat milk until it is steaming.

Using a wooden spoon and stirring vigorously, combine the sugar and the egg yolks in a saucepan. Gradually stir in the hot milk. Stir over low heat until the mixture coats a spoon but do not let the sauce actually boil.

Immediately pass the mixture through a fine strainer into a bowl. Cover and cool to lukewarm.

Stir in the vanilla. Cover and chill until ready to use.

Sauce Caramel

Caramel sauce

1 cup (250 g) granulated sugar
1¼ cups (2½ dL) boiling water
1½ cups (3 dL) crème fraîche or heavy cream

Preparation time: 15 min.
Cooking time: 10 min.
Yield: 3 cups (6 dL)

Cook the sugar, without stirring, in a small skillet or nonstick pan until it liquifies and becomes golden brown.

Slowly add the water to the hot caramel and bring to a boil. Cool.

Slowly stir in the cream and let boil for 2 minutes until slightly thickened. Cool and then chill until needed.

This sauce goes very well with such desserts as Cinnamon Christmas Cookies (page 258), Kougelhopf (page 216), and Pear Charlotte (page 236).

Sauce au Chocolat

Chocolate sauce

4 ounces (100 g) bitter chocolate
½ cup (1 dL) milk
1 tablespoon crème fraîche or heavy cream
2 tablespoons superfine sugar
1 tablespoon butter

Preparation time: 15 min.
Cooking time: 10 min.
Yield: 1¼ cups (2½ dL)

Melt chocolate over low heat or in a pan placed over hot water.

Meanwhile, bring the milk to a boil. Stir in the cream and return to a boil.

Remove from heat. Stir in the sugar, melted chocolate, and butter. Mix well and cook for a few seconds more or until smooth. Cool and then chill until needed. Serve hot or cold.

Serve with Vanilla Ice Cream Cakes (page 262).

Sauce Framboise, or Coulis de Framboises

Raspberry sauce or raspberry topping

2 pints (250 g) ripe raspberries
2 cups (250 g) confectioners' sugar

Preparation time: 10 min.
Yield: 1 quart (1 L)

Pass the raspberries through a sieve or food mill.

Stir in the sugar until the sugar has dissolved.

This sauce keeps very well in the refrigerator and enhances Pear Charlotte (page 236), Raspberries Baked in Cream (page 252), or Vanilla Ice Cream (page 261).

LIQUORS

Here we give you a few recipes especially representative of Alsace: some apéritifs, some liqueurs, and some fruits soaked in liquor. Yield or serving portion is given for each recipe.

Cherry Kirsch
Amer à la Bière

Quince Liqueur
Wild Strawberry Liqueur
Raspberry Wine

Brandied Black Currants
Brandied Cherries
Brandied Raspberries
Brandied Grapes

Apéritifs

Guignolet-Kirsch

Cherry Kirsch

Serves: 1

4 parts cherry brandy, chilled
1 part Kirsch, chilled

Chill an apéritif glass.
Slowly combine brandy with Kirsch and stir gently.
Let stand 1 minute.

This is a typical Alsatian preparation. Use only chilled ingredients to avoid having to add an ice cube, which would dilute the drink.

Inhale the delicate perfume exuding from the drink. Then sip it slowly to enjoy its full flavor.

Amer à la Bière

Serves: 1

1 cup (¼ L) Amer Picon
1½ cups (3 dL) good, foamy and chilled beer

In a very large glass, mix ingredients.

This is a typically Alsatian drink, though not very well known elsewhere. Either dark or light beer may be used, but the latter is preferred.

Drink this slowly to appreciate the bouquet.

Liqueurs

Liqueur de Coings

Quince liqueur

24 quince
Eau-de-vie equal in volume to the juice of the quince
3 cups (600 g) confectioners' sugar per quart (L) of juice obtained
1 cinnamon stick
3 whole nutmegs

Preparation time: 20 min.
Standing time: 3 to 4 days
Curing time: 2 months
Yield: 3 quarts (3 L)

Very ripe quince (with wrinkled skins) are preferred for this recipe. Wipe the fruit, but do not peel. Grate coarsely.

Put the pulp into a container and let stand, covered, in a cool, shady place for 3 or 4 days.

Using a jelly cloth or several thicknesses of cheesecloth, mash the pulp to extract every drop of juice that you can. Measure exactly the amount of juice obtained.

Pour juice into a jug and, for every quart (L) of juice, add precisely 1 quart (1 L) brandy, 3 cups (600 g) confectioners' sugar, a small piece of cinnamon, and 2 to 3 nutmegs.

Seal the jug and let steep for 2 months in a cool place.

Strain through several thicknesses cheesecloth and pour into airtight sterilized bottles or jugs.

Serve chilled.

Liqueur de Fraises des Bois

Wild strawberry liqueur

1¼ pounds (500 g) wild strawberries, hulled
1 quart (1 L) eau-de-vie
1 vanilla bean, split in half
1 cup (2 dL) water
1 pound (500 g) confectioners' sugar

Preparation time: 20 min.
Standing time: 1 month
Curing time: 2 to 3 weeks
Yield: 1½ quarts (1½ L)

Select the berries with much care. Wild strawberries have a very intense flavor; cultivated berries can be used but the liqueur will not be as flavorful.

Gently place fruit into a jug. Cover with the *eau-de-vie*. Add vanilla. Seal the jug and let stand in a cool place for a whole month.

Strain liquid through a jelly cloth or several thicknesses of cheesecloth.

Bring water and sugar to a boil. Remove from heat as soon as it comes to a boil. Let cool and add to the strained liquid from the berries. Mix well, stirring with a very clean wooden spoon. Pour into sterilized airtight jugs or jars.

Let stand for 2 to 3 weeks before using.

Serve chilled.

Vin de Framboise

Raspberry wine

2¼ pounds (1 kg) raspberries (wild, if possible)
1 quart (1 L) red or white wine (Pinot or Riesling)
1 pound (500 g) confectioners' sugar per quart (L) of liquid
¾ cup (1¾ dL) grain alcohol for 2 quarts (2 L) of ingredients

Preparation time: 2 hr.
Standing time: 2 days
Cooking time: 30 min.
Curing time: 3 months
Yield: 2 quarts (2 L)

Crush the berries and add 1 quart (1 L) of wine for every 2¼ pounds (1 kg) of fruit. Let stand in a cool place for 2 days.

Press this mixture through a food mill, then strain through several thicknesses of cheesecloth. To this liquid, add the sugar, allowing 1 pound (500 g) confectioners' sugar for every quart (L) of liquid.

Cook over very low heat, stirring constantly so that the sugar may dissolve gradually. Simmer for 5 minutes and remove from heat. Cool.

Stir in the alcohol, allowing ¾ cup (1¾ dL) alcohol for every 2 quarts (2 L) of liquid.

Let cool, and pour into sterilized airtight bottles. Allow to age for at least 3 months, in a cool, shady place. This is necessary before the wine can be used.

Raspberry Wine is served as an apéritif or as a dessert wine.

Spirited fruits

Cassis à l'Eau-de-Vie

Brandied black currants

2 pounds (1 kg) fresh black currants
2 cups (454 g) granulated sugar
1 quart (1 L) eau-de-vie, cooled

Preparation time: 45 min.
Curing time: 2 months
Yield: 6 cups (1½ L)

Remove the seeds from the currants, leaving them intact, and eliminate all the currants that do not appear thoroughly healthy. Wipe, but do not wash.

Put the currants into a sterilized 6-cup (1½-L) jar or jug.

In another container, stir the sugar into the brandy. When the sugar is partially dissolved, pour the liquid into the jug so as to cover the currants completely.

Put a stopper or cork into the jug and make sure it is completely airtight. Let stand in a cool place away from the sun.

Wait at least 2 months before eating. Chill prior to serving.

Cerises à l'Eau-de-Vie

Brandied cherries

2 pounds (1 kg) fresh sour cherries (Montmorency, if possible)
2 cups (250 g) confectioners' sugar
1 quart (1 L) Kirsch

Preparation time: 20 min.
Curing time: 3 months
Yield: 6 cups (1½ L)

Sterilize an airtight 6-cup (1½-L) jug or jar.

Wash the cherries but do not pit. Cut off the stems so they are only 1 inch (2½ cm) long. Dry thoroughly with an absorbent paper towel.

Put the cherries into the jug, making successive layers of them and alternating the layers of cherries with layers of confectioners' sugar. (Do not crowd the cherries together.) Pour in the Kirsch to cover cherries.

Seal the jug and let steep. From time to time, make sure that the liquid covers the cherries. Add more Kirsch, if necessary, so that the top layer of cherries remains covered at all times. Keep in a cool dry place.

Wait 3 months before using.

Serve chilled.

ramboises à l'Eau-de-Vie

Brandied raspberries 

2 pounds (1 kg) especially fine fresh raspberries
1 quart (1 L) eau-de-vie or vodka
2¾ cups (300 g) confectioners' sugar

Preparation time: about 15 min.
Curing time: 3 months
Yield: 2 quarts (2 L)

Sterilize a 2-quart (2-L) jug or 2 1-quart (1-L) jars.

Select the raspberries with special care, throwing away any that are bruised. Do not wash.

Gently place the raspberries into the jug, in layers. Sprinkle each layer with confectioners' sugar. Cover with liquor. Seal the container.

Since raspberries tend to settle a bit, open the jug after 2 weeks and add 1 or 2 layers of good raspberries, then sprinkle with confectioners' sugar to fill the container. Make certain that all the fruit remains covered with liquid at all times.

Let steep in a cool dry place at least 3 months before using. Serve chilled.

Baies de Raisin de Chasselas Macérées

Brandied grapes

2 pounds (1 kg) red or white table grapes, stemmed
½ cup (100 g) superfine sugar
3 cups (¾ L) eau-de-vie, made from Gewürztraminer grapes, or cognac

Curing time: 10 days
Yield: 1 quart (1 L)

Wash the grapes and drain well.

Remove the seeds, leaving the grapes intact, and place them into a sterilized container (preferably an airtight glass jar).

Mix the sugar and *eau-de-vie* until sugar is dissolved. Pour over grapes until covered.

Seal the jar and keep in the refrigerator.

Let stand 10 days or so. Serve chilled or as topping for Gewürztraminer Sherbet (page 264).

GLOSSARY OF CULINARY TERMS

The following glossary is offered as a further aid for those following the recipes in this book, although all the recipes in *The Cuisine of Alsace* have been adapted for the U.S. cook. In addition, as is always the case with a brief glossary such as this, bear in mind that definitions are capsulized for easy reference; for more information, we suggest you refer to a more extensive dictionary of cooking terms.

Apértif A before-dinner drink that stimulates the appetite; usually somewhat bitter.

Arrowroot A starch made from the roots and rhizomes of a plant from the West Indies; used to thicken sauces.

Baba A cake of leavened dough, studded with raisins; usually it is steeped in liquor after cooking.

Bain-marie A warming utensil in which a sauce or other food is placed in one container, which then fits into a larger container. The bain-marie differs from a double boiler in that it is used primarily for warming instead of cooking, and also that the water in the lower pot comes up and around the sides of the inside pan.

Bard To cover a piece of meat, poultry, etc., with a layer of fat before braising. Barding fat is usually thinly sliced fat bacon.

Blanch To boil something for a brief time in lightly salted water. Usually vegetables are blanched (parboiled) prior to freezing, or salt pork is blanched to eliminate excess salt before use with a roast.

Blind To bake a crust blind is to bake the shell empty, so as to have a crisper crust for filling.

Bouillon Stock or broth, usually made from veal, chicken, fish, or beef.

Bouquet garni A cluster of herbs, tied together with string or bound with cheesecloth. These are used to flavor stews, and bouquet is removed prior to serving.

Braise A method of cooking in which the meat or other food is cooked slowly in liquid, in a covered pot, for a long time.

Canapé Originally a slice of crustless bread; now also used to refer to a variety of hors d'oeuvre consisting of toasted or fried bread spread with forcemeat, cheese, and other flavorings.

Caramelize To coat with sugar which has been heated to the point of browning.
Caul The type of fat used usually for wrapping meats prior to braising or roasting.
Charlotte A dessert in which a dish is lined with sponge fingers and filled with custard or another filling.
Chaud-froid Preparation of a dish, usually poultry, that is cooked, then served cold.
Chemisier To line a mold with aspic.
Chinois A strainer in the shape of a cone.
Chou pastry Cream puff pastry.
Clarify To make a liquid clear, as in clarifying a stock.
Concasser To chop roughly, as with vegetables.
Court-bouillon A seasoned liquid in which fish or shellfish are usually cooked.
Croûton Bread that has been diced and fried in butter, used as an accompaniment to soups or as a garnish.

Daube A stew of meat, usually made with red wine; can also apply to poultry or game.
Deglaze To dissolve the pan juices and scrape up the brown particles clinging to the bottom of a pan in which meat or poultry has been cooked. The deglazed juices then form the basis for a sauce.
Dégorger To soak food (as with sweetbreads) in cold water prior to cooking to eliminate impurities.
Diable A utensil consisting of two earthenware pots, one inside the other, thus allowing the cook to prepare a dish without using additional liquid.
Digestif After-dinner liqueur.
Double boiler A two-pan pot, the top one fitting into the lower one. In contrast to a bain-marie, the water in a double boiler should not touch the inside pan.
Duxelles Cooked minced mushrooms, usually used for stuffing or garnish.

Émincer To slice finely.
Éponger To dry blanched vegetables on a cloth or paper towel to rid them of excess moisture.
Essence A concentrated liquid, usually made from herbs or flowers, but also from fish, game, mushrooms, and other foods.

Fish poacher A long, thin kettle with a removable grid which allows the fish to be raised and lowered into and out of the broth without breaking apart.
Flambé To burn off the alcohol by igniting with a match. Usually the brandies or other liqueurs to be flambéed are warmed first, then poured into the dish and lit.

Forcemeat A mixture of ingredients, chopped and seasoned, used to stuff meats, poultry, and fish.
Food mill A grinding utensil that reduces foods to a purée.
Fricassée Nowadays, the preparation of poultry in white sauce.
Fumet A more richly seasoned stock, used as a base for sauces.

Gratin The crust formed on top of a baked dish when browned in broiler or oven; also the dish in which such food is cooked.

Infuse To steep in boiling liquid until the liquid absorbs the flavor of the seasoning agent.

Julienne To cut foods, such as vegetables or chicken, into thin strips or shreds.

Lard To thread the meat with strips of fat for added moisture.

Maceration To steep foods in liquid, usually changing the composition of both foods and liquid. As an example, fruits are often macerated in sugar to allow them to release their juices.
Marinade Seasoned liquid in which food—usually meat—is soaked for several hours. The liquid seasons and tenderizes at the same time.
Medallion A slice of meat, fish, or poultry cut round or oval, usually to be cooked quickly.
Mignonnette Coarsely ground pepper.
Mince To chop finely.
Mirepoix A mixture of minced vegetables, and sometimes meats, to be added to sauces.

Paupiettes Stuffed and rolled thin slices of meat, which are then wrapped in bacon and braised.
Pincer To brown foods in fat before adding liquid for braising.
Poach To cook in a clear, seasoned liquid, as for eggs, fish, chicken, or vegetables.
Purée To mash certain foods until smooth. Puréeing can be done in a blender or food processor, depending upon how fine a purée is desired.

Quenelle A light dumpling made from puréed fish or other foods, then braised or poached and served with a sauce or as a garnish.

Ragoût A meat, fowl, or other stew.
Ramekin A tartlet itself, or the small, round dish in which such a tart is baked.
Reduce To cook down; to evaporate some of the liquid in a braising pot, thus obtaining a stronger brew.
Revenir To brown ingredients in fat or oil so as to seal in juices; to sear.

Roll out To spread pastry on a board to a given even thickness, using a rolling pin.
Roux A mixture of butter and flour, used to thicken sauces.

Salamander An oven in which dishes are glazed or browned on top, just prior to serving.
Salpicon A mixture of diced food, such as carrots or meat or fruit, blended with a sauce or syrup and used to fill pastry.
Sauté To fry quickly in butter or oil over high heat.
Scum The foam which forms on the surface of a boiling liquid, such as a stock.
Simmer To cook gently over a low heat.
Steep To soak in liquid.
Stock The broth made from meat, fish, or vegetables, used as a basis for soups and sauces.
Suprême Boneless breast and wing of chicken, flattened.

Tourte A sweet or savory tart.
Truffle A wild mushroom, noted for its unique flavoring characteristics.

Velouté A white sauce made with chicken, fish, or veal stock.

Zest The outer peel of citrus fruit, used for flavoring.

RECIPE INDEX

A

B

G

H

I

J

K

L

M

N

O

P

T

V

W

Y